CLEP* HISTORY OF THE UNITED STATES II

1865 TO THE PRESENT

Lynn Marlowe, M.A.

And the Staff of
Research & Education Association

Research & Education Association
Visit our website at: www.rea.com

Planet Friendly Publishing
✔ Made in the United States
✔ Printed on Recycled Paper
　Text: 10%　　Cover: 10%
Learn more: www.greenedition.org

At REA we're committed to producing books in an Earth-friendly manner and to helping our customers make greener choices.

Manufacturing books in the United States ensures compliance with strict environmental laws and eliminates the need for international freight shipping, a major contributor to global air pollution.

And printing on recycled paper helps minimize our consumption of trees, water and fossil fuels. This book was printed on paper made with **10% post-consumer waste**. According to the Environmental Paper Network's Paper Calculator, by using this innovative paper instead of conventional papers, we achieved the following environmental benefits:

Trees Saved: 3 • Air Emissions Eliminated: 600 pounds
Water Saved: 600 gallons • Solid Waste Eliminated: 177 pounds

Courier Corporation, the manufacturer of this book, owns the Green Edition Trademark. For more information on our environmental practices, please visit us online at **www.rea.com/green**

Research & Education Association
61 Ethel Road West
Piscataway, New Jersey 08854
E-mail: info@rea.com

CLEP History of the United States II: 1865 to the Present with Online Practice Exams

Printed in the United States of America

Library of Congress Control Number 2013930175

ISBN-13: 978-0-7386-1127-3
ISBN-10: 0-7386-1127-1

Cover image: © istockphoto.com/GBlakeley

REA® is a registered trademark of
Research & Education Association, Inc.

CONTENTS

ABOUT THE AUTHOR

Lynn Elizabeth Marlowe obtained her master's degree in history from New York University in 1995, specializing in Modern American and Modern European history. She has taught history at several Los Angeles-area colleges, including Los Angeles City College (American history), Pasadena City College (American history), and Chaffey College (world history, European history). She also holds a teacher's certificate in secondary history and English, and has taught English as a Second Language to adults in the Los Angeles Unified School District. She has contributed to several REA publications.

ABOUT RESEARCH & EDUCATION ASSOCIATION

Founded in 1959, Research & Education Association (REA) is dedicated to publishing the finest and most effective educational materials— including study guides and test preps—for students in middle school, high school, college, graduate school, and beyond.

Today, REA's wide-ranging catalog is a leading resource for teachers, students, and professionals. Visit *www.rea.com* to see a complete listing of all our titles.

ACKNOWLEDGMENTS

We would like to thank Pam Weston, Publisher, for setting the quality standards for production integrity and managing the publication to completion; John Paul Cording, Vice President, Technology, for coordinating the design and development of the REA Study Center; Larry B. Kling, Vice President, Editorial, for his supervision of revisions and overall direction; Diane Goldschmidt and Michael Reynolds, Managing Editors, for coordinating development of this edition; Transcend Creative Services for typesetting this edition; and Weymouth Design and Christine Saul, Senior Graphic Designer, for designing our cover.

CHAPTER 1

Passing the CLEP History of the United States II Exam

PASSING THE CLEP HISTORY OF THE UNITED STATES II EXAM

Congratulations! You're joining the millions of people who have discovered the value and educational advantage offered by the College Board's College-Level Examination Program, or CLEP. This test prep covers everything you need to know about the CLEP History of the United States II exam, and will help you earn the college credit you deserve while reducing your tuition costs.

GETTING STARTED

There are many different ways to prepare for a CLEP exam. What's best for you depends on how much time you have to study and how comfortable you are with the subject matter. To score your highest, you need a system that can be customized to fit you: your schedule, your learning style, and your current level of knowledge.

This book, and the online tools that come with it, allow you to create a personalized study plan through three simple steps: assessment of your knowledge, targeted review of exam content, and reinforcement in the areas where you need the most help.

Let's get started and see how this system works.

Test Yourself & Get Feedback	Score reports from your online diagnostic and practice tests give you a fast way to pinpoint what you already know and where you need to spend more time studying.
Review with the Book	Study the topics tested on the CLEP exam. Targeted review chapters cover everything you need to know.
Improve Your Score	Armed with your score reports, you can personalize your study plan. Review the parts of the book where you're weakest and study the answer explanations for the test questions you answered incorrectly.

THE REA STUDY CENTER

The best way to personalize your study plan and focus on your weaknesses is to get feedback on what you know and what you don't know. At the online REA Study Center, you can access two types of assessment: a diagnostic exam and full-length practice exams. Each of these tools provides true-to-format questions and delivers a detailed score report that follows the topics set by the College Board.

Diagnostic Exam

Before you begin your review with the book, take the online diagnostic exam. Use your score report to help evaluate your overall understanding of the subject, so you can focus your study on the topics where you need the most review.

Full-Length Practice Exams

These practice tests give you the most complete picture of your strengths and weaknesses. After you've finished reviewing with the book, test what you've learned by taking the first of the two online practice exams. Review your score report, then go back and study any topics you missed. Take the second practice test to ensure you have mastered the material and are ready for test day.

If you're studying and don't have Internet access, you can take the printed tests in the book. These are the same practice tests offered at the REA Study Center, but without the added benefits of timed testing conditions and diagnostic score reports. Because the actual exam is computer-based, we recommend you take at least one practice test online to simulate test-day conditions.

AN OVERVIEW OF THE EXAM

The CLEP History of the United States II exam consists of approximately 120 multiple-choice questions, each with five possible answer choices, to be answered in 90 minutes.

The exam covers the material one would find in the second semester of what is often a two-semester class in United States History. The covers the period of United States history form the end of the Civil War to the present and focuses on the twentieth century.

The approximate breakdown of topics is as follows:

35%	Political institutions and behavior and public policy
25%	Social developments
10%	Economic developments
15%	Cultural and economic developments
15%	Diplomacy and international relations

ALL ABOUT THE CLEP PROGRAM

What is the CLEP?

CLEP is the most widely accepted credit-by-examination program in North America. CLEP exams are available in 33 subjects and test the material commonly required in an introductory-level college course. Examinees can earn from three to twelve credits at more than 2,900 colleges and universities in the U.S. and Canada. For a complete list of the CLEP subject examinations offered, visit the College Board website: *www.collegeboard.org/clep*.

Who takes CLEP exams?

CLEP exams are typically taken by people who have acquired knowledge outside the classroom and who wish to bypass certain college courses and earn college credit. The CLEP program is designed to reward examinees for learning—no matter where or how that knowledge was acquired.

Although most CLEP examinees are adults returning to college, many graduating high school seniors, enrolled college students, military personnel, veterans, and international students take CLEP exams to earn college credit or to demonstrate their ability to perform at the college level. There are no prerequisites, such as age or educational status, for taking CLEP examinations. However, because policies on granting credits vary among colleges, you should contact the particular institution from which you wish to receive CLEP credit.

Who administers the exam?

CLEP exams are developed by the College Board, administered by Educational Testing Service (ETS), and involve the assistance of educators from throughout the United States. The test development process is designed and implemented to ensure that the content and difficulty level of the test are appropriate.

When and where is the exam given?

CLEP exams are administered year-round at more than 1,200 test centers in the United States and can be arranged for candidates abroad on request. To find the test center nearest you and to register for the exam, contact the CLEP Program:

CLEP Services
P.O. Box 6600
Princeton, NJ 08541-6600
Phone: (800) 257-9558 (8 A.M. to 6 P.M. ET)
Fax: (609) 771-7088
Website: *www.collegeboard.org*

OPTIONS FOR MILITARY PERSONNEL AND VETERANS

CLEP exams are available free of charge to eligible military personnel and eligible civilian employees. All the CLEP exams are available at test centers on college campuses and military bases. Contact your Educational Services Officer or Navy College Education Specialist for more information. Visit the DANTES or College Board websites for details about CLEP opportunities for military personnel.

Eligible U.S. veterans can claim reimbursement for CLEP exams and administration fees pursuant to provisions of the Veterans Benefits Improvement Act of 2004. For details on eligibility and submitting a claim for reimbursement, visit the U.S. Department of Veterans Affairs website at *www.gibill.va.gov.*

CLEP can be used in conjunction with the Post-9/11 GI Bill, which applies to veterans returning from the Iraq and Afghanistan theaters of operation. Because the GI Bill provides tuition for up to 36 months, earning college credits with CLEP exams expedites academic progress and degree completion within the funded timeframe.

SSD ACCOMMODATIONS FOR CANDIDATES WITH DISABILITIES

Many test candidates qualify for extra time to take the CLEP exams, but you must make these arrangements in advance. For information, contact:

College Board Services for Students with Disabilities
P.O. Box 6226
Princeton, NJ 08541-6226
Phone: (609) 771-7137 (Monday through Friday, 8 A.M. to 6 P.M. ET)
TTY: (609) 882-4118
Fax: (609) 771-7944
E-mail: ssd@info.collegeboard.org

6-WEEK STUDY PLAN

Although our study plan is designed to be used in the six weeks before your exam, it can be condensed to three weeks by combining each two-week period into one.

Be sure to set aside enough time—at least two hours each day—to study. The more time you spend studying, the more prepared and relaxed you will feel on the day of the exam.

Week	Activity
1	Take the Diagnostic Exam. The score report will identify topics where you need the most review.
2–4	Study the review chapters. Use your diagnostic score report to focus your study.
5	Take Practice Test 1 at the REA Study Center. Review your score report and re-study any topics you missed.
6	Take Practice Test 2 at the REA Study Center to see how much your score has improved. If you still got a few questions wrong, go back to the review and study any topics you may have missed.

TEST-TAKING TIPS

Know the format of the test. CLEP computer-based tests are fixed-length tests. This makes them similar to the paper-and-pencil type of exam because you have the flexibility to go back and review your work in each section.

Learn the test structure, the time allotted for each section of the test, and the directions for each section. By learning this, you will know what is expected of you on test day, and you'll relieve your test anxiety.

Read all the questions—completely. Make sure you understand each question before looking for the right answer. Reread the question if it doesn't make sense.

Annotate the questions. Highlighting the key words in the questions will help you find the right answer choice.

Read all of the answers to a question. Just because you think you found the correct response right away, do not assume that it's the best answer. The last answer choice might be the correct answer.

Work quickly and steadily. You will have 90 minutes to answer 120 questions, so work quickly and steadily. Taking the timed practice tests online will help you learn how to budget your time.

Use the process of elimination. Stumped by a question? Don't make a random guess. Eliminate as many of the answer choices as possible. By eliminating just two answer choices, you give yourself a better chance of getting the item correct, since there will only be three choices left from which to make your guess. Remember, your score is based only on the number of questions you answer correctly.

Don't waste time! Don't spend too much time on any one question. Remember, your time is limited and pacing yourself is very important. Work on the easier questions first. Skip the difficult questions and go back to them if you have the time.

Look for clues to answers in other questions. If you skip a question you don't know the answer to, you might find a clue to the answer elsewhere on the test.

Acquaint yourself with the computer screen. Familiarize yourself with the CLEP computer screen beforehand by logging on to the College Board website. Waiting until test day to see what it looks like in the pretest tutorial risks injecting needless anxiety into your testing experience. Also, familiarizing yourself with the directions and format of the exam will save you valuable time on the day of the actual test.

Be sure that your answer registers before you go to the next item. Look at the screen to see that your mouse-click causes the pointer to darken the proper oval. If your answer doesn't register, you won't get credit for that question.

THE DAY OF THE EXAM

On test day, you should wake up early (after a good night's rest, of course) and have breakfast. Dress comfortably, so you are not distracted by being too hot or too cold while taking the test. (Note that "hoodies" are not allowed.) Arrive at the test center early. This will allow you to collect your thoughts and relax before the test, and it will also spare you the anxiety that comes with being late. As an added incentive, keep in mind that no one will be allowed into the test session after the test has begun.

Before you leave for the test center, make sure you have your admission form and another form of identification, which must contain a recent photograph, your name, and signature (i.e., driver's license, student identification card, or current alien registration card). You will not be admitted to the test center if you do not have proper identification.

You may wear a watch to the test center. However, you may not wear one that makes noise, because it may disturb the other test-takers. No cell phones, dictionaries, textbooks, notebooks, briefcases, or packages will be permitted, and drinking, smoking, and eating are prohibited.

Good luck on the CLEP History of the United States II exam!

CHAPTER 2

American History Review: 1865 – Present

AMERICAN HISTORY REVIEW: 1865 – PRESENT

The following American History review covers the period of time from the end of the Civil War through the present day. The review is divided into eight sections as follows:

1: **Reconstruction**

2: **Expansion of the Nation**

3: **Imperialism and War**

4: **Prosperity and Depression**

5: **Isolation and War**

6: **The Cold War**

7: **Cold War Politics and Society**

8: **The Post–Cold War Period**

By thoroughly studying this course review, you will be well-prepared for the material on the CLEP History of the United States II exam.

1. RECONSTRUCTION

Johnson's Reconstruction Plan

The United States faced an unprecedented situation as the Civil War ended, for there were no guidelines, constitutional or historical, for restoring the body politic. Consequently, Andrew Johnson, who had become president upon Lincoln's assassination in April 1865, and Congress struggled over who would control reconstruction policy.

Because Congress was in recess, Johnson acted first. He appointed provisional governors who called constitutional conventions. The new constitutions had to outlaw slavery and repudiate secession. Once the constitutions were ratified, the states could elect new officials and return to full participation in the nation's political life, including representation in Congress. Johnson's plan also prohibited several groups of Southerners, including former Confederate military and political officers, from political activity. The president began pardoning many of these individuals, however, with the result that the old Southern leadership class controlled the new governments. Consequently, when Congress reconvened in December 1865, it refused to seat the new southern Congressional representatives and appointed a joint committee to reexamine Reconstruction policy.

The Congressional Reconstruction Plan

Divided among Democrats and conservative, moderate, and radical Republicans, Congress had no clear alternative to Johnson's plan. Because neither the Democrats nor Johnson were willing to work with the conservative and moderate Republicans, the radicals gained the ascendancy. After Johnson in 1866 vetoed an extension of the life of the Freedman's Bureau and a Civil Rights bill (both later passed over his veto), the Republicans moved to take charge of Reconstruction policy. As it took form, the following were chief elements:

Fourteenth Amendment (adopted 1868). The amendment included four major provisions: (1) all persons born or naturalized in the United States, including African Americans, are citizens of the United States; (2) if the right to vote was denied to any male citizens over the age of 21—except for participation in rebellion or other crimes—representation was to be reduced proportionately;

(3) individuals who had previously taken an oath to support the Constitution of the United States and then participated in rebellion were prohibited from taking office; and (4) the Confederate debt was null and void.

Reconstruction Act of 1867. The major elements of this act included (1) division of the South into five military districts until new governments had been established; (2) Confederate leaders disallowed from voting until new state constitutions were ratified; (3) African Americans guaranteed the right to vote in elections for constitutional conventions and all subsequent elections; and (4) southern states required to ratify the Fourteenth Amendment and their new constitutions which were then to be approved by Congress.

Fifteenth Amendment (adopted 1870). This amendment stated that citizens could not be denied the right to vote "on account of race, color, or previous condition of servitude."

Impeachment of President Johnson

Because of the conflict over Reconstruction policy, Congress passed several acts restricting the power of the president, among them the Tenure of Office Act, which required Senate approval for changes in the president's cabinet. When Johnson sought to remove Secretary of War Edward M. Stanton, the House of Representatives voted in 1868 to indict the president. The Senate fell one vote short of the two-thirds majority required for conviction.

Reconstruction Politics in the South

Republican State Governments. The Republican party emerged to power as the states elected representatives, including many blacks, to the constitutional conventions. The new constitutions included reforms, among them the removal of property requirements for voting and office-holding and provisions for public schools. After ratifying the constitutions, the states elected new governments, again with Republican majorities.

Democratic Charges. Within this context, conservative Democrats charged that blacks were dominating Southern governments and that northern immigrants to the South, whom they called "Carpetbaggers," were looting state treasuries. Southerners who cooperated with the Republicans were reviled as

"Scalawags." The emergence of the Ku Klux Klan, particularly after 1867, introduced a campaign of terror aimed at intimidating blacks and their white Republican allies. By 1870 conservatives had regained power in three states: Tennessee, Virginia, and North Carolina.

Social and Economic Changes. Although Congress did not redistribute land to the freedmen, Republicans and northern philanthropists made some efforts to improve their situation. Groups founding schools included the Freedman's Bureau, which operated over 4,000 schools and established Howard University, and the American Missionary Association, which created Fisk and Atlanta universities. As part of their community-building efforts, blacks formed their own churches. Because they had little money, however, the freedmen turned to share-cropping, wherein the landowner provided them with land, seed, and supplies in return for a portion, at first usually one-half, of the resulting crop. Unfortunately, over time the landowners manipulated this system so that the sharecroppers were perpetually in debt. To make matters worse, cotton prices generally declined in the late nineteenth century, pushing southern agriculture into depression.

The End of Reconstruction

Congress Weakens Reconstruction. After winning the presidential election of 1868, Ulysses S. Grant sought to avoid confrontation with the South. By 1874 only 4,000 federal troops were stationed in southern states outside of Texas (where they were primarily concerned with Indians). The emergence of the Liberal Republicans, who opposed federal intervention in the South, weakened Republican support for Reconstruction. Also, in 1872 Congress passed the Amnesty Act, which pardoned all but 500 former Confederates, thereby greatly strengthening the Democratic party. In 1874 the Democrats gained control of the House of Representatives and by January 1876 had retaken eight of the eleven former Confederate states.

Economic Issues. Voters in the North became interested in issues other than Reconstruction and the situation of the freedmen. The Panic of 1873 turned attention to economic issues, with arguments centering over whether to keep Civil War paper money—"greenbacks"—in circulation (basically to produce inflation) or whether to return to hard ("sound") money. In what later became known as the "Crime of '73," Congress voted that greenbacks were to be converted to gold after 1878.

Election of 1876. The Democratic candidate for president, Samuel J. Tilden, came one electoral vote short of victory over Rutherford B. Hayes, because of disputes over the nineteen votes from Louisiana, South Carolina, and Florida, as well as one from Oregon. Congress set up a special electoral commission, which voted along party lines, resulting in the election of Hayes. Although there does not seem to have been a bargain between Hayes's supporters and Southerners, Reconstruction essentially ended when the new president took office in 1877.

2. EXPANSION OF THE NATION

The West

Indian Wars. Although their cultures varied from nomadic to village-dwelling, the Native Americans on the Plains maintained a largely subsistence economy to which the buffalo was central. When whites began settling the Plains, they killed millions of buffalo so that by the 1880s only a few hundred were left. This destruction disrupted life on the Plains, increasing conflict among the Native American tribes and between whites and Native Americans. From the Sand Creek Massacre in 1862 to the so-called Battle of Wounded Knee in 1890, sporadic fighting took place between the United States Army and the Plains Indians.

Reservations and Reform. Meanwhile, in the 1860s and 1870s the government sought to push the Native Americans onto Reservations, specific territories that supposedly were protected from white settlement and where the indigenous peoples could be "civilized." Reformers in the East, such as the Indian Rights Association, protested this policy, arguing instead for a policy of assimilation. Helen Hunt Jackson's *A Century of Dishonor* (1881) dramatically recounted the history of white mistreatment of Indians. The Dawes Act (1887) embodied many of the reformers' ideas and replaced tribal with individual ownership of property. Unfortunately, the new policy was disastrous to the Native Americans, as much of the reservation land ended up in the hands of whites and tribal authority disintegrated.

Mining, Timber, and Cattle. The West had numerous natural resources. Individual prospectors sought gold and silver, but once the surface minerals had been taken, deeper veins, if they existed, could only be mined by large companies with the capital to invest in equipment and men. Passage of the Timber and Stone Act (1878) enabled private citizens to purchase 160-acre plots at a low price; lumber companies took advantage of this provision by financing individuals purchases that were then turned over to the corporations. The cattle industry developed alongside mining and timber, with the cattlemen using the grasslands of the Western prairies to feed their herds. But as farmers and sheepherders invaded the Great Plains, they took away grazing land, a process aided by Joseph Glidden's invention of barbed wire in 1873. These problems drove down profits that, together with the blizzards of 1885–86 and 1886–87 and their intervening droughts, brought the open-range cattle industry to an end.

Agriculture. Between 1865 and 1890 hundreds of thousands of people poured into the prairies of eastern Kansas, Nebraska, and the Dakotas and then spilled into the Great Plains, placing more acreage under cultivation than in all previous American history. Congress passed several laws that encouraged this migration. The Homestead Act (1862) provided 160 acres of free land in exchange for five years of settlement and cultivation. The Timber Culture Act (1873) offered an additional 160 acres on the condition that a quarter of it be planted in trees. The Desert Land Act (1877) provided potential irrigators with 640 acres for the low down payment of 25 cents an acre.

The Railroads

Begun in 1862, the first transcontinental railroad was completed on May 10, 1869, with the joining in Utah of the Central Pacific Railroad, extending from Sacramento, California, and the Union Pacific Railroad, which stretched from Omaha, Nebraska. Because of the depressed economy, no more transcontinental routes were created until the 1880s and 1890s, when the Santa Fe, Southern Pacific, Northern Pacific, and Great Northern railroads were established. All but the last depended heavily on government subsidies. The increase in track from 35,000 miles in 1865 to 200,000 in 1890 provided an efficient means of moving goods around the country, as well as stimulated the steel industry, established the four time zones that we use today, and encouraged the growth of cities such as Omaha, Kansas City, and Seattle.

The South

Crop-Lien System and Sharecropping. Although the number of farms in the South more than doubled between the Civil War and 1880, the number of landowners stayed about the same because farmers increasingly rented their land. The 1880 census revealed that about one-third of the farmers were sharecroppers, a number that doubled by 1920. The "crop lien" system, whereby merchants advanced credit to farmers for a portion of the upcoming crop, most often resulted in overcharges and permanent indebtedness. The term "debt peonage" is sometimes used to describe the state of farmers who worked to pay off what they had lost on past crops. Attempting to pay off their debts, farmers increasingly concentrated on cash crops, particularly cotton, which made them more dependent on the merchant for food items. Because this economic system oppressed both blacks and poor whites, landowners stirred racial fears to prevent the two groups from becoming political allies.

Industrialization. Railroads helped spur the industrialization of the United States, particularly through its demand for steel. Production of steel, centered in Ohio, Pennsylvania, and Alabama, rose from less than 3 million tons in 1880 to nearly 35 million in 1914. The petroleum industry also grew from virtually nothing in the mid-nineteenth century to become one of the pillars of industrial America. Northern and European capitalists found profitable opportunities in the South. In addition to the development of the steel industry in Alabama, between 1870 and 1900 over 400 textile mills were built in the cotton-growing region and by 1920 the South was overtaking New England in textile production. Considerable investments were made in the lumber, iron and steel, coal, and railroad industries; by 1900 the South was more economically subservient to the North than in 1860.

Labor

The Workforce. Increasing numbers of workers entered industry so that by 1880 nearly 5 million were employed in manufacturing, construction, and transportation. That same year about 2½ million women worked in both factories and offices, a number that would more than triple in the next twenty years. Children also were entering the workforce in significant numbers. In 1890, for instance, 18% often to fifteen year olds worked for pay. Injuries and disease were common, while workers and their families had no safety nets such as disability insurance and pensions. New York's Triangle Shirtwaist Company fire of 1911, which killed 146—mostly women—workers, was only the most dramatic event exemplifying the dangerous conditions industrial workers endured.

Early Labor Unions. Workers formed unions in an attempt to improve their lot. The National Labor Union, founded in 1866, disintegrated in the wake of widespread strikes in 1877 that were suppressed by state militias and federal troops. The Knights of Labor, begun in 1860, greatly expanded after Terence Powderly was elected Grand Master in 1879. Recruiting all workers, rather than the skilled workers of most previous unions, the Knights sought to replace competitive capitalism with cooperatives. Although it reached a peak membership of 730,000 in 1886, this union could not reach consensus regarding strikes. After Powderly called off the railway strikes without gaining concessions from the railroad companies, those wanting more militant action began to leave the union.

Haymarket Riot. Also in 1886, mass strikes led to a large labor demonstration in Chicago on May 1. Three days later a bomb went off during a confrontation between labor groups and police at Haymarket Square, killing seven police and injuring many others. Because of the role of anarchists, eight of whom were convicted for the bombing, in these events, public fear of radical influence on labor grew.

AFL. In contrast to the rejection of the capitalist system by the Knights of Labor and anarchists, the American Federation of Labor (AFL), a combination of several craft unions formed in 1886, accepted capitalism and sought the right to collective bargaining and better hours, wages, and working conditions. Under the leadership of Samuel L. Gompers, the AFL grew to 2½ million members by 1917. Although the AFL pointed to the future direction of American labor, more radical movements such as the American Railway Union, with its president, Eugene V. Debs (1893–97), the future Socialist presidential candidate, and Industrial Workers of the World ("Wobblies" or IWW) continued to be active.

Business Organization

Consolidation. In an effort to control their economic environment, businesses pursued consolidation in several ways. One form was *horizontal integration,* where a single company sought to monopolize one product by either buying or driving out the competition. Two popular devices for achieving these objectives were the "trust," whereby one individual would manage the financial affairs of another, and the "holding company," in which one company would own shares of other companies. John D. Rockefeller's Standard Oil Company used these business models to gain control of 90% of the petroleum industry. Another approach was *vertical integration*, whereby a company attempted to control all of the elements—including raw materials, transportation, and manufacture—involved in the production of a particular product. Gustavus Swift pioneered this approach in the meat-packing industry.

Defending Consolidation. Some businessmen and intellectuals justified the developing economic system on the basis of "social Darwinism." Combining Adam Smith's classical economic theory that government should not intrude into the economy with the Darwinian concept of natural selection, such individuals as Herbert Spencer in England and William Graham Sumner in the United States argued that the survival of civilization depended on unregulated economic competition.

Criticizing Consolidation. Critics of the new industrial system also raised their voices. In *Dynamic Sociology* (1883), Lester Frank Ward attacked social Darwinism, arguing that social advancement would result only from gaining increasing control over natural processes. Economists such as Richard Ely and John R. Commons denied that the economy operated according to economic laws with which humans could not interfere. Congress responded slowly to such criticisms. In 1890 it passed the Sherman Anti-Trust Act, which made unreasonable actions "in restraint of trade" illegal. The vague language of the law enabled the courts, however, to rule against most government efforts to break up monopolies.

URBANIZATION AND POLITICS, 1877–1920

Growth of Cities

Between the end of Reconstruction and 1920, the United States became an urban nation. The number of Americans living in cities increased from 10 million in 1870 to 54 million in 1920, the year that the census revealed that 51% of the nation's population lived in communities of more than 2,500 people. The number of cities with a population of more than 100,000 had increased from fifteen to sixty-eight and those with over 500,000 had moved from two to twelve.

Population

Immigration. The population of these growing cities came from two sources: the American countryside and Europe. Especially during the difficult times of the 1880s and 1890s, low crop prices and debts drove farmers, and especially their children, from rural areas to the cities. But even more significant, some 26 million immigrants arrived in America between 1870 and 1920, most—the "New Immigration"— coming from southern and eastern Europe, rather than northern Europe as had most earlier immigrants. Their Jewish or Catholic religious faith helped spark an increase in nativist activity such as the American Protective Association's campaign in the 1890s to stop immigration altogether. Also reflecting this nativist impulse, Congress passed the Chinese Exclusion Act in 1882, banning Chinese immigration for 10 years; renewals of the law kept the ban in place until 1943.

Urban Slums. Because of inadequate housing, this new urban population was crowded together into former single-family homes that were now divided into apartments and multi-apartment tenement houses. The Lower East Side of New York, for instance, had an average of 702 people per acre in 1890. Reformers such as Jacob Riis, who in *How the Other Half Lives* (1890) graphically exposed the living conditions of the urban poor, called for improved housing, but except for some laws regulating new construction, little was done to improve housing. Progress was made, however, on such things as water, sewage, street lighting and paving, and fire fighting.

Urban Culture

The growing population centers and increasing amounts of leisure time, particularly for the middle class, encouraged the development of commercial entertainment. A national tour of the Cincinnati Red Stockings in 1869 helped develop professional baseball into the nation's premier sport by the 1880s. Controversy over deaths in college football games led to the development of the Intercollegiate Athletic Association in 1906. Vaudeville variety shows originated in the cities and, with the advent of railways, traveled to small towns throughout America. Developed in the late nineteenth century, moving pictures gradually developed increasing sophistication through the work of directors such as D. W. Griffith, whose *Birth of a Nation* (1913) combined technical achievement with blatant racism. But perhaps the most characteristic aspect of urban culture was the mass-circulation newspaper. Joseph Pulitzer's *New York World* took advantage of the newly developed rotary press, which made cheap production of newspapers possible, and pioneered what became known as "yellow journalism," an approach that emphasized sensational stories. William Randolph Hearst copied Pulitzer's style, around which he developed a newspaper empire. Mass-circulation magazines such as *McClure's, Ladies Home Journal,* and *Saturday Evening Post* also took advantage of new printing techniques and eye-catching stories to attract large audiences.

Urban Politics and Reform

City Machines and Reform Efforts. The rapid growth of both urban populations and infrastructure produced what came to be known as the "city machine," highly organized political organizations that exchanged the provision of city services for power and wealth. The "bosses" of these machines aided the new, mostly immigrant, urban population with services such as jobs and legal help in return for votes. Contracts for public works usually included bribes and kickbacks. Reformers complained about corruption and inefficiency and sought to destroy the power of the machines. Structural changes such as city-manager and commission forms of government and nonpartisan city-wide elections were introduced beginning in the 1890s.

Social Reformers. Other reformers worked more directly with the urban population. Advocates of the "Social Gospel" such as Washington Gladden and Walter Rauschenbusch sought to apply Christian principles to labor-management relationships. Jane Addams and Florence Kelley led the settlement house movement that provided a wide range of services to the urban poor and began the modern social work profession. In time these women also engaged the political system, pushing for such things as public playgrounds, public health programs, and building safety codes.

National Political Issues

Waving the Bloody Shirt. For nearly thirty years after the Civil War, both Republicans and Democrats stirred war memories by "waving the bloody shirt" whenever they needed to gain a political edge. But other issues also called for attention.

Civil Service Reform. Scandals in the Grant administration spurred interest in civil service reform, which eventually led to formation of the National Civil Service Reform League in 1881. After a disgruntled job seeker shot President James A. Garfield that same year, Congress passed the Pendleton Civil Service Act (1882), which created a system of competitive examinations for about 10% of government jobs.

Railroad Regulation. Another issue was railroad regulation. Because of differences in the shipping prices charged by railroads, which usually favored large shippers, various groups, including farmers, began calling for government regulation. In 1887 the Interstate Commerce Act prohibited various discriminatory practices and created the Interstate Commerce Commission to oversee the railroads. Court rulings, however, greatly weakened the legislation.

The Tariff. Protective tariffs on a wide range of goods were creating a surplus in the federal treasury. In opposition to Republican support for such tariffs, Democrats argued that such tariffs were hurting farmers while unfairly benefitting manufacturers. The Democrats were unsuccessful in their efforts, however, as the McKinley Tariff (1890) and Dingley Tariff (1897) both raised rates.

The Silver Issue. During the economically difficult times of the late 1870s, farmers and silver producers sought to reverse the 1873 decision that stopped the government from purchasing and coining silver. Farmers, who were increasingly indebted to banks, saw the monetizing of silver as a way to inflate the money supply, thereby making it easier to pay off their debts. Neither the Bland-Allison Act (1878) nor the Sherman Silver Purchase Act (1890) went far enough to satisfy the backers of silver.

Women's Suffrage. The National Woman Suffrage Association and American Woman Suffrage Association, which combined in 1890 to form the National American Woman Suffrage Association, fought for both the right to vote and legal reforms for women. They achieved limited success; by 1890 women had achieved the right to vote in school elections in nineteen states and on tax and bond issues in three.

The Presidency

The period between 1877 and 1901 is generally regarded as a time when Congressional power eclipsed that of the President. Rutherford B. Hayes (1877–81), James Garfield (1881), Chester Arthur (1881–85), Grover Cleveland (1885–89 and 1893–97), Benjamin Harrison (1889–93), and William McKinley (1897–1901) had relatively little influence on domestic affairs. Neither the Democrats nor the Republicans were able to gain dominance; for only three two-year periods did the same party control both the presidency and the two houses of congress.

Populism

The Grange and Farmers' Alliances. A fall in wheat prices by about two-thirds between the mid-1860s and the mid-1890s eventually produced an agrarian revolt. Beginning in the 1860s, farmers organized Grange branches. At first primarily social organizations, Granges began establishing sales cooperatives and pressed legislatures to pass laws regulating the storage and transportation of grain but had little success and reverted to their largely social function by the 1880s. During that decade, starting in Texas but extending throughout the South and Midwest, the more politically active Farmers' Alliances emerged. They called on the government to build warehouses, called "subtreasuries," where farmers could store crops in exchange for notes worth 80% of the crops' market value.

The Populist Movement. When Alliance members in Kansas formed a People's (otherwise known as the Populist) party in 1890 and won the state elections, they stimulated development of a national party. Representatives from both Southern and Northern Alliances met in Omaha, Nebraska, in 1892, where they adopted a strongly reformist platform and nominated James B. Weaver, a former Union general, for president. The "cooperative commonwealth" they proposed included government ownership of the railroads, coinage of silver, and a graduated income tax.

The Depression

In 1893 a difficult period began; in that year bankruptcy hit some 500 banks and 1,500 businesses. During the ensuing depression, which lasted until 1897, about 20% of workers suffered significant job loss. Because the nation's gold reserves were dwindling, largely because the government was purchasing silver—which was declining in value as a result of increased production—with gold, Congress repealed the Sherman Silver Purchase Act in 1893 and later that year Cleveland arranged a deal whereby banker J. P. Morgan exchanged gold for government bonds. The depression, however, continued.

Election of 1896

After the Democrats nominated William Jennings Bryan of Nebraska, a supporter of silver, for the Presidency, the Populists followed a policy of "fusion," nominating Bryan—who was not a Populist—as their candidate as well. The Republicans nominated William McKinley, governor of Ohio, a staunch ally of business. Although Bryan campaigned widely, McKinley won the election. The Populists, however, were the real losers, for through fusion they had compromised their identity and with the return of prosperity in 1897 they lost their appeal. A sound-money president, McKinley supported the Gold Standard Act (1900) and through the Dingley Tariff (1897) sought to promote American industry.

The Progressive Era

Origins of Progressivism. Although the Populist movement achieved national attention in the 1890s, a number of urban-oriented reform movements (which came to be called "Progressive") arose about the same time, including the National American Woman Suffrage Association, the National Consumers

League, and the National Municipal League. Popular writers, whom Theodore Roosevelt derisively termed "muckrakers," revealed corruption and abuse in many quarters. Lincoln Steffens, for instance, in *The Shame of the Cities* (1904) exposed the big-city political machines, while Sinclair Lewis, although intending to promote socialism, revealed the adulteration of food in *The Jungle* (1906). Out of this reform impulse rose state political leaders. Governor Robert M. LaFollette of Wisconsin, for example, reformed the tax system, established railroad legislation, and helped democratize politics by instituting direct primaries. Also calling for change was W. E. B. Du Bois, a founder of the National Association for the Advancement of Colored People (1909), who opposed Booker T. Washington's policy of accommodation and pushed to end racial segregation.

Theodore Roosevelt. Theodore Roosevelt (1901–09) came to the presidency as a result of the assassination of McKinley. An advocate of a strong central government led by an educated and talented elite, Roosevelt broke up some trusts but favored government regulation. The Hepburn Act (1906) strengthened the Interstate Commerce Commission's authority to set railroad rates; the Meat Inspections Act (1906) provided oversight of the meatpacking industry; and the Pure Food and Drug Act (1906) required labeling of patent medicines. Concerned about protecting natural resources, Roosevelt also supported the National (Newlands) Reclamation Act (1902), which financed irrigation in the West, and increased the national forests by nearly 150,000 acres.

William Howard Taft. William Howard Taft (1909–13) succeeded Roosevelt but quickly became caught between the reformers and the old guard of the Republican party. The Paine-Aldrich Tariff (1909), which he signed, made protective tariff compromises that lost Taft support among the reformers and he angered conservationists by allowing land to be removed from protected status. Nonetheless, Taft supported the Mann-Elkins Act (1910), which strengthened the Interstate Commerce Commission, brought 80 anti-trust suits—compared to Roosevelt's 25, and removed more land from public use than had Roosevelt. Also, during Taft's presidency efforts began to enact constitutional amendments that legalized the income tax (Sixteenth—1913) and established direct election of senators (Seventeenth—1913).

Election of 1912. During the presidential election of 1912, the Republicans renominated Taft, after a challenge by Roosevelt who then became the candidate of the newly former Progressive ("Bull Moose") party. Governor Woodrow Wilson of New Jersey became the Democratic candidate. The campaign focused on different approaches to reform. Roosevelt advocated the "New Nationalism," which emphasized government regulation of big business. Wilson's "New Freedom," in contrast, proposed to break up monopolies and restore competition. With the Republican party divided, Wilson won the presidency.

Woodrow Wilson. As president (1913–21), Wilson supported several reform measures. The Clayton Anti-Trust and the Federal Trade Commission Acts (1914) gave the government increased authority over business and the Federal Reserve Act (1913) established a central banking system. The Underwood Tariff (1913) lowered tariffs and created a graduated income tax. The Federal Farm Loan Act (1916) aided agriculture and the Adamson Act (1916) established the eight-hour day for railroad workers. The entrance of the United States into World War I in 1917 largely ended domestic reform legislation, although the Eighteenth Amendment to the Constitution was approved in 1919 which, accompanied by the Volstead Act of the same year, prohibited the commercial manufacture and sale of alcoholic beverages. Also in 1919, women received the right to vote with the adoption of the Nineteenth Amendment.

3. IMPERIALISM AND WAR

Expansion of Trade and Investment

The foreign trade of the United States expanded rapidly in the decades following the Civil War. Exports grew from about $600 million in 1875 to $1.5 billion in 1900 and nearly $2.5 billion in 1914. During the same period, the United States also became one of the leading countries investing abroad. By 1914 nearly one-third of these investments, about $1.26 billion, was going to Latin America, with significant implications for American foreign policy.

Expansionism

Early Expansionism. Beginning soon after the Civil War, the United States took several steps to secure its interests outside North America. William H. Seward, Secretary of State from 1861 to 1869, started the process with the purchase of Alaska from Russia. Then in 1878 the United States obtained a naval station in Samoa; within ten years it had annexed a portion of the islands. During the 1880s Alfred T. Mahan began promoting the concept of a large navy, which in turn required colonies for fueling and repair. His *The Influence of Sea Power Upon History* (1890) carried this message far beyond navy circles. During the 1880s, the so-called "New Navy," built with steel and powered by steam, took form.

Hawaii. When in 1893 a cadre of wealthy American planters overthrew Queen Liliuokalani of Hawaii, incoming President Cleveland opposed annexation and sought to restore the monarchy. The American planters resisted Cleveland and continued to seek annexation, which they achieved in the midst of the Spanish-American War in 1898.

Venezuela. In 1895 Secretary of State James Olney strongly invoked the Monroe Doctrine when he warned Britain against taking territory from Venezuela with whom it was disputing the border with British Guiana. Largely ignoring Venezuela, Britain and the U.S. settled the dispute in 1896.

Spanish-American War

Origins of the War. Next, a crisis emerged in Cuba. For decades the Cubans had been in conflict with their Spanish colonizers. But when the Wilson-Gorman Tariff (1894) imposed heavy duties on Cuban sugar, ninety percent of which was exported to the United States, the Cuban economy was devastated. At that point José Martí began a revolution in 1895 that the Spanish sought to repress. American newspapers publicized the alleged atrocities of the Spanish. In January 1898, a pro-Spanish riot in Havana prompted the United States to send a battleship, the *Maine,* to Havana harbor, where an explosion sunk the ship on February 15. President McKinley, who had been criticized as "weak" by a Spanish diplomat, sent an ultimatum to Spain insisting, among other things, that he serve as an arbitrator to end the conflict. Although Spain made concessions, McKinley was dissatisfied and on April 11 asked Congress to authorize the use of force. On April 19, Congress declared that Cuba was independent and authorized war. The Teller Amendment stated that the United States would not annex Cuba.

Conduct of the War. With war declared, Assistant Secretary of State Theodore Roosevelt ordered Commodore George Dewey to attack the Spanish fleet in the Philippines. Dewey destroyed the fleet on May 1. Although the U.S. army was woefully unprepared, it first engaged the Spanish in Cuba on June 22 and by mid-July had largely achieved victory and then invaded Puerto Rico. The Spanish signed an armistice on August 12 and in December signed in Paris a treaty with the Americans. In return for a $20 million payment, the United States received Puerto Rico, while Guam and Cuba were granted independence.

Debate over Imperialism

The Treaty of Paris provoked an intense debate over imperialism. The anti-imperialists, led by such people as William Jennings Bryan, Mark Twain, and Jane Addams, argued that possession of colonies conflicted with American principles of freedom and would draw resources away from domestic concerns. In response, the imperialists stated that America must fulfill its duty as one of the civilized nations and that overseas possessions served the national interest. In February 1899, the Senate approved the Treaty of Paris.

Asia

China. For over half a century, the European nations had been establishing "spheres" in China giving them special trade rights. Fearing that opportunities would soon disappear, American businessmen pushed the American government to act. In 1899 Secretary of State John Hay sent a note to the European imperial nations, asking them to acknowledge that the United States had equal trading rights or an "Open Door" to China. Little came from this effort, but the Open Door became an important principle of American foreign policy.

The Philippines. While Hay was pursuing the Open Door in China, Emilio Aguinaldo proclaimed Philippine independence in January 1899, and engaged in an insurrection that lasted until 1902. In succeeding years, the United States sought to Americanize the Philippines but difficulties continued. The Jones Act (1916) promised the Philippines an independence that would not come until after World War II.

Japan. Wanting to protect the Philippines by maintaining peace in the region, President Theodore Roosevelt pursued a series of agreements with Japan. The Taft-Katsura Agreement (1905) and the Root-Takahara Agreement (1907) both gained Japan's recognition of American holdings in the region in return for similar recognition by the United States for Japan's interests. Also, after San Francisco attempted to segregate Asians in its public schools, Roosevelt in 1907 made a "gentleman's agreement" with Japan whereby the latter limited emigration to America and San Francisco reversed its segregation decision.

Latin America

Cuba. Although Cuba was ostensibly independent, the United States forced it to include the Platt Amendment in its new constitution, allowing the American government to approve all of its treaties with foreign nations. Also, political unrest on the island prompted the United States to send in troops three times over the next two decades. The Foraker Act (1900) established American control over Puerto Rico, although the islanders were granted citizenship in 1917.

Panama Canal. In addition to these matters left over from the Spanish-American War, Roosevelt also sought to build a canal that would enable ships in the Atlantic to quickly sail to the Pacific Ocean. He helped Panamanians successfully revolt against Colombia. Upon achieving independence, Panama then signed a treaty in 1903 giving the United States the rights to a canal zone. The canal reached completion in 1914.

Roosevelt's Corollary. Meanwhile, the United States continued to assert its hegemony over Latin America. In his Corollary to the Monroe Doctrine (1904), Roosevelt stated that the United States had the right to intervene wherever there was "chronic wrongdoing."

World War I

American Neutrality. After several weeks of international maneuvering following the assassination of Archduke Ferdinand, heir to the Austrian-Hungarian throne, in Bosnia, Germany declared war on Russia on August 1, 1914. Ultimately, Great Britain, France, Italy, Russia, and Japan (the Allied Powers) faced Germany and Austria-Hungary (the Central Powers). Although President Woodrow Wilson proclaimed American neutrality, continuing trade with the Allies made such neutrality difficult. When Germany proclaimed a war zone around the British Isles in February 1913, and warned all neutral ships to stay away, Wilson responded by telling Germany that it would be held accountable for any loss of American life and property. Then, on May 7, German U-boats (submarines) sank the British passenger ship *Lusitania*, killing over 1,000 people, including 128 Americans. Wilson insisted on the right of Americans to travel on belligerent ships and demanded that Germany halt its submarine warfare. Although Germany stopped attacking passenger ships for a time, in February 1917, it announced unrestricted submarine warfare, which meant that ships of all nations, belligerent or not, faced destruction if caught sailing within the war zone.

United States Enters the War. In reaction, Wilson broke off diplomatic relations with Germany. About the same time, Britain intercepted a telegram from the German Foreign Secretary, Arthur Zimmermann, to the Mexican government asking it to join the war against the Allies in return for help in recovering the territories lost in 1848 as a result of the Mexican War. When released to the American public on March 1, the telegram stirred outrage. As relations with Germany deteriorated, there was little surprise when Wilson asked Congress on April 2, 1917, to declare war on Germany, a request quickly approved.

America at War. Even before declaring war, the United States had taken some steps to improve its military readiness. In 1916 the National Defense and the Navy Acts enlarged the armed forces, and the Revenue Act established new taxes to pay for the expansion. Once war had been declared, the Selective Service Act (1917) introduced the draft. The American military, under General John J. Pershing, operated independently as an "associated" power and did not take significant military action until May 1918. Nonetheless, American participation seems to have tipped the balance of power toward the Allies and Germany agreed to an armistice that took effect on November 11, 1918. Despite its limited participation, the United States lost about 100,000 men in combat-related deaths, half of them due to disease.

The Home Front

The coming of war enlarged the federal government. The Food Administration controlled the price and distribution of food; the Fuel and Railroad Administrations addressed transportation issues; the War Industries Board coordinated supplies, prices, and production; the War Shipping Board oversaw shipbuilding; and the National War Labor Board dealt with labor-management relations. The work force changed as women moved into factory work and, more significantly, approximately 500,000 African Americans moved from the South to the North in what became known as the "Great Migration." The war also resulted in actions that threatened civil liberties, especially through the Espionage (1917) and Sedition (1918) Acts, which gave the government broad powers to limit criticism of the war, resulting in over 2,000 prosecutions. In *Schenck v. U. S.* (1919) the Supreme Court upheld the constitutionality of the Espionage Act. Even after the war ended, the suppression of dissent continued. After a series of bitter labor strikes, Attorney General A. Mitchell Palmer in 1919–20 launched a campaign (the "Red Scare") against radical groups, including socialists, communists, and the IWW that seriously eroded freedom of speech.

The Peace Settlement

In January 1918 Wilson had presented "Fourteen Points" on which, he believed, peace terms should be based. The points included freedom of the seas, open treaty making, and national self-determination, but in Wilson's mind the most important was the creation of an association of nations to keep the peace. The Paris peace conference, however, produced the Treaty of Versailles, which forced Germany to admit its war guilt and accept unspecified reparations. In Wilson's mind, these compromises were outweighed by the fact that the treaty included a League of Nations. Unfortunately for him, many members of the Senate opposed the League on the grounds that it compromised the sovereignty of the United States. Through the adroit political maneuvering of Henry Cabot Lodge and Wilson's refusal to compromise, the Senate rejected the treaty. Although the United States later signed a separate treaty with Germany, it never became a member of the League of Nations.

4. PROSPERITY AND DEPRESSION

The Republican Ascendency

Aiding Business. The progressive reform that had characterized most of the first two decades of the twentieth century went into retreat after World War I. The administrations of Warren G. Harding (1921–23) and Calvin Coolidge (1923–29) favored business interests and avoided interfering in the economy. In 1921 Congress reduced taxes for corporations and the wealthy, and the following year raised tariff rates with the Fordney-McCumber Tariff Act. In 1922 the Harding Administration put down major strikes by railroad workers and miners. Not surprisingly, union membership during the 1920s fell by about a third. Congress passed the Federal Highway Act (1921) to aid states in road building and, reflecting the earlier reform impulse and the new political influence of women, the Sheppard-Towner Act gave money to states for establishing maternity and pediatric clinics.

Agriculture. Agriculture did not share in the pro-business orientation of the federal government, for when Congress passed the McNary-Haugen Acts in 1927 and 1928 to provide price supports for farmers, Coolidge exercised his veto.

Immigration. Concerned also about the impact that immigration was having on American society, Congress passed the Johnson Act in 1921, restricting immigration by a 3% quota based on the 1910 census. In 1924 the Johnson-Reid Act lowered the quota to 2% based on the 1890 census and limited total annual immigration to 165,000.

Social Patterns

Prosperity. The gross national product increased by 40% between 1919 and 1929. Electricity now supplied two-thirds of American homes and apartments. Automobile ownership during the decade increased from 8 to 23 million, thereby providing mobility for both young and old and spurring economic development by its use of petroleum products and the need for road building. Over 10 million homes had radios by the end of the decade, enabling the new medium to effectively compete with newspapers for both audience and advertising.

Population Shifts. According to the 1920 census, for the first time a majority of Americans lived in communities with populations of over 2,500. Urbanization continued throughout the 1920s as some 6 million Americans left the farms for jobs in cities such as Detroit or Birmingham. Population also moved westward. California, for instance, grew by 67% during the decade. The "Great Migration" of African Americans from the South continued to grow, as some 1.5 million moved to such cities as Chicago, Detroit, and New York. The automobile also made possible the growth of suburbs, usually middle- or upper-class in character. The number of women in the work force increased by about 2 million, birth rates dropped, and the ratio of divorces to marriages edged upward.

Leisure-time Activities. With increased prosperity, more free time, and greater mobility, Americans nearly doubled the amount of money they spent on leisure-time activities. Weekly movie attendance increased from 40 million viewers in 1922 to over 100 million in 1930. Spectator sports, including team contests like college football and professional baseball and individual competitions such as golf, tennis, and boxing, attracted large audiences.

Literature and Music. The materialism and seeming triviality of American culture alienated many intellectuals and writers. Some members of the so-called "Lost Generation," among them Ernest Hemingway and F. Scott Fitzgerald, moved to Europe, while William Faulkner and Sinclair Lewis stayed at home. All nonetheless criticized America and modern culture through such books as Lewis's *Main Street* (1920) and Fitzgerald's *The Great Gatsby* (1925). With increasing numbers congregating in northern cities, African Americans experienced a cultural awakening known as the Harlem Renaissance, led by poets such as Langston Hughes and essayist Alain Locke. African Americans, including Louis Armstrong and Bessie Smith, also brought jazz, which increasingly gained a white audience, especially as white bandleaders like Paul Whiteman and composers such as George Gershwin brought it into the concert hall.

Reactions to Change

Ku Klux Klan. Not everyone accepted easily the changes occurring in American life. The Ku Klux Klan emerged once more, gaining perhaps 5 million members by 1923. Opposing new immigrants, Jews, and Catholics, as well as blacks, the Klan sought influence outside the South but scandals and the inherent limitations of its political appeal sent it into decline by the end of the decade.

Sacco-Vanzetti. The anti-radicalism left over from the Red Scare of 1919 probably helped convict Nicola Sacco and Bartolomeo Vanzetti for murder in 1921. Despite intense protests that the trial had been rigged and that the men were being persecuted for their anarchist political beliefs, the state of Massachusetts executed the two Italian immigrants in 1927.

Scopes Trial. Another notorious trial took place in 1925 when the state of Tennessee prosecuted John T. Scopes for teaching evolution. Although the prosecution won the case, the nation's newspapers generally presented the anti-evolution forces as ignorant, foolish, and attempting to stand in the way of intellectual progress.

Marcus Garvey. Among the African Americans moving to the northern cities, Marcus Garvey's Universal Negro Improvement Association with its promotion of black capitalism, separatism, and racial pride had considerable appeal. Before the Association went into decline in the mid-1920s, because of economic problems and legal actions against Garvey, the movement had gained over half a million members.

Economic Crash

When Herbert Hoover (1929–33) was elected president, it seemed that prosperity would last forever. But a few months later, on Thursday, October 24, 1929, the stock market fell sharply. Despite an influx of money from bankers, the market fell again the following Tuesday, October 29, ushering the nation into the "Great Depression." The market crash destroyed confidence in the economy, which had the following underlying weaknesses: (1) Income increases during the decade heavily favored the rich, with the result that workers were increasingly unable to purchase the products they were making. (2) Many corporations, especially in the utility and banking industries, had large debts and shaky organizational structures that were dependent upon continuing profits. (3) Stock market speculation had driven the prices of many stocks beyond any reasonable relationship to company profits, a situation encouraged by the policies of the Federal Reserve Board and the fact that significant amounts of stock purchases were facilitated by borrowed money. (4) Because America was more profitable, investors were putting less money into the European economy, with the result that Europe bought fewer American goods and began defaulting on debts acquired during World War I. (5) The American economy was overly dependent on a few major industries, while "sick industries" like family farming and coal faltered. These weaknesses, exacerbated by the Federal Reserve Board's decision to tighten the money supply, ultimately created the depression.

Hoover's Response

Pressure on Hoover. The depression quickly deepened. Between 1929 and 1932 over 5,500 banks collapsed, a situation exacerbated by the Federal Reserve's decision in 1929 to tighten the money supply. Meanwhile, unemployment increased, reaching a peak of one-quarter of all workers by 1933. Farmers also suffered, as prices dropped by 60% between 1929 and 1933. Not surprisingly, protest movements emerged.

Government Actions. Hoover encouraged private contributions for poor relief through the President's Organization on Unemployment Relief. The Federal Farm Board loaned money to cooperatives which could then purchase crops, thereby keeping them off the market. The federal government sponsored the National Credit Corporation that used private funds to assist banks. In 1931 Hoover declared a moratorium of European nations' World War I debts and reparations. The most important of Hoover's efforts, however, was the Reconstruction Finance Corporation (1932), which loaned money to banks, insurance companies, and railroads, which in turn loaned money to smaller companies. Unfortunately, none of these measures worked. Perhaps making things worse, Hoover supported the Hawley-Smoot Tariff (1930), which raised rates, and raised taxes through the Revenue Act (1932).

The First New Deal

Election of 1932. In the election of 1932, Governor Franklin D. Roosevelt of New York easily defeated Hoover.

Banking. Upon taking office on March 4, 1933, Roosevelt declared a bank holiday and called Congress into emergency session, the "Hundred Days." The Emergency Banking Relief Bill provided for the reopening of banks under Treasury Department oversight.

Agriculture. Roosevelt sought to aid agriculture through the Agricultural Adjustment Act (AAA), which paid farmers not to plant, thereby seeking to reverse overproduction, and the Farm Credit Act, which provided loans to farmers.

Unemployment. Addressing the issue of unemployment relief, Congress created the Civilian Conservation Corps (CCC) to employ young men in tree planting and building projects. The Federal Emergency Relief Act provided money to state and local governments to use in relief aid. And, most importantly, the National Industrial Recovery Act (NIRA) established the Public Works Administration (PWA), which oversaw the construction of such things as roads and public buildings, and the National Recovery Administration (NRA), which provided a structure for business to cooperate in limiting production and setting prices.

Labor Rights. Section 7(a) of the NIRA guaranteed the right of collective bargaining.

Monetary Policy. The Banking Act of 1933 established the Federal Deposit Insurance Corporation (FDIC), which insured bank deposits, and Roosevelt took the United States off the gold standard, bringing to fruition efforts that had been underway since the early 1920s.

TVA. Congress created the Tennessee Valley Authority (TVA), which through its dams and resulting power production and flood control applied economic planning to an entire region.

After the "Hundred Days." Further significant congressional actions included creation of the Commodity Credit Corporation (1933) to provide loans to farmers, and in 1934 the establishment of the Securities and Exchange Commission to regulate the stock market, the National Labor Relations Board to resolve labor disputes, and the Federal Housing Administration for building public housing. By 1936 unemployment had fallen by about one-quarter, while farm income and total manufacturing salaries and wages nearly doubled.

Opposition to the New Deal. Several important business leaders formed the American Liberty League in 1934, denouncing the New Deal for providing relief and thereby destroying individual initiative. Charles Coughlin, a Roman Catholic priest in Detroit, at first supported the New Deal in his radio sermons but then opposed the crop-limiting measures pursued by the AAA. In 1934 he organized the National Union for Social Justice, which became increasingly anti-Semitic. In California, Dr. Francis Townsend proposed the Old Age Revolving Pensions Plan in which all citizens over sixty would receive $200 a month on the condition that they would spend the money within the month they received it. Huey Long, a senator from Louisiana, proposed in 1934 a "Share Our Wealth Society," which through taxation would seize large incomes and inheritances and then distribute the money to American families. Long had presidential ambitions but was assassinated in 1935. The most serious criticism of the New Deal, however, came from the Supreme Court, which in 1935 struck down the NIRA and in 1936 the AAA.

The Second New Deal

Emphasis on Relief. The Emergency Relief Appropriation Act authorized large public works programs. Under this act the Works Progress Administration not only constructed highways and bridges but also brought plays and art to people throughout the country. Roosevelt also used the powers of this act to create the Resettlement Administration, Rural Electrification Administration, and the National Youth Administration. The National Labor Relations Act placed collective bargaining on a strong legal foundation. The Social Security Act established a system of old-age pensions and a system of unemployment insurance, a groundbreaking commitment by the government to social welfare. A revenue act raised taxes on the wealthy and "excess" corporate profits. Roosevelt easily won the ensuing election, establishing a coalition including labor, many farmers, and the South that would maintain the Democrats as the majority party into the 1960s.

"Court-Packing." Because the Supreme Court had overturned major elements of his program, Roosevelt sought to increase the number of justices with his own appointments. Criticized as "court-packing," this proposal failed in Congress. The Court may have received the message, however, for it began approving New Deal legislation such as the National Labor Relations Act.

Economic Downturn. Roosevelt, always committed to a balanced budget, began to limit public spending in 1937, about the same time that the Federal Reserve Board raised interest rates. The economy quickly took a downturn as unemployment increased by nearly 3 million over the next year. Roosevelt began deficit spending again, but it had little effect on unemployment.

The Depression and Society

Rural Areas. The AAA had the unintended result of encouraging landowners to shut down tenant farmers and sharecroppers and collect the money themselves for the crops that went unplanted. Between 1930 and 1940 the numbers of sharecropper farms dropped by nearly a third. On the southern Great Plains, drought parched the soil that was then stirred by winds into great dust storms. Over 350,000 farmers and their families gave up and migrated west to California, as chronicled by John Steinbeck in his novel *The Grapes of Wrath* (1939).

Labor. As the status of unionized labor improved significantly, the unskilled industrial unions within the AFL gained the most membership but felt neglected by the more powerful craft unions. Led by John L. Lewis of the United Mine Workers (UMW), the industrial unions formed the Committee for Industrial Organization (CIO). When in 1938 the AFL expelled the unions of the CIO, the latter reorganized as the Congress of Industrial Organizations. Already it had more members than the AFL and continued to grow through the remainder of the decade.

African Americans. In a notorious case, eight African Americans who were riding a freight train were arrested in 1931 near Scottsboro, Alabama, and—despite flimsy evidence—were later convicted for rape. Although Roosevelt frequently brought in African American advisors—the "Black Cabinet"—he never committed himself to the civil rights struggle because of his fear of losing white southern support. Once war in Europe began and defense jobs multiplied, A. Philip Randolph, president of the Brotherhood of Sleeping Car Porters, planned a march on Washington in 1941 demanding that defense industry jobs be equally available to blacks. As pressure mounted, Roosevelt issued Executive Order 8802 creating the Fair Employment Practices Committee. Randolph then called off the march.

Native Americans. The Indian Reorganization Act (1934) reestablished tribal ownership of lands and under John Collier the Bureau of Indian Affairs encouraged preservation of Native American cultures.

Women. During the 1930s the female work force increased by about one-third, but their jobs were largely confined to low-paying positions that had traditionally been identified as "women's work." Over 70 percent of working women were single, although the number of married working women increased during the 1930s. Women also gained more visibility in Washington, D.C., when Frances Perkins became the Secretary of Labor, the first female to hold a cabinet position.

Election of 1940

Foreign affairs was beginning to dominate the nation's concerns, and with war already under way in Europe, Roosevelt decided to run for an unprecedented third term in 1940. With the economy improving as a result of defense industry jobs and promising that he would not send American boys to fight foreign wars, Roosevelt defeated Republican Wendell Willkie.

5. ISOLATION AND WAR

Pursuing Peace

Their World War I experience soured Americans on military ventures. Peace groups such as the Women's Peace Union advocated alternatives to war; during the 1920s the United States government also sought peaceful approaches to international problems. Because the arms race was regarded both as an important cause of World War I and as economically destructive, at the Washington Conference (Nov. 1921–Feb. 1922), the United States Secretary of State Charles Evans Hughes proposed limits on the size of navies. Britain, the United States, Japan, France, and Italy agreed to reduce the size of their navies according to a ration that required the first three to destroy some of their ships. In 1928, the United States led in the development of the Kellogg-Briand Pact, ultimately signed by 62 nations, that renounced war as "an instrument of national policy."

The International Economy

World War I Debts. The United States came out of World War I a creditor nation to which Europeans owed about $13 billion. Partly because Americans were unwilling to forgive the debts as the Europeans requested, a complex relationship developed in which Germany borrowed money from the United States which it then used to pay its reparations to the Allied powers who in turn sent a portion of that money back to the United States. The Dawes Plan (1924) extended the payment period of Germany's reparations. But when American loans to Germany fell off in 1928 because of the financially more attractive domestic stock market, the whole system began to fall apart despite the effort of the Young Plan (1929) to fix the situation. By 1931, worsening economic conditions caused several nations to default on their loans. Hoover, bowing to the inevitable, declared a moratorium on further war debt payments.

Protective Tariffs. Despite the fact that it was the world's largest exporter, the United States increased its protective tariffs with the Fordney-McCumber Act (1922) and the Hawley-Smoot Act (1930).

After Franklin D. Roosevelt became president, Secretary of State Cordell Hull, who believed that revival of international trade was vital to combating the depression, tried to reverse this tariff policy. The Reciprocal Trade Agreements Act (1934) provided a framework for reducing tariff rates through agreements with individual nations. The Export-Import Bank (1934) also encouraged trade by making loans available for international purchase of American goods.

Latin America

American Intervention. American troops left the Dominican Republic in 1924 and Nicaragua the following year only to return to the latter in 1926, staying there until 1933. Haiti was occupied from 1913 to 1934, and American troops entered Honduras in 1924 to restore order. The United States also provided the backing for several dictatorships: Rafael Trujillo (Dominican Republic), Anastasio Somoza (Nicaragua), and Fulgencio Batista (Cuba). Between 1914 and 1929 both American investments and exports to Latin America tripled and American business controlled the national economies of such countries as Chile and Honduras. In Puerto Rico the Nationalist party called for the violent overturn of United States rule, engaging in armed conflict with the police in 1937. Mexico's adoption in 1917 of a new constitution that claimed national ownership of raw materials such as oil produced continuing diplomatic conflict with the United States. Then in 1938 Mexico nationalized foreign-owned petroleum companies, an action that Roosevelt ultimately accepted in 1942, after which the companies received compensation.

Good Neighbor Policy. Roosevelt attempted to pursue a nonmilitary relationship with Latin America which he called the "Good Neighbor" policy, announced in 1933. Significantly, in 1936 the United States adopted a policy of nonintervention at the Pan American Conference in Buenos Aires, an action that paved the way for the Declaration of Panama (1939) when Latin American countries declared their region off-limits to military aggressors.

Europe Moves Toward War

Outbreak of War. Adolf Hitler, who came to power in Germany in 1933, occupied the Rhineland in 1936, formed alliances with Italy and Japan, took over Czechoslovakia in 1938 and 1939, and invaded Poland on September 1, 1939. Only with the latter action did the other European nations respond militarily. With Britain and France declaring war on Germany on September 3, World War II was under way.

Neutrality Acts. Between 1935 and 1937 Congress passed a series of three Neutrality Acts, designed to prevent those things which it believed had led the United States into World War I: (1935) prohibition of arms shipments to nations at war once the president had determined a state of belligerency; (1936) prohibition of loans to belligerents; and (1937) belligerent nations could purchase with cash non-military items from the United States but must transport them in their own vessels, and prohibition of American passengers on ships of belligerent countries. After war began in Europe, Congress revised neutrality in the fall of 1939 to include cash-and-carry purchase of arms by belligerents.

Tensions in Asia

Japan launched its first step towards becoming an empire by invading Manchuria in 1931. In what became known as the "Stimson Doctrine," Secretary of State Henry L. Stimson declared that the United States would not recognize such seizures from China. In 1937 the Sino-Japanese War broke out but Roosevelt did not officially recognize a state of belligerency so that China could purchase weapons. When the Japanese sank the American gunboat *Panay,* Roosevelt demanded and received an apology but tensions continued. In 1939 the United States abrogated a trade treaty signed with Japan in 1911.

Movement Toward War

Aiding Britain. As France fell in mid-1940 and Great Britain seemingly stood at the brink of defeat, the president acted. In May 1940 the United States sold surplus military equipment to Britain and France. The following September, Roosevelt traded fifty American destroyers to Britain in exchange for naval bases. That same month Congress approved the Selective Training and Service Act, which introduced the first peacetime draft in American history. In March 1941, Roosevelt pushed through Congress the Lend-Lease Act, which enabled the United States to send arms to Britain. The following August, Roosevelt and Winston Churchill, Prime Minister of Great Britain, signed the Atlantic Charter agreeing to war aims. As an undeclared naval war broke out with Germany that fall, Congress further revised the neutrality policy to allow shipment of war materials to Britain in armed American merchant ships.

Tensions with Japan. While attention was focused on Europe, tensions with Japan increased. Roosevelt embargoed airplane fuel and scrap metal shipments to Japan in September 1940, after the latter signed the Tripartite Pact with German and Italy. He then froze Japanese assets in the United States after Japan invaded French Indochina in July 1941. Finally, in the early morning of December 7, 1941, Japanese bombers attacked the American naval base at Pearl Harbor, Hawaii. The following day Congress voted to declare war on Japan. On December 11 Germany and Italy in turn declared war on the United States. The war now spanned the globe.

The European Theater

Germany had invaded the Soviet Union in June 1941, which carried most of the burden of the European War for the next three years. Stalin argued for opening a second front on the European continent; Churchill, however, convinced Roosevelt that a joint American-British attack on North Africa would be better, an assault which took place in November 1942. Meanwhile, the Soviets were defeating the Germans in the bitter battle of Stalingrad (September 1942–January 1943). American and British forces then invaded Italy, in September 1943. Although the Italians surrendered that same month, Germans continued to defend the peninsula. On June 6, 1944, Allied forces invaded France at Normandy, pushing through to Paris by August. Despite a December counterattack by the Germans in Belgium's Aardennes Forest, the Allies crossed the Rhine on March 7. Soviet forces, meanwhile, moved eastward across Poland and met the American military at the Elbe River on April 25. Germany surrendered on May 8.

War Refugee Board

In January 1944 the United States established the War Refugee Board to attempt to save refugees scattered across German-occupied Europe from the hands of the Nazis and almost certain death. The board began its work after the Nazis had already systematically killed millions, mostly Jews, in concentration and extermination camps. The board's effectiveness, however, was hampered by a late start, limited resources, and bureaucratic conflicts among U.S. agencies. The board was formed after Treasury Secretary Henry Morgenthau, Jr., turned up damning evidence of State Department inaction which he shared with President Roosevelt.

The Pacific Theater

After Pearl Harbor Japan advanced in the Pacific, gaining control of Singapore in February 1942, and the Philippines in May. At the Battle of the Coral Sea, May 7–8, American forces stopped the Japanese move toward Australia and at Midway, June 3–6, sank four Japanese aircraft carriers in what would prove to be the turning point of the Pacific war. Developing a strategy of "island-hopping," American forces between 1942 and 1944 moved through the Pacific, eventually defeating the Japanese forces at the Battle of the Philippine Sea (June 19–20, 1944). Severe fighting took place at Iwo Jima (February-March 1945) and Okinawa (April-June 1945), which convinced American leaders that an attack on the Japanese homeland would cost many American lives. When Harry S. Truman, who had become president upon Roosevelt's death on April 12, 1945, learned in July that an atomic bomb had been tested, he approved its use to end the war. American planes dropped the new bomb on Hiroshima on August 6 and Nagasaki on August 9. Five days later Japan surrendered. World War II was over; the United States had lost 405,399 lives, a small percentage of the more than 40 million people killed worldwide.

The Home Front

Economy and Government. In January 1942 Roosevelt created the War Production Board, which supervised the conversion of the economy from civilian to military production. The War Manpower Commission (1942) assisted in this conversion by recruiting workers for those areas where labor was most needed. During the war years production of durable goods nearly tripled; large corporations such as General Motors received the bulk of the government contracts. The Army's Manhattan Project, charged with developing an atomic bomb, worked closely with universities. Because a revived economy might bring inflation, Roosevelt created the Office of Price Administration, which imposed price controls and rationed key commodities. With the number of manufacturing jobs increasing, unions also grew, nearly doubling in size between 1940 and 1945. The National War Labor Board (NWLB) sought to prevent labor-management conflicts. When strikes developed in 1943, especially in the coal industry, Congress passed the War Labor Disputes Act in June which authorized the president to seize plants closed by strikes and authorized the NWLB to settle labor disputes.

Racial Issues. Longstanding prejudice against Asians combined with security fears once war began with Japan led to the internment in 1942 of about 120,000 Japanese Americans. More than a million African Americans moved from the segregated South (the armed forces were segregated as well) to the North and West seeking defense jobs. As in World War I, tensions between blacks and whites mounted, especially in 1943 when forty-seven cities, including Detroit, experienced violent racial conflicts. An increasing Hispanic population, partly caused by the *bracero* program, which beginning in 1942 brought short-term workers from Mexico, also led to tensions that led to Los Angeles's "zoot-suit" riots of 1943.

Women. Some 6 million women entered the work force during the war, 2.5 million of them in manufacturing. Because this employment impacted families, the government provided some aid through the Lehman Act (1940), which aided communities experiencing large influxes of population. In addition to helping with sewers and hospitals, the act also provided for childcare and recreation centers. Marriages, divorces, and the birthrate all increased significantly.

Politics. In 1942 the Republicans increased their representation in the House and Senate. Seeking a fourth term in 1944, Roosevelt chose Harry S. Truman of Missouri as his vice-presidential candidate, for he could hold the support of the South, urban bosses, and political liberals. Roosevelt defeated Republican Thomas Dewey of New York, but his death in April brought the inexperienced Truman to the presidency.

Diplomacy

Churchill and Roosevelt agreed at the Casablanca Conference (1943) on a policy of "unconditional" surrender for all enemies. Later that year, at the Tehran conference Roosevelt called for development of a new international organization to replace the League of Nations. The following year, the Dumbarton Oaks conference developed a preliminary agreement for an organization that would have a Security Council which included five permanent members— United States, Great Britain, Soviet Union, France, and China—each of whom had veto power, and a relatively weak General Assembly. At Yalta (February 1945), the Allied powers decided to divide Germany into temporary zones of control. With the war in Europe over and Truman now president, the Potsdam conference (July 1945) brought the conflicting interests of the United States and the Soviet Union into the open.

6. THE COLD WAR

Emergence of Containment

Concern over Communism. The tensions between the Soviet Union and the United States erupted into the open during the next few years. First, in 1945 the Soviet Union kept conservatives out of the Communist government they instituted for Poland. Then they supported Communist control of Romania and Hungary (1947) and Czechoslovakia (1948). Soviet suspicions of American goals led to the U.S.S.R.'s refusal to participate in the Baruch Plan to establish an international agency for control of atomic energy and the World Bank and International Monetary Fund, established at the Bretton Woods Conference in 1944. In a speech at Fulton, Missouri, early in 1946 Winston Churchill graphically described an "iron curtain" descending between western and eastern Europe.

The Truman Doctrine. When Great Britain asked the United States for aid to defend the conservative government in Greece against a leftist insurgency, on March 12, 1947, Truman asked Congress for funds, stating that America must support free peoples anywhere who were resisting Communist takeover. This position became known as the "Truman Doctrine" and shaped American foreign policy for several decades. The State Department's George F. Kennan wrote an article calling for vigorous "containment" of Communism, thereby both developing the theory of the policy and giving it a name.

Marshall Plan. In June 1947, Secretary of State George C. Marshall announced a plan for the reconstruction of Europe that would be financed by the United States. Between 1948 and 1951 the Marshall Plan invested $12.4 billion in Europe, for the purpose of promoting prosperity that in turn would undermine the appeal of Communism.

National Security Act. Through the National Security Act (1948), Congress established the Department of Defense and the Central Intelligence Agency.

Berlin Airlift. After France, Britain, and the United States had combined their occupation zones into the Federal Republic of Germany (West Germany), the Soviet Union in June 1949, blockaded Western access to the jointly occupied city of Berlin, which lay within the Soviet zone. Truman ordered an airlift of supplies that continued until the Soviets lifted their blockade in May 1949; shortly thereafter the Soviets formed the German Democratic Republic (East Germany).

NATO. Meanwhile, in April the United States developed the North Atlantic Treaty Organization (NATO), involving most Western European nations, Canada, and the United States in a defensive alliance.

The Korean War

Outbreak of War. In China the conflict between the Nationalist government of Jiang Jieshi (Chiang Kai-shek) and Mao Zedong's Communists antedated World War II. The Chinese civil war ended when in 1949 Jiang took his forces to Formosa (Taiwan) and Mao announced the People's Republic of China. The Truman administration refused to recognize the new government. Then on June 25, 1950, North Korean troops moved south across the 38th parallel, which had been established after World War II as a temporary division of the country. The United States quickly obtained U.N. Security Council approval (the Soviet delegate had recently stormed out of the council in anger) of military action with General Douglas MacArthur as commander. Although at first the mostly American forces did poorly, MacArthur launched an invasion at Inchon on September 15 that soon pushed the North Koreans back across the 38th parallel.

China Enters War. After American soldiers moved deep into North Korea, on November 26 Chinese forces came across the border pushing the Americans back to the 38th parallel.

MacArthur and Truman. MacArthur publicly criticized Truman and called for an attack on China; Truman fired him in April 1951.

Armistice. Although armistice talks began in July 1951, the war continued until the Eisenhower administration took office and signed an agreement in July 1953, which established the boundary between North and South Korea near the 38th parallel. The United States had lost about 34,000 soldiers among the nearly 2 million people killed in the war.

The Eisenhower Administration

Soviet Union. The nuclear arms race did intensify as both the United States and the Soviet Union developed the hydrogen bomb, the Americans first detonating theirs in 1952 and the Soviets the following year. In 1957 the Soviets launched the first man-made satellite, *Sputnik,* into space. In response, the United States put both long-range (ICBM) and intermediate-range missiles in place and in 1958 formed the National Aeronautics and Space Administration (NASA). Despite disarmament talks, a summit meeting in 1955 between Eisenhower and the new Soviet leader Nikita Khrushchev and a suspension of atmospheric nuclear testing in 1958, tensions continued to mount. In 1955 the Soviets crushed a Hungarian revolt and three years later announced that East Germany would take control of all of Berlin unless the United States negotiated reunification. A summit meeting scheduled for Paris in 1960 to discuss these issues was scuttled when the Soviet Union shot down a CIA spy plane.

China. Conflict also built up between the United States and China, particularly over the islands of Jinmen (Quemoy) and Mazu (Matsu), which Jiang used as launching sites for raids against mainland China. After the Chinese fired on the islands in 1954, Congress passed the Formosa Resolution in 1955, authorizing the president to protect the islands with force. The issue of the islands continued to simmer, prompting China to produce its own atomic bomb in 1964.

Middle East. Largely because Gamal Abdul Nasser, president of Egypt, refused to side with the United States in the Cold War, the Eisenhower administration in 1956 withdrew financing from Egypt's Aswan Dam project. Nasser responded by nationalizing the Suez Canal, owned by Britain. On October 29 Israel attacked Egypt; Britain and France entered the war two days later. Eisenhower, who had not been consulted, demanded that the invaders withdraw, which they did, but Middle Eastern nationalism emerged the true victor. In 1957 Eisenhower announced that the United States would come to the aid of any Middle Eastern government threatened by a Communist takeover. Under this Eisenhower doctrine, in 1958 American forces invaded Lebanon to settle a governmental crisis.

The Kennedy Administration

Soviet Union. John F. Kennedy came to the presidency in 1961 as a thorough-going cold-warrior. The Soviet Union ended its moratorium on atmospheric nuclear testing in the fall of 1961 and the United States greatly increased the number of its nuclear weapons. The Limited Test Ban Treaty signed in 1963 banned all but underground nuclear testing but did little to curb the arms race. After Kennedy refused to negotiate the status of Berlin, the Soviet Union constructed a wall between East and West Berlin.

Cuba. Cuba was another source of conflict. In 1959 Fidel Castro had driven out the dictator Fulgencio Batista, establishing a revolutionary government that developed ties with the Soviet Union and—in response to the United States cutting its sugar purchases—nationalizing American companies. In April 1961, 1,400 Cuban exiles sponsored by the CIA invaded Cuba at the Bay of Pigs. Unfortunately for them, the people of Cuba did not rise in support of the invasion and Cuban forces shortly captured virtually all of the invaders. The United States continued to harass Cuba, including attempting to assassinate Castro.

Cuban Missile Crisis. These American threats led Cuba to rely more heavily on the Soviet Union, which began to install military weapons on the island. When an American spy plane brought back photographs of missile installations, Kennedy—after intense debate among his advisors—publicly demanded on October 22 that the Soviets remove the missiles, placed the American military on a global alert, and sent naval ships into the Caribbean to intercept Soviet military shipments. After exchanges of messages with the American president, Khruschev on October 28 announced that he would remove the missiles in return for Kennedy's pledge not to invade Cuba.

The Johnson Administration

Latin America. Lyndon B. Johnson continued the American tradition of intervention in Latin America when in 1965 he sent American troops to the Dominican Republic to prevent a leftist government from taking office. In the Johnson doctrine, he stated that the United States would keep Latin America free from future Communist governments.

Origins of the Vietnam War. In 1946 the Vietminh, under the leadership of Ho Chi Minh, a Communist, rebelled against French colonization of Vietnam. Beginning in 1950, first the Truman and then the Eisenhower administrations provided financial support to the French cause, primarily to gain French cooperation in NATO. In 1954, however, the French signed the Geneva Accords, which temporarily divided the country at the 17th parallel, giving the north to Ho Chi Minh and the south to Bao Dai, whom the French supported, with unification elections to take place in 1956. The United States, believing that Vietnam would go Communist, enabled Ngo Dinh Diem, a Catholic Vietnamese nationalist, to oust Bao Dai, supported Diem financially, and refused to allow the agreed-on elections. As Diem became increasingly authoritarian and corrupt, resistance developed within the south, with the Communists organizing the National Liberation Front (Vietcong). American military advisors had been in the country since the mid-1950s; with resistance to Diem building, Kennedy sent additional advisors, reaching more than 16,000 by 1963. Disillusioned with the South Vietnamese government, however, the United States supported a military coup that ended in Diem's death in November 1963.

Johnson's Escalation. After the *U.S.S. Maddox* was allegedly attacked by a North Vietnamese gunboat in August 1964, Congress approved the Gulf of Tonkin Resolution, which President Lyndon B. Johnson used to justify retaliating militarily. The president began a bombing program that extended into both neighboring Laos and North Vietnam. In July 1965, he began sending more ground troops to Vietnam, a number that would reach more than 500,000 by 1969. As the war dragged on with no apparent success, organized protests emerged in the United States, including 100,000 who marched on Washington in October 1967. When widespread Vietcong and North Vietnamese attacks took place during Tet, the Vietnamese new year (January 1968), penetrating even the American embassy in Saigon, political support for the war seriously eroded. Johnson announced on March 31 that he was halting the bombing, proposed negotiations to end the war, and dropped out of the presidential race. Although peace talks began in May, the war continued.

The Nixon Administration

Vietnamization. After Richard M. Nixon became president in 1969 he pursued a policy of "Vietnamization," which meant that the South Vietnamese— with financial help from the United States—increasingly bore responsibility for the war. Nixon gradually withdrew American troops and at the same time increased the bombing of the North.

Cambodia. After Nixon's decision in April 1970 to broaden the war by sending troops into Cambodia, protests erupted on college campuses, most significantly at Ohio's Kent State University, where the National Guard killed four individuals.

Pentagon Papers. In June 1971, the *New York Times* began publishing the *Pentagon Papers,* a secret government study leaked to the paper which revealed that American leaders had often misled Congress and the American people as they escalated the Vietnam War.

Cease-Fire. With the peace talks making no progress, Nixon ordered heavy bombing of the North in December 1972. Finally, the United States and the North Vietnamese signed a cease-fire on January 27, 1973, in which the U.S.

agreed to remove all troops within sixty days and that South Vietnam would form a coalition government which included the Vietcong.

Fall of South Vietnam. Soon after American troops pulled out, civil war broke out again and, despite American aid, the South Vietnamese government fell to the North on April 29, 1975. Overall, the United States had lost more than 58,000 soldiers and spent more than $150 billion on a war that failed in its objective of preserving the independence of a non-Communist South Vietnam, sharply divided the American people, and caused a host of diplomatic problems.

War Powers Resolution. Because Johnson had justified his prosecution of the war on the basis of the Gulf of Tonkin Resolution rather than a congressional declaration of war, Congress in 1973 had passed the War Powers Resolution, which stated that the president had to obtain congressional approval for committing American troops longer than sixty days. This action, it was hoped, would prevent future Vietnams.

Détente. While trying to find a way out of the Vietnam War, Nixon in 1972 made a surprise visit to China, which led to eventual diplomatic recognition of that country in 1979 and pushed the Soviet Union toward limited cooperation and acceptance of a balance of power with the United States. In 1972 the Soviet Union and the United States signed a trade agreement for American grain and a Strategic Arms Limitation Talks Treaty that placed limits on each nation's number of antiballistic missiles.

Middle East. The Cold War also affected the Middle East as the United States supported Israel and the Soviet Union supported the Arabs. In 1967 Israel's "Six-Day War" against Jordan, Egypt, and Syria resulted in Israeli possession of the West Bank, Jerusalem, the Golan Heights, and the Sinai peninsula. Syria and Egypt sought to recover their lost territories by attacking Israel in October 1973 (Yom Kippur War), which ended when Henry Kissinger arranged a cease-fire. Meanwhile, the Organization of Petroleum Exporting Countries (OPEC) placed an embargo on oil shipments to the United States that lasted until March 1974. Through his "shuttle diplomacy," Kissinger in 1975 arranged for a United Nations peacekeeping force to be placed in the Sinai.

Latin America. Nixon regarded the Marxist president of Chile, Salvador Allende, as a threat to the stability of Latin America. The CIA seems to have played a role in supporting the coup that resulted in Allende's death and the military dictatorship of Augusto Pinochet.

The Carter Administration

The Cold War Intensifies. President Jimmy Carter's administration negotiated the SALT II treaty, which established new limits on bombers and long-range missiles. When the Soviets invaded Afghanistan in 1979, however, Carter withdrew the treaty from the Senate, where it was already in trouble. Because of the invasion, Carter also stopped wheat shipments, boycotted the summer Olympics in Moscow, and provided covert assistance to the Afghani resistance.

Middle East. In 1978 Carter personally negotiated an agreement— the "Camp David Accords"—between Egypt and Israel, signed the following year, in which the latter agreed to withdraw from the Sinai. After the Soviet Union invaded Afghanistan, Carter in 1980 announced the "Carter Doctrine," pledging that the United States would intervene militarily against any Soviet aggression in the Persian Gulf region. But Iran became the most difficult problem after a radical cleric, Ayatollah Ruhollah Khomeini, in 1979 led the overthrow of the Shah, long backed by the United States. When the Shah entered the United States that same year for medical treatment, anti-American Iranians captured the American embassy, taking more than fifty hostages, and demanded the return of the Shah and his wealth. Carter refused to accede to the demands, froze Iranian assets in the United States, and in April 1980 broke off diplomatic relations. The hostages did not gain their freedom until after Carter left office.

Latin America. In 1977 the United States signed treaties with Panama in which it agreed to return the Canal Zone in 2000 but retained the right to defend the canal. When Nicaragua's Sandinistas overthrew Anastacio Samoza in 1979, Carter recognized the new government. Shortly before leaving office in 1981, however, he stopped American aid to Nicaragua because of increasing concerns over the radical direction of the Sandinistas.

The Reagan Administration

Anti-Communism. In addition to strengthening the military's weapon systems, Ronald Reagan proposed the Strategic Defense Initiative that would establish a space-based antimissile defense system. In what became known as the "Reagan Doctrine," he announced in 1985 that the United States would support "freedom fighters" against Communist regimes. Reagan reached an agreement in 1987 with the new Soviet leader Mikhail Gorbachev to ban all land-based intermediate-range missiles in Europe.

Latin America. Soon after taking office, Reagan provided aid to the government of El Salvador in its battle against leftist insurgents. Simultaneously, the United States began training counter-revolutionaries ("Contras") to overthrow the leftist Sandinista government in Nicaragua. In 1984, however, Congress voted to ban aid to the Contras but reversed the decision two years later. Meanwhile, the Reagan administration continued to help the Contras through "humanitarian" aid and a complex arrangement whereby arms were secretly sold to Iran and the profits sent to the Contras. In addition to these interventions, in 1983 Reagan sent troops into the Caribbean island of Grenada to overthrow a leftist government.

Middle East. After Israel invaded Lebanon, already suffering from civil war, to destroy Palestine Liberation Organization camps located there, Reagan in 1982 sent marines to be part of a peacekeeping mission. The following year a terrorist bombing killed 240 American soldiers; shortly thereafter Reagan removed the American forces. After the Palestinian uprising (Intifada) on the West Bank of the Jordan River began in 1988, the United States began to negotiate with PLO leader Yasser Arafat, but peace remained elusive.

Africa. Pressure built upon the Reagan administration to enact economic sanctions that would force South Africa to abandon its segregation policies known as "apartheid." After first attempting to convince the South African government to change its ways voluntarily ("constructive engagement"), in 1986 the administration adopted economic sanctions. Two years later, the administration negotiated the removal of Cuban troops from Angola and black majority rule for Namibia.

Collapse of Soviet Communism

During the 1980s internal economic and political pressures pushed Mikhail Gorbachev to attempt to reform the Soviet economy ("perestroika") and open up the political system ("glasnost"). These changes in the Soviet Union in turn set loose forces in Eastern Europe that the Soviets could no longer contain. In 1989 East Germany's Communist government fell and with it went the Berlin Wall, long a symbol of Cold War divisions. East and West Germany united the following year while around them Communist regimes fell throughout eastern Europe: Poland (1989), Hungary (1989), Czechoslovakia (1989), Romania (1989), Bulgaria (1990), and Albania (1990). Beginning with the breakaway of Lithuania in 1990, the Soviet Union soon disintegrated. After a failed coup by old-line Communists against Gorbachev in August revealed the weakness of the central state, most of the remaining republics declared their independence. The Soviet Union no longer existed; the Cold War was over.

Bush Foreign Policy

Russia. As the Cold War ended, President George H.W. Bush proclaimed a "New World Order." In 1991 the United States signed the START I treaty with Russia, followed in 1992 by START II, which reduced the nuclear arsenals of both nations.

Latin America. In 1989 American troops invaded Panama, overturning Manuel Noriega, who had established a dictatorship based largely on drug money. After Central American presidents in 1989 had arranged for free elections in Nicaragua, the United States supported the National Opposition Union which defeated the Sandinista Front at the polls in 1990. Two years later, El Salvador's civil war also ended through negotiations pushed by the United States.

NAFTA. In 1992 the United States, Canada, and Mexico signed the North American Free Trade Agreement (NAFTA), which proposed a largely tariff-free trading community. The Senate ratified the agreement in 1994.

Persian Gulf War. In the Middle East, when Iraq invaded oil-rich Kuwait in 1990, Bush organized an international coalition that began an air assault in January 1991, followed by ground forces about a month later that pushed the Iraqis from Kuwait in about four days. This "Persian Gulf War" ended in April when the United Nations Security Council approved a cease-fire.

Africa. In 1992 Bush sent American troops into Somalia to oversee distribution of humanitarian aid in the midst of public disorder; the following year a United Nations peace-keeping force took over the operation.

7. COLD WAR POLITICS AND SOCIETY

Postwar Economic Conversion

Demobilization. With World War II over, the defense industry declined and by March 1946 over 2.5 million people were unemployed. The rapid demobilization of the military from 12 million in 1945 to 3 million in 1947 also placed tremendous pressure on the economy. Some help came from the fact that Congress had passed the Readjustment Act (popularly called the "G. I. Bill of Rights") in 1944 which provided aid for veterans to attend college; more than one million former soldiers took advantage of the program in 1946.

Employment and Inflation. Congress passed the Employment Act of 1946 which established the Council of Economic Advisors and committed the government to achieving "maximum employment." As it turned out, however, inflation—which reached 18 percent in 1946 after the Office of Price Administration lifted price controls—proved to be the major problem, as consumers spent savings accumulated during the war years.

Labor Unrest. Workers, whose incomes often were less than during the war because they were working fewer hours, began striking in large numbers. In May 1946, a strike by the United Mine Workers led to a temporary government takeover of the coal mines and Truman threatened further such seizures.

The Eightieth Congress. Congress responded to the labor strife by passing—over Truman's veto—the Taft-Hartley Act (1947), which severely limited the power of unions by prohibiting the "closed shop," i.e., a workplace open only to union members. Congress also weakened price supports for agriculture and rejected legislation ranging from health insurance to the minimum wage, thereby alienating the voting public, which surprisingly returned Truman to the presidency in the election of 1948. Although Truman continued to push for his "Fair Deal," a coalition of congressional southern Democrats and Republicans prevented most of his proposals from becoming law.

Civil Rights

Responding to mounting racial tensions that developed as African American soldiers returned home, Truman appointed in 1946 a Presidential Committee on Civil Rights. The committee's published report, *To Secure These Rights,* called for federal laws against lynching and segregation, among other things, but Congress had no interest. Truman, however, used the power of the presidency to order the desegregation of the armed forces and "fair employment" in the federal civil service. Through suits brought by the NAACP, the Supreme Court began to chip away at segregation laws, most significantly banning whites-only primaries and segregation of interstate bus transportation.

Anti-Communism

Spurred by the Soviet Union's pressure on Eastern Europe and China's fall to Communism, America's long-standing fear of Communism emerged strongly in the 1940s and 1950s. Questions about the possible existence of spies within the government led Truman to order a loyalty investigation of United States government employees. In 1950 Alger Hiss, a former State Department officer, was convicted for lying to a grand jury when he denied passing classified documents to a Communist spy in the 1930s. Then a British court convicted Klaus Fuchs, a scientist who had worked on the atomic bomb project at Los Alamos, for passing nuclear secrets to Soviet agents. While these trials were in progress, Senator Joseph McCarthy in February 1950 announced that he had a list of Communists in the State Department, stirring a frenzied search for domestic Communists that would last until the Army-McCarthy hearings of 1954 which discredited the senator. Meanwhile, in 1950 Congress passed the Internal Security Act, which required members of "Communist-front" organizations to register with the government.

The Eisenhower Administration

Dynamic Conservatism. Republican Dwight D. Eisenhower, who had overseen the Allied invasion of Europe, easily defeated Democrat Adlai Stevenson in the 1952 presidential election. Advocating "Dynamic Conservatism," Eisenhower cautiously sought to change the New Deal legacy in some areas while building on it in others.

Agriculture. His administration attempted to wean agriculture from government price supports in favor of the free market in various farm bills enacted between 1954 and 1958 but with little success.

Native Americans. The Eisenhower administration also reversed the New Deal support for Native American reservations in favor of "termination," enacted by Congress in 1953, and an end to federal services.

Social Security and Public Works. Eisenhower expanded Social Security in 1954 and through the Housing Act of that same year funded the construction of homes for low-income families. The government also launched major public works projects with the approval in 1954 of the St. Lawrence Seaway, a canal linking Montreal and Lake Erie, and the Highway Act of 1956, which provided funds for construction of the Interstate Highway System.

Deficit Budgets. Although one of Eisenhower's goals during his presidency was to balance the federal budget, he was able to do so only three of the eight years he was in office.

Civil Rights

School Desegregation. In 1954 the NAACP won a major victory before the Supreme Court in *Brown v. Board of Education of Topeka*, which determined that racially segregated school facilities are inherently unequal. As resistance to the decision grew in the South, Eisenhower responded ambiguously. Events came to a head when Orval Faubus, governor of Arkansas, attempted in 1957 to block the integration of Little Rock High School. When violence threatened, Eisenhower nationalized the Arkansas National Guard and sent in paratroopers to protect the children. In turn, Little Rock closed its high schools in 1958 and 1959 rather than endure desegregation.

Montgomery Bus Boycott. While these events were taking place in Arkansas, African Americans were conducting a bus boycott in Montgomery, Alabama, sparked by Rosa Parks' refusal in 1955 to give up her seat to a white man. Baptist minister Martin Luther King, Jr., emerged as the leader of the boycott, which overcame resistance after the Supreme Court in 1957 declared Alabama's desegregation laws unconstitutional, and in 1957 King became president of the Southern Christian Leadership Conference (SCLC).

Civil Rights Act and Sit-Ins. Although Congress passed a Civil Rights Act in 1957, it proved ineffectual. In 1960 African Americans adopted a more aggressive tactic when students in North Carolina refused to leave a Woolworth's lunch counter, thereby beginning the sit-in movement that spread to other cities and resulted in the organization of the Student Nonviolent Coordinating Committee (SNCC).

The Affluent Society

Economic Growth. Beginning in 1945 the United States entered a 25-year period of steady economic growth averaging 3.5% annually. Per-capita real income grew 6% between 1945 and 1950, and an additional 15% in the 1950s and 32% in the 1960s. Part of the increase was fueled by a dramatically increased birthrate, the "baby boom," between 1946 and 1957, which impacted the construction and automobile industries. Military spending also helped produce the strong economy, standing at $10 billion in 1947 and over $50 billion in 1953.

Suburbs. With the growth of families and the availability of automobiles, suburbs grew rapidly, nearly equaling city population by 1960 and surpassing it ten years later. The government provided low-interest loans to veterans that produced a new housing boom. Much of the new population growth took place in the "Sunbelt," the area running from the southern Atlantic Coast through the south and southwest to southern California. Cities such as Atlanta, Houston, Phoenix, and San Diego became key economic centers.

Other Social Developments. Although families were growing bigger, women continued to work outside the home, their number increasing from 17 million in 1945 to 32 million in 1972. College enrollments, encouraged by the veterans' benefits and the loans offered by the National Defense Education Act, dramatically increased from 2.3 million in 1950 to 3.6 million in 1960 and nearly doubled again by 1970. Affluence also improved public health as infant mortality was improved by a third and in turn the life span increased from 67 years in 1946 to 71 years in 1970. Jonas Salk's polio vaccine, introduced in 1955, was perhaps the most dramatic public health breakthrough.

Entertainment. Having money to spend and increased leisure time, Americans searched for entertainment. Television, which had been invented prior to World War II, became common in the American home. The 8,000 televisions in 1946 increased to 46 million in 1960. Movie attendance dwindled from 60 million weekly in 1960 to 40 million ten years later, and radio lost its audience for soap operas and other dramas; both mediums responded by increasingly focusing on young people as a teenage subculture began to take form around "rock 'n' roll" music and nonconformist movie themes. This rebellion against conformity also expressed itself through the Beat movement, an underground cultural movement of jazz musicians, poets, and novelists. Works such as Allen Ginsberg's *Howl* (1956) and Jack Kerouac's *On the Road* prepared the way for the youth rebellion of the 1960s.

Poverty. As revealed by Michael Harrington's *The Other America* (1962), not all Americans participated in the post-war prosperity. Nearly one in four Americans in 1962 earned less than $4,000 a year for a family of four, the government's definition of "poor." African Americans living in the nation's inner city ghettoes, Mexican American migrant farm workers, Appalachian whites, Native Americans, and the elderly ineligible for Social Security were among the major groups making up this "other America."

The Kennedy Administration

Domestic Legislation. Senator John F. Kennedy narrowly defeated Vice President Richard M. Nixon. Although he was able to gain congressional approval for limited measures, such as increasing the minimum wage and expanding public housing, the conservative coalition of Republicans and southern Democrats blocked more expansive proposals, including a new Department of Urban Affairs and Medicare for the aged.

Civil Rights. As the Civil Rights movement gained momentum through actions such as the "Freedom Rides," in which integrated groups traveled by bus into the South, Kennedy gradually committed himself to the cause. In 1962 he ordered first federal marshals and then the National Guard to protect James Meredith, the first African American to enroll at the University of Mississippi. The following year Kennedy proposed legislation that would end segregation in public accommodations. In August 250,000 people marched in Washington in support of this law and listened to Martin Luther King give his "I Have a Dream" speech. Nonetheless, the bill languished in Congress. Violence also hit the civil rights movement that year, culminating in the September bombing of a Baptist Church in Birmingham in which four girls were killed.

Kennedy's Assassination. Two months later, on November 22, Kennedy himself fell to an assassin's bullet while beginning his reelection campaign in Dallas, Texas. No one would ever know the motives of the alleged killer, Lee Harvey Oswald, for he too was murdered two days later.

Lyndon Johnson and the "Great Society"

Kennedy's death brought Vice President Lyndon B. Johnson to the presidency. Johnson effectively drew on Kennedy's memory to push through Congress in 1964 the Civil Rights Act, which banned racial discrimination in both public accommodations and employment, and the Economic Opportunity Act, which provided nearly $1 billion to begin a "War on Poverty." After winning the presidency in his own right over conservative Republican Barry Goldwater in 1964, Johnson put forward his ambitious "Great Society" program. Large Democratic majorities in both houses of Congress enabled the administration in 1965 and 1966 to gain approval of a sweeping reform program, including Medicare, federal aid to education, voting rights, establishment of a Department of Housing and Urban Development, and a range of anti-poverty programs. The Vietnam War, however, eroded Johnson's political base and drew his attention away from domestic affairs during his last two years in office.

Black Activism

Black activists in Mississippi organized the Mississippi Freedom Democratic party that went to the Democratic convention in 1964 but could not gain Johnson's support to unseat the regular Mississippi delegation. In 1965 an African American riot erupted in Watts, a Los Angeles ghetto; over the next three years, similar riots took place in northern cities, including Newark, New Jersey, and Detroit, Michigan. The frustration expressed through these riots also appeared in the growing visibility of the Black Muslims and the Black Panther Party.

The Youth Revolt

The organization of Students for a Democratic Society (SDS) in 1962 and the Free Speech Movement at the University of California, Berkeley, in 1964 marked the beginning of youth activism. Fueled by concerns over racism, the Vietnam War, and American capitalism, a "New Left" of young activists emerged, although they were divided organizationally and ideologically. Other disaffected young people "dropped out" of mainstream society in favor of the "counterculture." The assassinations of Martin Luther King, Jr., and Robert Kennedy in 1968 further stirred the political alienation of the young. At the Democratic convention of that year, violence broke out in the streets of Chicago between police and youthful protestors.

Other Rights Movements

The Civil Rights movement and changing views among the young regarding sexual behavior provided an environment in which homosexuals could also claim rights, beginning with a riot against police harassment in 1969 in Greenwich Village in New York. The feminist movement, however, was more immediately visible, marked by the publication of Betty Friedan's *The Feminine Mystique* (1963) and the formation of the National Organization for Women (NOW) in 1966. Focusing on such issues as equality in both employment opportunities and pay, the feminist movement also won a major victory with the Supreme Court's ruling in *Roe v. Wade* (1973) legalizing abortion.

The Nixon Administration

Economic Problems. Republican Richard Nixon defeated Democrat Hubert Humphrey in the 1968 election. In the midst of continuing social and political instability, Nixon also faced high inflation, fueled by Johnson's effort to fund both social programs and the Vietnam War, and Nixon's own 1969 tax cut. In 1971–74 Nixon initiated wage and price controls in an effort to curb inflation.

Environment and Revenue Sharing. Democrats, who continued to dominate Congress, gained the president's approval of the Clean Air (1970) and Clean Water (1972) Acts. In 1972, Nixon began a program of "Revenue Sharing," whereby the federal government gave funds to the states to spend as they wished.

Watergate Scandal. During the presidential campaign of 1972, however, the Nixon forces engaged in illegal activities that came to light after a failed attempt to break into the Democratic headquarters at the Watergate apartment complex. Nixon's subsequent efforts to cover up these activities led to Congressional hearings, appointment of a special "Watergate" prosecutor, and finally an impeachment effort in the House that was cut short by Nixon's resignation on August 9, 1974. Gerald Ford, who had been appointed vice president after the resignation of Spiro T. Agnew in 1973, became president.

Economic Problems and the Ford Administration

The inflation spurred by domestic spending and the Vietnam War received another boost when the Organization of Petroleum Exporting countries (OPEC) established an oil embargo in 1973 that lasted for five months. Domestic oil prices more than tripled and the automobile industry went into decline. With inflation at 11% in 1974, Gerald Ford promoted a voluntary approach to energy use and inflation control with little effect. When the Federal Reserve Board raised interest rates, the worst recession since the 1930s hit the United States in 1975, with unemployment reaching over 8%. Complicating the economic situation, American productivity had been falling since the mid-1960s, reaching a low of 0.2% in the late 1970s.

The Carter Administration

Jimmy Carter, former governor of Georgia, defeated Gerald Ford by a small margin in the 1976 election. The new president established cabinet-level departments of education and energy, created a "superfund" for cleaning up chemical waste dumps, and deregulated the transportation industries. But inflation continued to ravage the economy, reaching 13% by 1979, while unemployment stood at more than 7%. Economic troubles, stalemate over Americans being held hostage in Iran, and the decline in presidential power resulting from the Watergate scandal led to Carter's defeat in 1980 by Ronald Reagan, former governor of California.

The Reagan Administration and the Economy

Ronald Reagan, a movie actor who had come to political notice during the 1964 Goldwater campaign, helped bring together the anti-Communist, anti-New Deal, and social conservatives—among them pro-life activists and evangelical Christians—into a new conservative coalition. Once in office, Reagan quickly obtained the Budget Reconciliation Act (1981), which cut $39 billion from social programs such as food stamps and public housing, and, in 1983, a 25% tax cut spread over three years. As the Federal Reserve Board lowered interest rates, inflation fell below 7 percent in 1982. Recession continued, however; by 1982 unemployment moved above 10%. Annual budget deficits more than tripled during Reagan's first presidential term. The combination of lower inflation, interest rates, and taxes began taking effect, however; by 1984 unemployment had fallen to 8%. The Tax Reform Act of 1986 lowered tax rates again, this time abandoning the policy of progressive taxation—the higher the income, the higher the percentage taken in taxes—in favor of two tax rates. By 1986 inflation had fallen to near 2% and unemployment to about 6%.

Social Issues

Affirmative Action. Caucasians had complained ever since the 1960s that "affirmative action" programs, which sought to increase African American representation in higher education and the workplace, resulted in "reverse discrimination." In *Bakke v. University of California* (1978), the Supreme Court overturned the use of quotas to achieve racial balance and in subsequent decisions further weakened the legal viability of affirmative action.

Feminism. Although Reagan appointed the first woman justice of the Supreme Court, Sandra Day O'Connor, his administration generally opposed feminist goals. The Equal Rights Amendment, approved by Congress in 1972, fell three states short when the ratification deadline of 1983 arrived.

Immigration. More than 9 million immigrants came into the United States during the 1980s, double the number who had arrived during the previous decade. Latin America provided the bulk of these immigrants, but others came from southeast Asia and the Caribbean. The Immigration Reform and Control Act (1986) placed sanctions on employers who hired undocumented workers but did little to slow illegal immigration from Mexico.

AIDS. Beginning in 1981 Acquired Immune Deficiency Syndrome (AIDS) appeared and spread rapidly among intravenous drug users and male homosexuals. By 1988 about 57,000 cases had been reported, over half of which had ended in death.

The Bush Administration

Election of 1988. In 1988 Vice President George H.W. Bush defeated Democrat Michael Dukakis by maintaining Reagan's coalition of white Southerners, the Western states, and sufficient numbers of "Reagan Democrats" who enabled him to win northern industrial states.

The Economy. With deficits continuing to mount, Bush negotiated an agreement with Congress in 1990 raising taxes and cutting Medicare and other domestic programs. Meanwhile, the economy fell into recession; in 1991 unemployment reached 6.8% and median household income fell by 3.5%. It was generally believed that Bush did little to address the recession.

Savings and Loan Crisis. The savings and loan industry reached a crisis in 1989, largely because of bad real estate loans, which resulted in the sale or closure of 350 institutions and a government bailout.

Disabilities Act. Bush supported the Americans with Disabilities Act (1990), which forbade discrimination because of physical impairments or disease.

Rodney King Affair. In March 1991, following an automobile chase, police in Los Angeles were caught on videotape violently beating an African American driver named Rodney King. After an all-white jury acquitted the police officers in April 1992, a violent riot broke out in South Central Los Angeles that lasted for three days. After 51 people were killed and more than $750 million in property destroyed, the Bush administration provided emergency aid.

8. THE POST–COLD WAR PERIOD

BILL CLINTON AND THE 1990s

Election of 1992

Although George H.W. Bush had gained high approval ratings during the Persian Gulf War, the economic problems at home made him vulnerable by the time the presidential campaign of 1992 began. To make matters worse, a Texan billionaire, H. Ross Perot, ran as a third-party candidate who claimed that he could bring his business expertise to government. Bill Clinton, governor of Arkansas, ran as a "New Democrat," who would take a more centrist approach to political issues than the liberals who had dominated the party since the 1960s. Perot, who gained 19% of the vote, may have made the difference in the race, as Clinton defeated Bush 43.2% to 37.7%.

Domestic Issues

Gays in the Military. After controversy following his January 1993 announcement that he was suspending the ban on gays in the military, Clinton negotiated an agreement with Congress in which the military would not ask questions about sexual orientation and servicemen and women would not volunteer such information. Homosexual acts by service personnel also would be prohibited.

Health Care. Though Clinton's proposal for universal health care coverage was defeated, some of its elements were made law. Health insurance for children was subsidized under CHIP (Children's Health Insurance Program).

Family and Medical Leave Act. Passed in 1993, the Family and Medical Leave Act required most employers who had fifty or more workers to provide up to twelve weeks of unpaid leave for family emergencies, such as the birth or adoption of a child, or the illness of an immediate family member. Employers were also required to continue providing health insurance to the employee during the leave of absence.

The Deficit. In 1993 Clinton proposed an economic plan to Congress to address the mounting federal deficit through a combination of increased taxes, raising the top rate from 31% to 36%, and reducing federal jobs and other government spending. A highly partisan debate ensued, but Clinton's main proposals passed by a narrow margin.

Anti-crime Legislation. Despite strong lobbying by the National Rifle Association (NRA), Congress passed in 1993 the Brady Handgun Violence Prevention Act, which required a five-day waiting period before anyone could purchase a handgun, during which a background check for criminal convictions would be made. The bill also provided funds to develop a computerized system that when completed would make the background checks nearly instantaneous. In 1994 Congress adopted a crime bill proposed by Clinton that provided over $8 billion for the hiring of 100,000 new police officers and the building of new prisons. It also banned nineteen types of assault weapons.

1994 Congressional Elections. Accusations that the Clintons had been involved in a questionable Arkansas land deal—"Whitewater"— led Congress to appoint a special prosecutor. Also, rumors emerged that Clinton had made improper sexual advances on women while governor. These suggestions of scandal together with the debate over gays in the military and the health care proposals enabled Republicans to gain control of both houses of Congress in the 1994 elections. Led by Congressman Newt Gingrich, they had signed a ten-point "Contract with America" that promised a smaller, more efficient government.

Welfare Reform. Proposed by Republicans and modified through negotiation by Clinton, the Welfare Reform Act (1996) replaced the federal welfare program with block grants to the states that were given the responsibility to design their own programs. The bill also required that the heads of all families receiving assistance must obtain employment within two years or lose their benefits.

Election of 1996. Through skillful maneuvering and a prospering economy, Clinton was able to rebuild his popularity and defeated Republican Senator Robert Dole. Republicans, however, maintained control over the House and the Senate.

Impeachment. Early in 1998 Clinton was accused of having a sexual relationship with Monica Lewinsky, a White House intern. After Clinton denied the charges under oath, the Whitewater prosecutor, Kenneth Starr, recommended that he be impeached and sent a lengthy report to the House of Representatives. Although the House eventually voted impeachment on grounds of perjury and obstruction of justice, the Senate voted against conviction. In the aftermath of this failure, Speaker of the House Newt Gingrich resigned.

The Economy

The Computer. Between 1946 and the mid-1970s mainframe computers became increasingly common as businesses used them to track records such as payroll and billing. The development of microprocessors then made possible the invention of the small personal computer, which over the next two decades replaced the mainframe for business work and came into common use among the American public. The development of the Internet, which originated with the Department of Defense in the 1960s, and the Worldwide Web, which enabled users to easily access the Internet, created a global communication medium. These technological developments brought into existence entirely new industries and opened the possibility of new ways of conducting business.

Prosperity. The economy was growing at an annual rate of 4% by 2000. At the same time, unemployment dropped to 4.7%. Both productivity and inflation hovered around 2%. Nearly half of the new industrial growth came from the information revolution introduced by the personal computer. The value of the stock market quadrupled between 1992 and 1998, much of the growth coming from the fact that 37% of American households in 1997—as compared to 6% in 1980—owned stocks and bonds, mostly through retirement accounts encouraged by tax law changes. Prosperity also brought the federal government a $70 billion surplus for the 1998 fiscal year and projections of further surpluses.

American Society

School Shootings and Popular Culture. Several school shooting incidents in 1998–99, especially in Littleton, Colorado, where two students killed twelve classmates and a teacher, further stirred an already existing debate over the values propagated by popular culture.

Racial Tensions. The acquittal in 1995 of former football star O. J. Simpson of charges of murdering his former wife and a male friend revealed America's racial divide; most African Americans believed that the Los Angeles police department had framed Simpson while most whites thought that he was guilty. Affirmative action continued to be an issue as well. In 1996 California approved a law banning preferences based on sex or race in state college admissions or state government contracts and employment.

The Branch Davidians. Concerned that a religious group known as the Branch Davidians was stockpiling weapons, the Bureau of Alcohol, Tobacco, and Firearms raided their compound near Waco, Texas, on February 28, 1993. After a battle in which four government agents were killed, the Federal Bureau of Investigation (FBI) took over the operation, which turned into a 51-day siege. On April 19 armored vehicles attacked the main building, which soon began burning, resulting in the death of 86 persons including Branch Davidian leader David Koresh.

Domestic Terrorism. Two years after the Waco incident, a bomb blast on April 19, 1995, destroyed the Alfred P. Murrah Federal Building in Oklahoma City, killing 168 people. Subsequently, investigators discovered that the perpetrator was a Persian Gulf veteran, Timothy McVeigh, who held the United States government responsible for the Branch Davidian disaster. The bombing brought to public attention the increasing number of right-wing militia groups, many of them advocating conspiracy theories which portrayed the government as a threat to individual rights.

Foreign Policy

Africa. Inheriting the presence of American troops in Somalia, Clinton expanded their mission from humanitarian aid to combating the warring clans. After soldiers were killed in October 1993, Clinton withdrew American forces, which were replaced by United Nations peacekeepers.

Haiti. After a military coup had overthrown Jean-Bertrand Aristide, the elected president of Haiti, Clinton applied diplomatic pressure to restore Aristide. Not until he threatened the use of military force, however, did the junta give up power.

Free Trade. Clinton supported NAFTA, negotiated by the Bush administration, which the Senate ratified in 1994. That same year Congress also approved the General Agreement on Tariffs and Trade (GATT), involving 117 nations who agreed to cut or eliminate many tariffs. GATT also established the World Trade Organization (WTO) to resolve trade disputes among nations.

The Balkans. Following declarations of independence by Slovenia, Croatia, and Bosnia-Herzegovina in 1991, Yugoslavian President Slobodan Milosevic attacked Croats and Muslims living in areas largely populated by Serbs. NATO airplanes entered the conflict in 1994 against Milosevic forcing a peace agreement between Bosnia, Croatia, and Serbia the following year. Clinton then committed American troops as part of a multinational peacekeeping force. Milosevic then attacked Kosovo, where ethnic Albanians were seeking independence. After Serbia refused to sign a peace agreement with the Kosovars, in 1969 NATO intervened militarily, forcing Milosevic to withdraw his forces.

Iraq. Problems with Saddam Hussein continued after the Persian Gulf War. In 1994 Clinton sent American troops to the Gulf when it appeared that Hussein might threaten Kuwait. In 1996 the United States launched air strikes against Iraqi missile sites when Hussein increased military operations against rebels in northern Iraq. After Hussein refused to cooperate with United Nations weapons inspectors, the United States and Great Britain bombarded Iraq in December 1998, but had little effect on the Iraqi leader's actions.

Terrorism. In 1993 Muslim terrorists bombed the World Trade Center in New York City, killing five people and injuring over a thousand. Terrorists also hit an American military barracks in Saudi Arabia in 1996, American embassies in Kenya and Tanzania in 1998, and the *U.S.S. Cole* while refueling in Yemen. American leaders believed that Osama bin Laden, a radical Saudi millionaire, was ultimately responsible for these attacks.

A NEW CENTURY BEGINS

The Election of 2000

The Democrats nominated Albert Gore, Clinton's Vice President, while the Republicans nominated George W. Bush, son of the former president and governor of Texas. A third-party candidate, Ralph Nader of the Green Party, became increasingly important during the campaign, for his candidacy threatened to siphon off liberal voters in key states. Although Gore held the lead in the popular vote, Florida provided the electoral votes that would determine the winner. Because of recounts, however, the final tally was not certified until November 27 when Bush was declared the winner. Gore then contested the Florida count until the Supreme Court on December 12 ruled 5 to 4 against another recount.

Tax Cut

In April 2001, Congress approved a tax cut of $1.2 trillion spread over ten years. This was slightly smaller than the cut proposed by George W. Bush.

Islamic Terrorism Strikes the United States

On September 11, 2001, Muslim terrorists hijacked four passenger airliners, flying two of them into the World Trade Center in New York, killing nearly 3,000 people, and a third one into the Pentagon in Washington, D. C. A fourth airliner crashed in a Pennsylvania field, apparently after passengers took action against the hijackers.

War on Terrorism. President Bush quickly proclaimed a "war against terrorism." After developing an international coalition, including support from Pakistan, on October 7 the United States began military action against the Taliban government in Afghanistan, which had provided a haven for Osama bin Laden's Al Queda terrorist network. The Taliban fell in November and in the following month an interim government, supported by the international coalition, took power. The hunt for bin Laden and his terrorists continued, however, and political stability in Afghanistan was an open question.

National Defense Efforts

Also in the fall of 2001, Congress overwhelmingly passed the USA PATRIOT Act to expand the powers of the federal government in regards to monitoring suspected terrorist activities. The act greatly expanded government powers to allow eavesdropping on personal telephone or electronic communications, the monitoring of financial transactions, and the enforcement of stricter regulations on domestic and international travel, among other provisions. The act quickly came under fire as civil liberties watchdogs asserted that it infringed on Fourth Amendment rights against unreasonable search and seizure and that it granted too much unsupervised power to federal law enforcement agencies. Nevertheless the law withstood challenges in the U.S. Supreme Court and won congressional reauthorization in 2006 and 2011.

Along with the USA PATRIOT Act, President Bush sought to strengthen U.S. national security through the creation of the Department of Homeland Security. This department brought together under one umbrella existing federal agencies, including the U.S. Customs and Border Patrol, the Transportation

Security Administration (TSA), and the Federal Emergency Management Agency (FEMA).

Wars in Afghanistan and Iraq

The 2001 terrorist attacks also led the United States into two major foreign wars. The first began in Afghanistan in October 2001 as U.S. and British forces worked with Afghan allies to topple the fundamentalist Taliban government, which had permitted al-Qaeda to use the nation as its base of operations. Although the Taliban was quickly removed from formal governance, the war stretched on for several years as U.S. troops continued to fight the remnants of the Taliban and as new leaders sought to establish a stable democratic government. In 2009, a new administration supported a troop surge aimed at ending the insurgency; plans were also announced to fully withdraw U.S. troops and turn over the handling of the war to Afghan security forces by 2014. The war was hard-fought and marked by heavy civilian casualties. One major success in the conflict came in May 2011 when U.S. Special Forces successfully attacked Osama bin Laden's secret compound in nearby Abbottabad, Pakistan, killing the terrorist leader.

In 2003, U.S. troops also invaded the Middle Eastern nation of Iraq, ostensibly in retaliation for that nation's construction of weapons of mass destruction (WMDs). Later reports, however, confirmed that no such weapons had ever existed. By the end of the year, U.S. troops had captured Iraqi dictator Saddam Hussein, who was executed by Iraqi authorities in 2006. The war continued until 2011, though, as U.S. troops sought to establish a friendly democratic government and rebuild the war-torn nation. As time went on, the war—and the Bush administration that supported it—became increasingly unpopular at home, and a new administration oversaw the removal of the last U.S. troops from Iraq in December 2011.

DOMESTIC AFFAIRS

Hurricane Katrina

The most severe natural disaster to affect the United States in many years, Hurricane Katrina devastated the Louisiana and Mississippi coastlines in the fall of 2005. The storm flooded much of the city of New Orleans, forcing residents to evacuate or to take shelter in temporary emergency sites. Federal emergency response to the damage caused by the storm was slow, and both President George W. Bush and FEMA were strongly criticized for the handling of the response efforts. The hurricane resulted in approximately $80 billion in damage and caused the population of New Orleans to drop from approximately 445,000 in 2004 to just over 212,000 in 2006.

The Housing Bubble and Financial Crisis

Throughout much of the early 2000s, housing prices nationwide experienced strong growth fueled by low-cost, easily granted subprime mortgages. Housing prices grew at an average of more than five percent per year between 2000 and 2006, peaking at approximately 12 percent in 2005. This explosive growth was later determined to be a real estate bubble; home prices began to plummet in 2007, leaving many homeowners with mortgages in excess of their homes' values and dramatically raising the numbers of home foreclosures. Federal tax credits in 2010 helped spur home sales somewhat, but the market remained generally sluggish for years after the housing crash.

The decline of the housing market carried severe consequences for the larger financial industry. A complex network of mortgage-related securities and insurance products had contributed to huge banking profits for several years, but these financial instruments went on to create great losses for major banks as the housing stock that backed them lost value. In the fall of 2008, President Bush signed into law the Troubled Asset Relief Program (TARP), a series of measures designed to prevent the collapse of the U.S. banking system, including authorization for the U.S. government to purchase up to $700 billion in faltering mortgage-based and other assets from U.S. banks. Although the program did protect several banks from collapse, it failed to revive the stumbling U.S. credit market, and consumers faced ongoing problems getting mortgages and other loans.

The Election of 2008

The presidential election of 2008 saw a number of historic firsts. The Republican Party nominated its first female vice-presidential candidate, Alaska Governor Sarah Palin, and the Democratic Party nominated the first major party African American candidate, Barack Obama, who became the first African American U.S. president.

Rise of the Tea Party

Shortly after President Obama's inauguration, a conservative political move-ment known as the Tea Party arose to counter federal government efforts to stimulate the economy through large spending programs and support of flag-ging banks and auto companies. The movement generally called for a smaller, less powerful federal government and so attracted a mixture of small-govern-ment supporters, former Republicans, and individuals who believed Obama to have been born outside of the United States, to be secretly Muslim, or to be a left-wing radical despite all evidence to the contrary. Tea Party-supported candidates largely set the tone of the 2010 midterm elections, and the over-all Republican Party became somewhat more conservative in response to this populist movement.

Health Care Reform

President Obama and the Democratic Congress dedicated much of 2009 to the creation and passage of a major health care reform law—the Patient Protec-tion and Affordable Care Act. Popularly called Obamacare, the controversial law required health care companies to offer coverage to all applicants, to charge women and men the same premiums, and to allow young people to remain on their parents' insurance plans until age 26, among other provisions. The act also required businesses with more than 40 employees to offer health insurance coverage to their staff and mandated that most individuals purchase health care coverage or pay a tax. The law was strongly opposed by Republicans and the Tea Party movement, who believed it to be an excessive intrusion by the federal government into business and personal affairs, and it faced numerous political challenges even after the U.S. Supreme Court upheld nearly all of its provisions in 2012.

The Arab Spring

During the spring of 2011, pro-democracy movements swept through parts of North Africa and the Middle East. These popular uprisings led to regime changes in nations including Yemen, Egypt, and Libya, where U.S. air forces supported rebels seeking to overthrow long-time dictator Muammar al-Qaddafi. It was not immediately apparent whether the new governments in these nations would be more or less friendly to U.S. interests than their predecessors. Unrest spread to Syria by late 2011, opening the possibility of U.S. intervention in that region.

Immigration

What was perceived as a mounting problem of illegal immigration remained a contentious national issue throughout the 2000s. In 2010, the U.S. Census Bureau calculated the foreign-born population at approximately 13 percent of the overall population, with slightly more than half of those individuals originating in Latin America and the Caribbean, particularly Mexico. Estimates placed the number of undocumented immigrants at approximately 11 million in 2010, with illegal immigration tapering slightly due to a U.S. recession. Politicians on both sides of the spectrum proposed numerous reforms to address the issue of illegal immigration, including increased border security, stricter enforcement of existing laws, and the construction of a large border fence between the United States and Mexico. In Arizona, a controversial state law permitted law enforcement officers to check the citizenship papers of anyone that they believed to be an undocumented immigrant for any reason.

One measure supported by the Obama administration was the Dream Act, a proposed law that would allow undocumented young people brought to the United States as children to pursue a path to citizenship upon completion of a college degree or a stint of military service. Although the act failed to garner sufficient congressional support to achieve passage, the administration issued an executive order deferring deportation of such young people for at least two years.

Spread of New Technology

Mobile and wireless technology improved greatly during the early twenty-first century, with more and more Americans connected to the Internet not only through personal computers but also through tablets and smartphones. In 1997, less than 20 percent of all U.S. households had access to the Internet at home; by 2009, that figure had grown to nearly 70 percent.

By 2011, an estimated 83 percent of all Americans owned a cell phone, and about 35 percent owned a smartphone capable of connecting to the Internet. Text messaging, photo taking, and posting to popular social network websites such as Facebook were common uses of smartphone technology. At the same time, reliance on traditional landline communication decreased, with one-quarter of all U.S. households relying exclusively on mobile phones.

The Election of 2012

Economic concerns, particularly issues of job growth and federal spending, were at the heart of the presidential race between the incumbent, Democrat Barack Obama, and Republican challenger Mitt Romney, a former governor of Massachusetts. Foreign affairs played a smaller role, although a September 2012 terrorist attack on the U.S. Embassy in Benghazi, Libya, generated national discussion about the role of U.S. military strength in the world. When voters went to the polls in November, they ultimately put their faith in Obama to continue leading the nation.

Citizens United v. Federal Election Commission

The election was the first presidential campaign to show the effects of the 2010 U.S. Supreme Court decision in *Citizens United v. Federal Election Commission*, which overturned existing campaign finance laws to allow corporations and unions to spend unlimited amounts of money on political campaigning. Individuals, corporations, unions, and special interest groups spent more than one billion dollars on the presidential race alone. The decision also allowed for the creation of a new political body known as the super PAC, or super political action committee, which could accept and spend unlimited money from any source without disclosing its sources of revenue. However, like traditional political actions committees, super PACs were legally barred from directly coordinating their efforts with specific political campaigns. Still, in practice, most super PACs promoted similar messages to those of mainstream party committees.

PRACTICE TEST 1

CLEP History of the United States II: 1865 to the Present

Also available at the REA Study Center (*www.rea.com/studycenter*)

This practice exam is also available at the REA Study Center. To closely simulate your test-day experience with the computer-based CLEP exam, we suggest that you take the online version of the practice test. When you do, you'll also enjoy these benefits:

- **Timed testing conditions** – helps you gauge how much time you can spend on each question
- **Automatic scoring** – find out how you did on the test, instantly
- **On-screen detailed explanations of answers** – gives you the correct answer and explains why the other answer choices are wrong
- **Diagnostic score reports** – pinpoint where you're strongest and where you need to focus your study

PRACTICE TEST 1

CLEP History of the United States II: 1865 to the Present

(Answer sheets appear in the back of the book.)

TIME: 90 Minutes
120 Questions

DIRECTIONS: Each of the questions or incomplete statements below is followed by five possible answers or completions. Select the best choice in each case and fill in the corresponding oval on the answer sheet.

1. Place the following in the correct chronological order, from the earliest event to the most recent.

    I. *Brown v. Board of Education*
    II. Voting Rights Act
    III. Greensboro sit-In
    IV. *Plessy v. Ferguson*

    (A) I, II, III, IV
    (B) IV, I, III, II
    (C) II, III, IV, I
    (D) III, IV, II, I
    (E) III, II, I, IV

2. At the time President George H. W. Bush spoke of building "a new world order" in 1990–91, the most significant international situation confronting him was

    (A) the outbreak of civil war throughout the Balkans and the Caucasus
    (B) Afghanistan's harboring of terrorists
    (C) the rapid disintegration of Soviet control over Eastern Europe
    (D) the conflict between Israel and Egypt
    (E) the Chinese takeover of Hong Kong

3. Which of the following best characterizes the methods of Martin Luther King, Jr.?

   (A) Nonviolent defiance of segregation
   (B) Armed violence against police enforcing segregation laws
   (C) Patience while developing the skills that would make blacks economically successful and gain them the respect of whites
   (D) A series of petitions to Congress calling for correction of racial abuses
   (E) Call for reparations to reimburse African Americans for slavery

4. Which of the following best describes the agreement that ended the 1962 Cuban Missile Crisis?

   (A) The Soviet Union agreed not to station troops in Cuba, and the United States agreed not to invade Cuba.
   (B) The Soviet Union agreed to withdraw its missiles from Cuba, and the United States agreed not to invade Cuba.
   (C) The Soviet Union agreed not to invade Turkey, and the United States agreed not to invade Cuba.
   (D) The Soviet Union agreed to withdraw its missiles from Cuba, and the United States agreed not to invade Turkey.
   (E) The Soviet Union agreed to withdraw its missiles from Cuba, and the United States agreed to withdraw its missiles from Western Europe.

5. The "new immigrants" coming to America from Eastern and Southern Europe during the late nineteenth century were most likely to

   (A) settle in large cities in the Northeast or Midwest
   (B) settle on farms in the upper Midwest
   (C) seek to file on homesteads on the Great Plains
   (D) migrate to the South and Southwest
   (E) return to their homelands after only a brief stay in the U.S.

6. Which of the following had the greatest effect in moving the United States toward participation in World War I?

   (A) The German disregard of treaty obligations in violating Belgian neutrality
   (B) Germany's declaration in 1917 of its intent to wage unrestricted submarine warfare
   (C) A German offer in 1917 to reward Mexico with U.S. territory should it join Germany in a war against the United States
   (D) The beginning of the Russian Revolution in 1917
   (E) The rapidly deteriorating situation for the Allies

7. The main idea of Theodore Roosevelt's proposed "New Nationalism" was to

   (A) make the federal government an instrument of domestic reform by regulating big business
   (B) develop an American colonial empire
   (C) increase economic competition by breaking up all trusts and large business combinations
   (D) establish government ownership of basic industries such as coal, steel, and railroads
   (E) take an isolationist position in foreign policy that largely ignored international affairs

8. Franklin D. Roosevelt's New Deal program contained all of the following EXCEPT

   (A) the attempt to raise farm prices by paying farmers not to plant certain crops
   (B) the attempt to encourage cooperation within industries to control production so as to raise prices generally
   (C) support for the creation of the Reconstruction Finance Corporation
   (D) effectively eliminating the gold standard as it had previously existed
   (E) the attempt to restore confidence in the banking system by establishing government regulation

9. The Haymarket Affair of 1886 involved

   (A) a riot between striking workers and police
   (B) a scandal involving corruption within the Grant administration
   (C) allegations of corruption on the part of Republican presidential candidate James G. Blaine
   (D) a disastrous factory fire that killed 146 workers, mostly young women
   (E) an early challenge to the authority of states to regulate the railroad industry

10. Which of the following was a goal of the Populist movement?

   (A) Free coinage of silver
   (B) Reform of child labor laws
   (C) Using modern science to solve social problems
   (D) Eliminating the electoral college as a method of choosing the nation's president
   (E) National legislation outlawing racial discrimination

11. This cartoon from the early twentieth century suggests that

   (A) Theodore Roosevelt is ignoring the trusts
   (B) the trusts are defeating Theodore Roosevelt
   (C) Theodore Roosevelt is taming the trusts
   (D) Theodore Roosevelt is in league with the trusts
   (E) the trusts are ignoring Theodore Roosevelt

12. Which of the following statements is true of the SALT I treaty of 1972?

   (A) It brought sharp reductions in the number of ballistic missiles in both the U.S. and Soviet arsenals.
   (B) It was intended to encourage the deployment of defensive rather than offensive strategic weapons.
   (C) It indicated U.S. acceptance of the concept of Mutual Assured Destruction.
   (D) It was never ratified by the U.S. Senate.
   (E) It created basic equality in the number of ballistic missiles on each side.

13. All of the following were parts of Andrew Johnson's plan for Reconstruction EXCEPT

   (A) recommending to the Southern states that the vote be extended to the recently freed slaves
   (B) requiring ratification of the Thirteenth Amendment
   (C) requiring payment of monetary reparations for the damage caused by the war
   (D) requiring renunciation of secession
   (E) requiring repudiation of the Confederate debt

14. Which of the following words best describes the spirit of American intellectuals in the 1920s?

   (A) Alienation
   (B) Complacency
   (C) Romanticism
   (D) Patriotism
   (E) Pietism

15. In reaction to the arrest of U.S. sailors and a perceived insult to the U.S. flag and in order to hasten the downfall of Mexican leader Victoriano Huerta, in 1914 President Woodrow Wilson

   (A) ordered General John J. Pershing to take U.S. troops across the border into northern Mexico
   (B) withdrew previously granted diplomatic recognition of Huerta's regime
   (C) ordered the occupation of Mexico City by U.S. troops
   (D) ordered U.S. forces to occupy the Mexican port city of Vera Cruz
   (E) sent a strong diplomatic protest

16. All of the following were part of Woodrow Wilson's Fourteen Points EXCEPT

   (A) self-determination
   (B) open diplomacy
   (C) freedom of the seas
   (D) a League of Nations
   (E) a restoration of the balance of power

17. Which of the following was among the objectives of Booker T. Washington?

    (A) To keep up a constant agitation of questions of racial equality
    (B) To encourage blacks to be more militant in demanding their rights
    (C) To encourage blacks to work hard, acquire property, and prove they were worthy of their rights
    (D) To urge blacks not to accept separate but equal facilities
    (E) To form an organization to advance the rights of blacks

18. When President Andrew Johnson removed Secretary of War Edwin M. Stanton without the approval of the Senate, contrary to the terms of the recently passed Tenure of Office Act, he

    (A) was impeached and removed from office
    (B) came within one vote of being impeached
    (C) was impeached and came within one vote of being removed from office
    (D) resigned to avoid impeachment and was subsequently pardoned by his successor
    (E) was impeached, refused to resign, and his term ended before a vote could be taken on his removal from office

19. By the Compromise of 1877 the Democrats agreed to allow the Republican candidate to become president in exchange for

    (A) a promise that they would be allowed to win the next two presidential elections
    (B) an end to Reconstruction
    (C) large personal bribes to leading Democrats
    (D) a substantial lowering of protective tariffs
    (E) retroactive compensation for freed slaves

20. Which of the following was passed into law during the presidency of Woodrow Wilson?

    (A) The Pure Food and Drug Act
    (B) A progressive income tax
    (C) A high protective tariff
    (D) A national old-age pension
    (E) The Sherman Antitrust Act

21. At the Casablanca Conference in January 1943, President Franklin Roosevelt and British Prime Minister Winston Churchill agreed

   (A) to concentrate on beating the Germans first before dealing with the Japanese
   (B) to shift Allied efforts from the European to the Pacific theater of the war
   (C) to demand unconditional surrender of the Axis powers
   (D) to grant a general amnesty to Axis leaders who would surrender
   (E) to land troops in France in the summer of 1943

22. The Farmers' Alliances of the 1880s appealed primarily to

   (A) small farmers in the Northeast who found themselves unable to compete with large Western farms
   (B) Southern and Great Plains farmers frustrated with low crop prices and mired in the share-cropping and crop-lien systems
   (C) established and well-to-do farmers who desired to limit production in order to sustain high prices
   (D) owners of the giant "bonanza" farms of the northern plains states who sought special advantages from the government
   (E) former plantation owners in the South who sought to strengthen their share-cropping and crop-lien systems

23. During the period of Reconstruction, most of the states of the former Confederacy, in order to regain admission to the Union, were required to

   (A) grant blacks all the civil rights that Northern states had granted them before the war
   (B) ratify the Fourteenth Amendment
   (C) provide integrated public schools
   (D) ratify the Sixteenth Amendment
   (E) provide free land and farming utensils for the recently freed slaves

24. The primary function of the Food Administration during World War I was to

(A) keep farm prices high by limiting the amount of food produced on American farms
(B) insure an adequate supply of food for American needs by arranging for imports from America's British and French allies
(C) oversee the production and allocation of foodstuffs to assure adequate supplies for the army and the Allies
(D) monitor the purity and wholesomeness of all food items shipped to France to feed the American Army there
(E) create and operate large-scale, government-owned farms

25. The purpose of the Truman Doctrine was to

(A) aid the economic recovery of war-torn Europe
(B) prevent European meddling in the affairs of South American countries
(C) aid countries that were the targets of Communist expansionism
(D) reduce the dependence of the European economy on overseas empires
(E) expand the Monroe Doctrine to include Eastern Asia

26. Government subsidies for the building of transcontinental rail roads during the nineteenth century mainly took the form of

(A) special tax breaks based on the mileage of track built
(B) a one-time blanket appropriation for the building of each separate transcontinental line
(C) generous land grants along the railroad's right-of-way
(D) the option of drawing supplies and materials from government depots
(E) the provision of large amounts of convict labor at no charge to the railroad company

27. A member of the Social Gospel movement would probably

(A) consider such social sins as alcohol abuse and sexual permissiveness to be society's most serious problems
(B) assert that the poor were themselves at fault for their circumstances
(C) maintain that abuses and social degradation resulted solely from a lack of willpower on the part of those who committed them
(D) hold that religion is an entirely individual matter
(E) argue that Christians should work to reorganize the industrial system and bring about international peace

28. In its decision in the case of *Plessy v. Ferguson*, the Supreme Court held that

    (A) separate facilities for different races were inherently unequal and therefore unconstitutional

    (B) no black slave could be a citizen of the United States

    (C) separate but equal facilities for different races were constitutional

    (D) Affirmative Action programs were acceptable only when it could be proven that specific previous cases of discrimination had occurred within the institution or business in question

    (E) imposition of a literacy test imposed an unconstitutional barrier to the right to vote

29. The Spanish-American War spurred the building of the Panama Canal by

    (A) demonstrating the need to shift naval forces quickly from the Atlantic to the Pacific

    (B) demonstrating the ease with which Latin American countries could be overcome by U.S. military force

    (C) discrediting congressional opponents of the project

    (D) removing the threat that any possible canal could be blockaded by Spanish forces based in Cuba and Puerto Rico

    (E) demonstrating that such tropical diseases as malaria and yellow fever could be controlled

30. This 1919 cartoon suggests that the United States

THE CHILD WHO WANTED TO PLAY BY HIMSELF

PRESIDENT WILSON: "Now come along and enjoy yourself
with the other nice children. I promise that you'd be the
life and soul of the party.

London Punch, 1919

(A) strongly supported Wilson's internationalism
(B) favored Great Britain over France
(C) took an aggressive stance against Europe
(D) opposed participation in the League of Nations
(E) favored the European continental nations over Great Britain

31. Which of the following is true of W. E. B. Du Bois?

(A) He helped found the National Association for the Advancement of Colored People.
(B) He was the chief author of the Atlanta Compromise.
(C) He was an outspoken critic of the Niagara Movement.
(D) He believed that blacks should temporarily accommodate themselves to the whites.
(E) He worked closely with Booker T. Washington.

32. The primary underlying reason that Reconstruction ended in 1877 was that

    (A) Southerners had succeeded in electing anti-Reconstruction govern-
    ments in all the former Confederate states
    (B) all the goals set by the Radical Republicans at the end of the Civil
    War had been accomplished
    (C) leading Radicals in the North had become convinced that Reconstruc-
    tion had been unconstitutional
    (D) Northern voters had grown weary of the effort to reconstruct the
    South and generally lost interest
    (E) Republican political managers had come to see further agitation
    of North-South differences arising from the Civil War as a political
    liability

33. The Marshall Plan was

    (A) a strategy for defeating Germany
    (B) a strategy for defeating Japan
    (C) an American economic aid program for Europe
    (D) an American commitment to give military and economic aid
    to any nation resisting Communist aggression
    (E) a civil-defense plan for surviving a Soviet nuclear strike

34. All of the following statements are true of John Dewey EXCEPT

    (A) he strove to alter radically both the content and purpose of schooling
    (B) he strove to strengthen the child's respect for parental and other tradi-
    tional authorities
    (C) he substituted the authority of the peer group for that of the teacher
    so that the child would be socialized and schooling would be made
    relevant to him
    (D) he was much influenced by William James
    (E) he has been called the father of Progressive Education

35. This cartoon, drawn during the period leading up to the Spanish-American War, presents McKinley as

ANOTHER OLD WOMAN TRIES TO SWEEP BACK THE SEA

(A) a strong influence on public opinion
(B) having control over Congress
(C) ignoring public opinion
(D) an effective leader
(E) ultimately overwhelmed by public opinion and Congress

36. Which of the following expresses the first policy taken by the federal government toward the Indians of the Great Plains?

(A) The Indians should be confined to two large reservations, one north of the Platte River and the other south of it.
(B) Since the Great Plains are a desert anyway, the Indians may be allowed to keep the entire area.
(C) Indians should be given individual parcels of land by the government rather than holding land communally as tribes.
(D) Indians are subhuman and ought to be exterminated.
(E) The Indians should be induced to accept permanent residence on a number of small reservations.

37. Georgia O'Keeffe, Thomas Hart Benton, and Edward Hopper were all

    (A) American painters of the 1920s
    (B) pioneers in the field of a distinctly American music
    (C) known for their abstract paintings of flowers and other objects
    (D) pioneers in the building of skyscrapers
    (E) American literary figures of the first decade of the twentieth century

38. The 1944 Dumbarton Oaks Conference involved primarily

    (A) the trial and punishment of Nazi war criminals
    (B) the decision on whether or not to use the atomic bomb
    (C) startling revelations of the Nazi atrocities against Jews
    (D) American plans for redrawing the map of Eastern Europe
    (E) the formation of the United Nations

39. What was the OVERALL U.S. unemployment rate during the worst periods of the depression?

    (A) 10%
    (B) 25%
    (C) 40%
    (D) 60%
    (E) 90%

40. Which battle was the turning point in the Pacific war between Japan and the U.S.?

    (A) Leyte Gulf
    (B) Pearl Harbor
    (C) Coral Sea
    (D) Midway
    (E) Guadalcanal

41. The United States Supreme Court case of *Brown v. Board of Education of Topeka* was significant because it

    (A) prohibited prayer in public schools on the grounds of separation of church and state
    (B) legally upheld the doctrine of "separate but equal" educational facilities for blacks and whites
    (C) clarified the constitutional rights of minors and restricted the right of school administrators to set dress codes or otherwise infringe on students' rights
    (D) upheld school districts' right to use aptitude and psychological tests to "track" students and segregate them into "college prep" and "vocational" programs
    (E) ordered the desegregation of public schools, prohibiting the practice of segregation via "separate but equal" schools for blacks and whites

42. One of the major effects of the industrial revolution of the late nineteenth century in the United States was

    (A) an increased emphasis on worker health and safety issues
    (B) an increased emphasis on speed rather than quality of work
    (C) an increased emphasis on high-quality, error-free work
    (D) an increase in the number of small industrial facilities, which could operate more efficiently than larger, more costly industrial plants
    (E) a decrease in worker productivity as a result of continuous clashes between unions and management

43. The American hostage crisis in Iran was precipitated by

    (A) the American government allowing the deposed Shah of Iran to come to the United States for cancer treatment
    (B) Jimmy Carter's involvement in arranging the Camp David Accords between the Egyptians and the Israelis
    (C) American air strikes against Iran's ally Libya
    (D) American support for Israel's 1980 invasion of southern Lebanon
    (E) American attempts to overthrow the newly established government of Ayatollah Khomeini

44. The thrust of Roosevelt's "Good Neighbor" policy was to

    (A) retreat from the military interventionism and blatant economic domination, which had characterized previous American policy toward Latin America
    (B) guarantee the protection of Latin America and South America from European aggression by permanently stationing U.S. forces in the region
    (C) promise "Good Samaritanism" in the United States by encouraging people who still owned their own homes to provide temporary housing for their neighbors who had become homeless because of the Great Depression
    (D) force Latin American countries to cooperate peacefully with each other and end their petty border disputes or face United States military intervention
    (E) supply Britain with the goods and nonmilitary essentials they needed to maintain their struggle against Nazi Germany

45. Reaganomics is most closely associated with

    (A) the "trickle-down" theory
    (B) the "controlled growth" theory
    (C) the "bubble up" theory
    (D) a "planned" economy
    (E) the "pump-priming" theory

46. What proposal did President Woodrow Wilson make in 1918 that convinced the Germans they would be treated fairly if they surrendered?

    (A) The Twenty-One Demands
    (B) The Fourteen Points
    (C) The Sussex Pledge
    (D) The Balfour Declaration
    (E) The "New Freedom" policy

47. U.S. presidents between 1876 and 1900 are generally considered among the weakest in American history. A major reason for their reputation was that

    (A) none of them served more than one term in office
    (B) they considered themselves caretakers, not dynamic initiators of new legislation
    (C) Congress enacted several new laws restricting presidential power during this period
    (D) they were the products of machine politics, political followers who were typically incompetent leaders
    (E) they were limited in their actions by the overwhelming Populist sentiment of their time

48. This Currier and Ives print strongly suggests that the way to prosperity is through

THE WAY TO GROW POOR.   ✻   THE WAY TO GROW RICH.

(A) gambling
(B) stock speculation
(C) politics
(D) credit
(E) hard work

49. In what way did the muckrakers contribute to the rise of Progressivism in the early years of the twentieth century?

(A) Their lurid stories of European abuses led directly to American isolationism until World War I.
(B) Their stories glorifying the rich and famous led to the supremacy of laissez-faire economic theories during this period.
(C) Their horror stories of Marxist infiltration into workers' unions led to public support for crackdowns against reform-minded unions and alliances.
(D) Their exposes of government and business corruption, abuse, and mismanagement led to widely supported public demands for effective reform.
(E) They created a repugnance for the national press that developed into a general distrust for all government and business institutions

50. All of the following were characteristic of the 1920s EXCEPT

    (A) voting rights for women
    (B) prohibition and bootlegging
    (C) consumerism and easy credit
    (D) Progressivist reform and union growth
    (E) Ku Klux Klan power and popularity

51. All of the following "New Deal" agencies were created during the Great Depression to provide jobs for the unemployed EXCEPT the

    (A) Farm Security Administration (FSA)
    (B) Civil Works Administration (CWA)
    (C) Civilian Conservation Corps (CCC)
    (D) Works Progress Administration (WPA)
    (E) National Youth Administration (NYA)

52. The most important factor in the destruction of the Plains Indians' societies by whites in the late nineteenth century was

    (A) the use of modern weapons by white soldiers and cavalrymen
    (B) the destruction of the buffalo herds by whites
    (C) the introduction of alcohol by whites to Indian society
    (D) the encroachment of railroads into Indian lands
    (E) the use of reservations by whites to limit the movement of Indians

53. The sharecropping system in the South following Reconstruction had the effect of

    (A) allowing many former slaves and poor white tenant farmers, who could have never otherwise owned land, to buy their own farms
    (B) moving many former slaves and poor white tenant farmers into the middle class
    (C) pushing tenant farmers and poor independent farmers into deep levels of debt to large landowners and merchants
    (D) helping to limit the power of former plantation owners and northern business interests
    (E) changing the basic attitudes of whites and blacks who were now forced to work side by side farming the same land

54. The Interstate Commerce Act of 1887 was aimed primarily at

    (A) increasing interstate trade by forbidding states from levying tariffs on goods transported from other states
    (B) curbing abusive pricing and hauling policies by the nation's railroads
    (C) increasing interstate trade through government assistance in efforts to build new canals, roads, and railroads
    (D) curbing abusive pricing and hauling policies by the nation's ocean-going, river-going, and canal-going shipping companies
    (E) increasing interstate commerce by offering financial incentives to companies that operated offices or manufacturing plants in more than one site

55. The only dominant, broad-based labor union in the United States from 1870–90 was the

    (A) National Labor Union
    (B) Industrial Workers of the World (IWW)
    (C) American Federation of Labor (AFL)
    (D) Congress of Industrial Organizations (CIO)
    (E) Knights of Labor

56. The political machines such as Tammany Hall that ran American cities in the late nineteenth century derived their strongest support from

    (A) industrial leaders and business elites
    (B) organized religion
    (C) wealthy landowners living in rural areas outside the cities
    (D) the middle class
    (E) poor immigrants and ethnic communities in the inner city

57. The combination of European musical influences with African musical influences came together in 1890s New Orleans to form a new distinctly American musical style called

    (A) gospel
    (B) jazz
    (C) folk
    (D) country
    (E) blues

58. In 1968, Vietcong guerrillas and North Vietnamese regulars launched a massive series of attacks which failed militarily, but succeeded in ending U.S. hopes for an early end to the Vietnam War. This episode of the war became known as the

    (A) Pleiku Offensive
    (B) NLF Offensive
    (C) Gulf of Tonkin Incident
    (D) Battle of KheSanh
    (E) Tet Offensive

59. What event triggered President Truman to announce the "Truman Doctrine"?

    (A) The overthrow of the Czechoslovakian government by Soviet Communists
    (B) Russian actions in Iran
    (C) The Greek Civil War
    (D) The Hungarian Revolution
    (E) The Korean War

60. Place the following in the correct chronological order, from the earliest event to the most recent.

    I. election of Franklin D. Roosevelt
    II. U.S. stock market crash
    III. National Labor Relations Act
    IV. Hawley-Smoot tariff

    (A) II, IV, III, I
    (B) I, II, III, IV
    (C) II, III, I, IV
    (D) III, IV, II, I
    (E) II, IV, I, III

61. What was the reaction in the U.S. Senate to the terms of the 1918 Treaty of Versailles?

    (A) The Senate overwhelmingly supported the major provisions of the treaty and only demanded a few minor adjustments before ratifying it.

    (B) The Senate felt that in many ways the treaty was too harsh on Germany, but that overall it was a good plan for postwar peace.

    (C) The Senate was angry at Wilson for the way he handled the negotiations, but felt that the treaty was too important to be destroyed by partisan politics. As a result, the Senate narrowly passed the ratification measure making the treaty official.

    (D) The Senate was angry at Wilson for the way he handled the negotiations and had problems with several treaty articles. As a result, the Senate didn't ratify the treaty until the second time Wilson sent it to them. Even then, the Senate refused to ratify the provisions calling for U.S. membership in a League of Nations.

    (E) The Senate was angry at Wilson for the way he handled the negotiations and for the treaty that the peace conference produced. Wilson refused to compromise on various treaty provisions and the Senate rejected the treaty both times it was sent to them.

62. The "Lost Generation" refers to

    (A) those young adults whose lives and families were devastated by the Great Depression of the 1930s

    (B) the millions of young men killed in the senseless trench warfare of World War I

    (C) young writers disillusioned by the materialism, decadence, and conformity dominating 1920s America

    (D) the thousands of workers killed or injured in efforts to form and promote worker safety in turn-of-the-20th century America

    (E) the generation of young Americans caught up in the turmoil of war protests and moral collapse during the 1960s

63. In this cartoon Thomas Nast presents Boss Tweed as

(A) a politician ruled by greed
(B) a benefactor of the public
(C) a political reformer
(D) a politician corruptly influenced by business
(E) a politician who rejected business influence

64. All of the following contributed to the Great Depression EXCEPT

(A) excessive stocks and securities speculation
(B) protectionist trade measures
(C) huge farm debts resulting from collapsed crop prices
(D) lack of credit to help consumers sustain economic growth
(E) an imbalance of distribution of wealth in which the rich controlled far too much of the available income

65. The Indian Reorganization Act of 1934 sought to

(A) end federal subsidies to landless Indian tribes and force them to support themselves
(B) prohibit the division of tribal lands into allotments and allow Indians to resume using their own tribal languages and rituals on their lands
(C) requisition desirable lands from Indian tribes and force those tribes to relocate on smaller jointly occupied reservations, in which several tribes would reside, intermingle, and share the same land
(D) break up tribal reservations into individual allotments of land that could be occupied by Indians or purchased by whites
(E) prohibit Indians from using tribal languages or practicing ancient tribal religions on government reservations

66. Lyndon Johnson's Great Society program was aimed primarily at

    (A) spurring advances in American science and technical education and increasing funding to high-tech research facilities
    (B) sending American volunteers to impoverished foreign nations to help educate their people and build their economic base
    (C) securing civil rights for all Americans and eliminating poverty
    (D) providing minimum wage jobs for all unemployed Americans and shifting tax dollars from the military to the civilian sector of the economy
    (E) retraining adults who had dropped out of school and increasing the number of Americans who attended college

67. "Jim Crow" laws were laws that

    (A) effectively prohibited blacks from voting in state and local elections
    (B) restricted American Indians to U.S. government reservations
    (C) restricted open-range ranching in the Great Plains
    (D) established separate segregated facilities for blacks and whites
    (E) restricted the consumption and distribution of alcohol within the limits of pro-temperance communities

68. The Smoot-Hawley Tariffs and other protectionist trade measures had the long-term effect of

    (A) improving the competitiveness of U.S. industry in foreign markets
    (B) improving U.S. economic strength in the long-term, although short-term economic performance was weakened
    (C) making little difference in the economies of Europe and the U.S
    (D) sparking retaliatory measures from Europe that weakened both their economies and ours
    (E) providing European leaders with the incentive to finally put their differences aside and form an economic confederation, which would eventually evolve into the European Common Market

69. The Iran-Contra Affair upset most Americans because it involved

    (A) illegal support for the Contra rebels in Nicaragua
    (B) illegal support for government-backed "death squads" in El Salvador
    (C) a presidential coverup similar to and, to some extent, worse than the Watergate Affair
    (D) trading arms to Iran for release of American hostages
    (E) providing funding for Contra rebels to be trained by Iranians in terrorist tactics to be used against the Nicaraguan government

70. Between 1860 and 1910, the area of the United States that underwent the largest PERCENTAGE increase of population was

    (A) the Northeast
    (B) the Old South
    (C) the Mid-Atlantic
    (D) the Far West
    (E) the Great Plains

71. The Fourteenth Amendment to the Constitution was important because it

    (A) prohibited slavery within the United States
    (B) guaranteed equal protection under the law for every American citizen
    (C) prohibited any state from denying an American citizen the right to vote based on race/ethnic background, color, or having previously been a slave
    (D) prohibited any state from denying women the right to vote
    (E) provided Congress with the power to establish and collect income taxes

72. The Watergate scandal led to Richard Nixon's downfall primarily because

    (A) of his role in planning and coordinating the Watergate break-in and other illegal campaign activities
    (B) the press, the Democrats, and some liberal Republicans united to rid themselves of Nixon and his conservative philosophy
    (C) he was already so unpopular because of his Vietnam War policies that virtually anything he did wrong would have been used as an excuse to remove him from office
    (D) of his role in directing the cover-up of the Watergate Affair
    (E) of his involvement with organized crime in carrying out political "dirty tricks" against his Democratic opponent, George McGovern

73. The Atlantic Charter

    (A) set collective war strategy and long-term war goals for Britain and the United States
    (B) guaranteed American neutrality in World War II as long as American warships stayed out of British territorial waters
    (C) pledged South and Central American neutrality after Germany and Japan declared war on the United States
    (D) provided Britain with 50 World War I vintage American destroyers in return for American control of British military bases in the Caribbean and the Mid-Atlantic
    (E) repealed the American arms embargo and allowed Britain and France to buy American war materials on a cash-and-carry basis

74. The Japanese surprise attack on Pearl Harbor succeeded for all of the following reasons EXCEPT

   (A) a conspiracy by the United States government to let the Japanese attack Pearl Harbor by surprise so America would have a legitimate excuse to enter World War II

   (B) commanders at Pearl Harbor were convinced that the only real threat to the base was from local saboteurs, not a Japanese naval attack

   (C) a message ordering the base on maximum war alert was sent via commercial telegraph rather than military cable and did not arrive until the day after the attack

   (D) Americans did not believe the Japanese would dare attempt such a risky attack and did not believe the Japanese COULD pull it off if they tried

   (E) interservice rivalry effectively kept the military intelligence services from sharing and coordinating the information they had collected which could have allowed them to anticipate the Pearl Harbor attack

75. The decline of "open range" ranching in the West resulted primarily from

   (A) low beef prices that made "open range" ranching unprofitable

   (B) government policies giving priority use of the range to sheepherders, thus denying cattlemen equal access to the open range

   (C) overgrazing and intense competition for use of the land between ranchers and farmers

   (D) the increased use of sharecropping techniques by cattle ranchers which lessened their need for open range policies

   (E) the high cost of replacing cattle that constantly wandered off in the open range

76. Joseph Pulitzer was a pioneer in the development of

   (A) new journals aimed exclusively at the upper class and social elites in America

   (B) weekly journals focusing exclusively on economic news

   (C) yellow journalism

   (D) ethics in journalism laws to prevent slanderous news stories that often ruined innocent peoples' lives

   (E) the nation's first national "wire service," the United Press

77. In the 1880s, the issue of tariffs on imported goods became a major contro-versy because

    (A) the free trade policies in effect at that time were allowing underpriced foreign goods to destroy fledgling American industries and virtually eliminate American crop exports to Europe

    (B) individual states refused to give up their right to enact tariffs on goods brought across state lines from neighboring states

    (C) high tariffs were resulting in unnecessarily high prices on manufac-tured goods, hurting both farmers and consumers while protecting several wealthy manufacturers

    (D) Democrats forced the enactment of free trade legislation in the U.S., but European countries responded by raising their tariffs on U.S. manufactured goods, throwing the U.S. economy into a depression

    (E) Democrats allowed tariffs to be enacted only on imported farm goods, which protected American farmers but left U.S. manufacturers vulner-able to European tariffs

78. Industrial committees that helped mobilize the country's war efforts during World War I were

    (A) instrumental in preventing corruption and labor dissension from crip-pling the mobilization campaign

    (B) so dominated by greedy businessmen cashing in on the war they were disbanded and replaced by the War Industries Board

    (C) the key to an efficient war effort following the collapse of the War Industries Board

    (D) ruled unconstitutional by the conservative Supreme Court and were forced to reorganize as unfunded private consulting groups

    (E) not formed until so late in the war effort that they had little impact other than to streamline the process for the transfer of men and equip-ment from the United States to France

79. The Scopes Trial had the effect of

    (A) eliminating state restrictions on the teaching of evolution in schools
    (B) highlighting the intolerance of religious fundamentalism and its conflict with contemporary science and secularism
    (C) emphasizing the importance of the First Amendment when a person's ideas are not popular among the majority of Americans
    (D) pointing out the necessity of preventing the state from interfering in religious matters
    (E) reestablishing the predominance of fundamentalist religious ideas over secular scientific pronouncements which had dominated American thought throughout the early 1920s

80. In 1948, what city did the U.S., Britain, and France have to keep supplied for over 300 days in a massive airlift due to the Soviets cutting off all land-based supply routes in an effort to drive the Westerners out of the city?

    (A) Helsinki
    (B) Warsaw
    (C) Bonn
    (D) Berlin
    (E) Prague

81. The philosophy behind the New Deal was primarily to

    (A) restore the laissez-faire capitalism that had worked so well in the early 1920s
    (B) eliminate the massive federal deficit that had led to the Great Depression by mandating a balanced federal budget
    (C) establish a socialist system in which government would takeover private industry, set all prices, and guarantee employment for workers
    (D) cut down the size of government, which had become a massive drain on the nation's economy, and return more power to the states so they could each deal with their specific economic problems in their own way
    (E) expand the role of the federal government in providing jobs, relief for the unemployed, better wages, and regulation of industry to control the abuses of the past that had led to the current depression

82. The Taft-Hartley Labor Act of 1947 had the effect of

   (A) prohibiting strikes by government employees
   (B) granting railroad workers the right to strike and to organize unions
   (C) extending the right to strike and to organize unions, previously allowed to railroad workers only, to all workers
   (D) allowing unions to force management into binding arbitration when contract negotiations broke down
   (E) forbidding unions from closing shops to nonunion employees

83. Which of the following was the MAJOR reason Truman used to justify his decision to drop the atomic bomb on Hiroshima in August 1945?

   (A) He believed it would shorten the war and eliminate the need for an invasion of Japan
   (B) He believed it would end up saving Japanese civilian lives, when compared to the casualties expected from an invasion of Japan
   (C) He wanted to send a strong warning message to the Russians to watch their step in the Pacific after Japan was defeated
   (D) He believed it would be an appropriate revenge for the Japanese attack on Pearl Harbor
   (E) Once the bomb was completed, Truman felt he had to use it in order to justify the huge investments in time, resources, scientific expertise, and expense involved in its development

84. Jane Addams was a turn-of-the-20th century activist most well known for her work in

   (A) settlement houses
   (B) the temperance movement
   (C) nursing home care for war veterans
   (D) the suffrage movement
   (E) children's literature

85. The internment of Japanese-Americans by the United States during World War II was primarily because

    (A) of evidence and suspicions that they were involved in treasonous activity

    (B) they were Japanese

    (C) of desires by business leaders to grab valuable Japanese-owned properties in California

    (D) many of them openly supported Japanese government poli-cies, even after Pearl Harbor, although none of them actuallyengaged in treasonous behavior

    (E) most of them refused to take oaths of loyalty to the UnitedStates even though they also publicly denounced Japanesegovernment actions and condemned the Pearl Harbor attack

86. Which of the answer choices best expresses the point of view of this cartoon?

RE-CONSTRUCTION,
OR "A WHITE MAN'S GOVERNMENT".

    (A) Southern whites and blacks can never be reconciled.

    (B) Southern whites would willingly be reconciled with blacks.

    (C) Blacks have no interest in reconciliation with Southern whites.

    (D) The president must take a forceful role in reconciling Southern whites and blacks.

    (E) Reconciliation of Southern whites and blacks is simply a matter of recognizing the new realities.

87. The agreement that ended most trade barriers among the United States, Canada, and Mexico was

    (A) SALT
    (B) START
    (C) NAFTA
    (D) WIN
    (E) SDI

88. The first female justice named to the Supreme court was

    (A) Ann Richards
    (B) Ruth Bader Ginsberg
    (C) Madeleine Albright
    (D) Sandra Day O'Connor
    (E) Margaret Chase Smith

89. Louis Sullivan's pupil who opposed the construction of skyscrapers and favored a form of architecture in harmony with natural surroundings was

    (A) Ernest Hemingway
    (B) Virgil Thomson
    (C) Victor Herbert
    (D) James T. Farrell
    (E) Frank Lloyd Wright

90. William M. Tweed of New York City

    (A) headed a "ring" of politicians that cheated New York City of $100 million through fraudulent city contracts and extortion
    (B) was an outspoken supporter of fiscal integrity in municipal government
    (C) pioneered the regulation of tenement house construction and sanitation
    (D) urged the New York state legislature to adopt the governmental reforms advocated by the Progressives
    (E) served as Secretary of Interior in President Ulysses Grant's administrations

91. Marcus Garvey, leader of the Universal Negro Improvement Association, argued for

    (A) equal rights
    (B) a return to Africa
    (C) racial desegregation
    (D) violence in the cities
    (E) more representation in Congress for Washington, D.C.

92. When the United States Supreme Court failed to rule favorably on New Deal legislation, President Franklin Roosevelt

    (A) introduced a judiciary reorganization bill that would increase the number of Supreme Court justices
    (B) attempted to circumvent the Court by having cases involving New Deal legislation appealed to state supreme courts
    (C) called for the election of federal judges
    (D) used his emergency powers and appointed three new justicesto the Supreme Court
    (E) threatened to have Congress reduce the justices' salaries

93. The Roosevelt Corollary to the Monroe Doctrine, enunciated by President Theodore Roosevelt in his annual message to Congress in May 1904 did all of the following EXCEPT

    (A) assert that the United States would take action to guarantee that Latin American nations paid their debts
    (B) stated that the United States could intervene in the affairs of Western Hemisphere nations to forestall the intervention of other powers
    (C) was preceded by Roosevelt's assertion that the Monroe Doctrine prohibited Europeans from using force in the Americas
    (D) led to protracted intervention in Santo Domingo and, subsequently, to intervention in Haiti, Nicaragua, and Cuba
    (E) proposed a massive foreign aid program to stabilize the governments of Latin America

94. McCarthyism in the 1950s was an attempt to reveal

    (A) Communist infiltration in the United States government
    (B) corruption in the Truman administration
    (C) the plot to sell weapons to belligerent nations
    (D) misuse of corporate funds for political purposes
    (E) the dangers of nuclear energy

95. The United States' policy of Lend-Lease in 1940 benefitted what allied nation the most?

(A) France
(B) Great Britain
(C) Denmark
(D) Finland
(E) Sweden

96. The controversy over the presidential election in 1876 between Samuel J. Tilden and Rutherford B. Hayes arose because

(A) the Greenback-Labor party's presidential candidate prevented either Tilden or Hayes from winning a majority of the electoral votes
(B) No candidate received a majority of the popular vote as required by the Constitution
(C) three Southern states—South Carolina, Louisiana, and Florida—submitted contested electoral votes
(D) the Democratic party withdrew its nomination of Tilden
(E) Union military forces still occupied the South

97. Helen Hunt Jackson's book entitled *A Century of Dishonor* (1881) recounted

(A) American imperialism and its effects on the middle class
(B) discriminatory practices employed by the United States government against African Americans
(C) the atrocities of the Spanish-American War
(D) the long record of broken treaties and injustices against American Indians
(E) the abuses involving big business trusts in America

98. The Nineteenth Amendment, added to the United States Constitution in 1920, did which of the following?

(A) Limited the president to two terms
(B) Created the federal income tax
(C) Outlawed the sale and transportation of alcoholic beverages
(D) Enfranchised women
(E) Ended prohibition

99. "There is no right to strike against the public safety, anywhere, any time," was said by

    (A) Rutherford B. Hayes with regard to the Great Railroad Strike of 1877
    (B) Grover Cleveland on sending federal troops to help put down the Pullman strike
    (C) Calvin Coolidge on calling out the Massachusetts National Guard during the Boston police strike
    (D) Senator Robert A. Taft speaking in favor of the Taft-Hartley Act
    (E) Ronald Reagan with regard to the air traffic controllers' strike

100. Under the crop lien system, a farmer

    (A) borrowed money against his next harvest in order to buy more land
    (B) borrowed money against the previous year's harvest, which was stored in warehouses until the market was favorable for selling
    (C) was likely to diversify the crops he planted
    (D) mortgaged his next harvest to a merchant in order to buy seed and supplies and support his family
    (E) could usually become completely debt-free within seven to ten years

101. All of the following were New Deal reforms EXCEPT

    (A) the National Industrial Recovery Act
    (B) the Tennessee Valley Authority
    (C) the Reconstruction Finance Corporation
    (D) the Agricultural Adjustment Act
    (E) the Works Progress Administration

102. Which of the following statements is LEAST true about immigration to the U.S. between 1880 and 1900?

    (A) Most immigrants were unskilled day laborers.
    (B) Immigration increased steadily during these years.
    (C) Immigrants tended to be Catholic, Eastern Orthodox, or Jewish.
    (D) Most immigrants came from northern and western Europe.
    (E) Chinese immigrants were excluded by law during most of this time.

103. Which of the following gave the president the most power in directing American foreign policy during the post–World War II era?

    (A) The Tonkin Gulf Resolution
    (B) The Civil Rights Act of 1964
    (C) The Boland Amendments of 1982 and 1984
    (D) The War Powers Act
    (E) The Good Neighbor Policy

104. Which of the following would NOT have supported the late nineteenth century drive for bimetallism in the United States?

    (A) Those who thought inflation would benefit the economy
    (B) Those who owned stock in silver mines
    (C) Those who held large amounts of government securities
    (D) Those who were deeply in debt
    (E) Those who came from predominantly agricultural states

105. Which of the following was NOT associated with the Harlem Renaissance literary movement?

    (A) Countee Cullen
    (B) James Baldwin
    (C) Langston Hughes
    (D) Alain Locke
    (E) Zora Neale Hurston

106. Which of the following circumstances was most significant in bringing an end to Reconstruction in 1877?

    (A) The installation of a Republican administration
    (B) The deaths of many leading Radical politicians in the North
    (C) The increasing interest in economic issues rather than racial or sectional ones
    (D) The violent resistance of Southerners in such organizations as the Ku Klux Klan
    (E) The Northern electorate's fatigue with the effort to remake southern society

107. The purpose of Franklin D. Roosevelt's "Four Freedoms" speech was to

    (A) obtain a congressional declaration of war against Germany
    (B) gain support for his Lend-Lease program
    (C) obtain a congressional declaration of war against Japan
    (D) assert complete American neutrality in the war in Europe
    (E) set forth the terms under which Germany's surrender would be accepted

108. Which of the following did the U.S. annex during the Spanish-American War?

    (A) Alaska
    (B) Hawaii
    (C) Cuba
    (D) California
    (E) New Mexico

109. Lincoln Steffens' *The Shame of the Cities* specifically denounces

    (A) corruption in big-city politics
    (B) poverty in large cities
    (C) the growth of large cities
    (D) dominance of state governments by urban voters at the expense of farmers
    (E) the increasing reliance of urban economies on manufacturing rather than trade

110. The urban riots of the mid-1960s were primarily triggered by

    (A) opposition to the Vietnam War
    (B) the needs of the rioters for food and clothing
    (C) opposition to runaway government spending
    (D) racial tensions
    (E) the conflicting concerns of the counterculture and traditional society

111. The "Crime of '73" refers to the

    (A) demonetization of silver
    (B) incursion of whites into treaty-guaranteed Sioux lands in the Black Hills
    (C) assassination of President James A. Garfield
    (D) failure of Congress to pass civil service legislation in that year
    (E) attempt by Jay Gould and others to corner the gold market

112. All of the following are true about presidential elections between 1876 and 1900 EXCEPT

    (A) twice, the candidate who polled the most popular votes failed to gain a majority of the electoral vote
    (B) the Democrats had the most success with "waving the bloody shirt"
    (C) factional infighting within the Republican party produced several "compromise" candidates
    (D) the Republican party won most of these elections
    (E) the major third-party force was eventually absorbed by the Democrats

113. What was the significance of the Immigration Acts of 1921 and 1924?

    (A) They limited immigration from Mexico for the first time.
    (B) They created a category of "special immigrants," which included relatives of U.S. citizens living abroad.
    (C) They made immigration requirements qualitative, rather than quantitative.
    (D) They set quotas on immigration from certain areas of Europe, Asia, and Africa.
    (E) They based annual quotas on a flat one-sixth of one percent of the national population in 1920.

114. All of the following were cardinal features of U.S. foreign policy during the Harding and Coolidge administrations EXCEPT

    (A) a strong interventionist policy in Latin America
    (B) an aversion to involvement in European political conflicts
    (C) a concrete naval disarmament treaty
    (D) rigidity in demanding repayment of Allied war debts
    (E) the negotiation of independence for the oil-rich Middle Eastern nations

115. Which of the following would most likely have drawn this cartoon?

(A) A Republican

(B) A member of the Grange

(C) A Populist

(D) An advocate of the monetization of silver

(E) A supporter of paper money

116. Henry Kissinger is most closely associated with the

(A) "Vietnamization" of the war effort in Indochina

(B) flexible response policy

(C) policy of detente

(D) U.S. rapprochement with China

(E) Watergate break-in

117. In general, state governments in the South during Reconstruction

    (A) were ineffective compared to pre–Civil War governments because they were dominated by freed slaves and others who were not competent to hold office

    (B) were ineffective compared to pre–Civil War governments because of the restrictive rule of the Union military bureaucracy, which kept a tight reign on state governments

    (C) accomplished some notable achievements, but basically squandered their opportunity to effectively rebuild the South because of the greed and corruption of scalawags and Yankee carpetbaggers

    (D) were much more successful than the pre–Civil War governments that preceded them

    (E) accomplished some notable achievements and were comparable in their effectiveness to the pre–Civil War governments that preceded them

118. The establishment of transcontinental rail lines and the construction of America's massive rail network had all of the following effects EXCEPT

    (A) rapid industrialization of the Old South following the CivilWar

    (B) rapid distribution of goods throughout the country

    (C) spurring a series of important technical advances

    (D) making the country smaller by dramatically reducing thetime needed to traverse the continent

    (E) the establishment of standardized time zones throughout thecountry

119. The Washington Conference of 1921–22 resulted in agreements between European powers, the United States, China, and Japan that

   I. established a ratio for capital ships among the five great naval powers.

   II. stabilized the postwar title to islands previously held by Germany.

   III. conformed to the standards of the Reparations Commission established at the Versailles Peace Conference.

   IV. reaffirmed the integrity and independence of China.

   V. recognized Manchuria as a Japanese sphere of influence.

    (A) I and III only

    (B) III and IV only

    (C) I, II, and IV only

    (D) I, II, and V only

    (E) I, II, III, IV, V

120. The "Red Scare" of 1919 was primarily caused by

    (A) the release of the Zimmermann papers
    (B) bombings of government facilities and industrial plants by agents of the Comintern
    (C) Lenin's promise to bury capitalism, starting with the United States
    (D) a rash of massive labor strikes and disputes affecting millions of American workers
    (E) the invasion of Poland by Soviet military forces

PRACTICE TEST 1

Answer Key

1.	(B)	31.	(A)	61.	(E)	91.	(B)
2.	(C)	32.	(D)	62.	(C)	92.	(A)
3.	(A)	33.	(C)	63.	(A)	93.	(E)
4.	(B)	34.	(B)	64.	(D)	94.	(A)
5.	(A)	35.	(E)	65.	(B)	95.	(B)
6.	(B)	36.	(B)	66.	(C)	96.	(C)
7.	(A)	37.	(A)	67.	(D)	97.	(D)
8.	(C)	38.	(E)	68.	(D)	98.	(D)
9.	(A)	39.	(B)	69.	(D)	99.	(C)
10.	(A)	40.	(D)	70.	(E)	100.	(D)
11.	(C)	41.	(E)	71.	(B)	101.	(C)
12.	(C)	42.	(B)	72.	(D)	102.	(D)
13.	(C)	43.	(A)	73.	(A)	103.	(A)
14.	(A)	44.	(A)	74.	(A)	104.	(C)
15.	(D)	45.	(A)	75.	(C)	105.	(B)
16.	(E)	46.	(B)	76.	(C)	106.	(E)
17.	(C)	47.	(B)	77.	(C)	107.	(B)
18.	(C)	48.	(E)	78.	(B)	108.	(B)
19.	(B)	49.	(D)	79.	(B)	109.	(A)
20.	(B)	50.	(D)	80.	(D)	110.	(D)
21.	(C)	51.	(A)	81.	(E)	111.	(A)
22.	(B)	52.	(B)	82.	(E)	112.	(B)
23.	(B)	53.	(C)	83.	(A)	113.	(D)
24.	(C)	54.	(B)	84.	(A)	114.	(E)
25.	(C)	55.	(E)	85.	(B)	115.	(A)
26.	(C)	56.	(E)	86.	(E)	116.	(C)
27.	(E)	57.	(B)	87.	(C)	117.	(E)
28.	(C)	58.	(E)	88.	(D)	118.	(A)
29.	(A)	59.	(C)	89.	(E)	119.	(C)
30.	(D)	60.	(E)	90.	(A)	120.	(D)

PRACTICE TEST 1

Detailed Explanations of Answers

1. **(B)** All of these events relate to the contraction and expansion of civil rights for African Americans. The order, from the earliest event to the most recent event, is as follows:

   1. *Plessy v. Ferguson* (1896)

   2. *Brown v. Board of Education* (1954)

   3. Greensboro sit-In (1960)

   4. Voting Rights Act (1965)

2. **(C)** The rapid democratization of the Soviet bloc caused an avalanche of change. The Union of Soviet Socialist Republics broke up into separate nations beginning in 1990. The rise of nationalism in areas of repression caused the outbreak of civil wars in the Balkans (A) later in the1990s. Afghanistan was in the midst of civil war and its harboring of terrorists was not yet a matter of concern (B). The conflict between Israel and Egypt (D) had been settled by a treaty in 1978. China took over Hong Kong (E) in 1997.

3. **(A)** Martin Luther King's methods were characterized by nonviolent defiance of segregation. King's commitment to nonviolence required his rejection of armed violence (B) as called for by such groups as the Black Panthers. At the same time, he promoted civil disobedience rather than the patience advocated by Booker T. Washington in the late nineteenth century. Petitions to Congress (D) were characteristic of nineteenth century abolitionism rather than the twentieth century civil rights movement. Calls for reparations (E) developed in the late twentieth century after King's death.

4. **(B)** The agreement ending the Cuban Missile Crisis called for the Soviet Union to withdraw its missiles from Cuba while the United States agreed not to overthrow Castro's regime. The Soviet Union objected to U.S. missiles in Turkey, but that issue was not included in the agreement (C) and (D). The agreement also said nothing with regard to Soviet troops in Cuba (A) or U.S. missiles in Europe (E).

5. **(A)** For whatever reasons, immigrants of the "New Immigration" tended to settle in the large cities of the Northeast and Midwest. Very few of them settled on farms (B), filed on homesteads (C), or migrated to the South and

Southwest (D). While some eventually returned to their countries of origin, the majority did not (E).

6. **(B)** Germany's 1917 declaration of its intent to wage unrestricted submarine warfare was the most important factor in bringing the United States into World War I. German violation of Belgian neutrality in 1914 (A) did nothing to aid Germany's cause in America, and revelation of German's suggestions to Mexico (C) was even more damaging, but neither of these had the impact of the U-boats. The fall of the tsar and beginning of the Russian Revolution (D) may or may not have had an influence on President Woodrow Wilson, and the deteriorating situation for the Allies (E) was not fully known.

7. **(A)** Roosevelt's New Nationalism pertained to domestic reform. Unrelated was the fact that Roosevelt favored development of a form of colonial empire (B) and rejected an isolationist approach to foreign affairs (E). Though he gained a reputation as a trust-buster, Roosevelt was by no means in favor of breaking up all trusts and large business combinations (C). He rejected the socialist call for government ownership of basic industries (D).

8. **(C)** It was FDR's predecessor, Herbert Hoover, who in 1932 established the Reconstruction Finance Corporation. In doing so, he broke withmany leaders in the Republican party, including Secretary of the Treasury Andrew Mellon, who believed the government had no choice but to let the business cycle run its course. Roosevelt's New Deal incorporated every other element listed.

9. (A) The Haymarket Affair involved the throwing of a bomb at Chicago police and a subsequent riot involving police and striking workers. There were plenty of scandals within the Grant administration (B), but this was not one of them. Allegations of corruption on the part of Republican presidential candidate James G. Blaine (C) were contained in the Mulligan Letters. The disastrous fire that pointed out the hazardous working conditions in some factories (D) was New York's Triangle Shirtwaist factory fire in 1911. An early challenge to the authority of states to regulate the railroad industry (E) was contained in the Supreme Court case of *Munn v. Illinois* in 1877.

10. **(A)** The Populists desired free coinage of silver. They also desired direct election of U.S. Senators, not necessarily an end to the electoral college (D). The Progressive movement, which followed Populism, favored the reform of child labor laws (B) and the use of modern science to solve social

problems (C). In general, Populists were more likely to favor racial discrimination than to oppose it (E).

11. **(C)** Drawing on circus imagery, this cartoon presents Roosevelt as a trust tamer.

12. **(C)** The SALT I Treaty indicated U.S. acceptance of the concept of Mutual Assured Destruction. It was ratified by the U.S. Senate (D)— unlike the SALT II Treaty—but did not bring substantial reductions in the number of missiles on either side (A), nor did it require the Soviet Union to reduce the number of its missiles to a level of equality with the United States (E). It discouraged the deployment of defensive weapons (B).

13. **(C)** Johnson did not require former Confederate states to pay reparations. He did, however, recommend they extend the franchise to blacks (A), and he did require them to ratify the Thirteenth Amendment (B), renounce secession (D), and repudiate the Confederate debt (E).

14. **(A)** Many American intellectuals of the 1920s expressed a sense of alienation for a country whose manners and direction they found distasteful. They tended to be more cynical than either romantic (C) or complacent (B), and many became expatriates while few if any could be called patriotic (D) or pietistic (E).

15. **(D)** In response to a perceived insult to the U.S. flag and in order to hasten the downfall of Mexican leader Victoriano Huerta, Wilson ordered U.S. forces to occupy the port of Vera Cruz where the original incident had occurred. Anxious to be rid of Huerta, Wilson would probably not have considered a diplomatic protest (E) strong enough, though he did respond with such protests to German U-boat activities in the First World War. Wilson ordered Pershing into Mexico (A) two years later after Mexican bandit Pancho Villa had raided across the border into the United States. Wilson had never granted diplomatic recognition to Huerta's regime (B), and U.S. troops have not occupied Mexico City (C) since the end of the Mexican War in 1848.

16. **(E)** Restoration of the balance of power was not a part of Wilson's Fourteen Points. Instead Wilson favored collective security. Self-determination (A), open diplomacy (B), freedom of the seas (C), and a League of Nations (D) were all advocated in the Fourteen Points.

17. **(C)** Booker T. Washington encouraged his fellow blacks to work hard, acquire property, and prove they were worthy of their rights. Washington's

contemporary and critic W.E.B. Du Bois urged his fellow blacks to agitate questions of racial equality (A), be more militant in demanding their rights (B), not accept separate but equal facilities (D), and form an organization to advance the rights of blacks (E).

18. **(C)**   Johnson was impeached but was never removed from office (A) and (B). He did not resign, was not pardoned, and was never charged with a criminal offense (D). The vote on his removal from office was in fact taken (E) but fell short by one vote.

19. **(B)**   The Democrats were promised an end to Reconstruction as part of the Compromise of 1877. Protective tariffs remained high (D), compensation was not paid for freed slaves (E), bribes were neither sought nor given (C), and, of course, no promise was made concerning future elections (A).

20. **(B)**   Wilson encouraged the passage of the Revenue Act of 1913, which established the graduated income tax. The Pure Food and Drug Act (A) was passed under Theodore Roosevelt, and the Sherman Antitrust Act (E) under Benjamin Harrison. The old-age pension (D) had to wait for Franklin Roosevelt. High protective tariffs (C) have existed at a number of times throughout U.S. history. The Underwood Tariff passed under Wilson represented a lowering of tariff rates.

21. **(C)**   At Casablanca, Roosevelt and Churchill agreed to demand unconditional surrender. Far from granting amnesty to Axis leaders (D), they determined to hold them responsible for their crimes. The decision to concentrate on the Germans first (A) had already been made and was not changed (B). It was held to be still too risky to land troops in France in the summer of 1943 (E).

22. **(B)**   Farmers of the Great Plains and the South often saw the Alliance movement as the only way to get out of the seemingly endless cycle of debt (crop liens), sharecropping, and/or low commodity prices. Small farmers in the Northeast could not, in fact, compete with Western farms, but they had no need to since they could concentrate on production of perishable items for nearby metropolitan areas (A). This was also the age of the giant "bonanza" farms of the northern Plains, but neither the owners of such farms (D) nor established, well-to-do farmers (C) had any need for the kind of government help the Farmers' Alliances sought. There were also a number of Chinese immigrants in the Western states at this time, not, however, in the Farmers' Alliances.

23. **(B)** Southern states were required to ratify the Fourteenth Amendment. Actually, blacks had not always been granted full civil rights even in northern states before the Civil War and after (A). Integrated public schools were more than a century away (C). The Sixteenth Amendment (D), allowing a federal income tax, was ratified in 1913. Some radicals talked of providing land to the freed slaves (E) but nothing ever came of it.

24. **(C)** The primary function of the World War I Food Administration was to oversee the production and allocation of foodstuffs to assure adequate supplies for the army and the Allies. It did not become involved in operating farms (E) nor did it, as a general rule, specially monitor the food produced (D). Farm prices were considered to be high enough already (A), and the U.S. would hardly have imported food from its somewhat undernourished Allies (B).

25. **(C)** The purpose of the Truman Doctrine was to aid countries that were the targets of Communist expansionism. Preventing European meddling in the affairs of South American countries (B) was the essence of the Monroe Doctrine, which was not directly related to the Truman Doctrine (E). It was the Marshall Plan, also instituted during Truman's presidency, that aided the economic recovery of Europe from the Second World War (A).

26. **(C)** Subsidies to transcontinental railroads generally took the form of land grants along the railroad's right-of-way. Occasionally, loans, rather than tax breaks (A), were granted on a per-mile basis. Blanket appropriations (B) and provision of supplies and materials (D) were generally not used. In the southeastern U.S., convict labor was sometimes rented to railroads (E), but not for the transcontinental railroads; much of their track lay, of necessity, far from centers of population.

27. **(E)** A member of the Social Gospel movement would probably argue that Christians should work to reorganize the industrial system and bring about international peace. He would probably not be very concerned about such "ordinary" sins as alcohol abuse and sexual permissiveness (A), nor would he hold the poor at fault for their plight (B) or suggest that those who committed abuses simply lacked willpower (C)—all this was society's fault. He did not see religion as an individual (D) but rather a social matter.

28. **(C)** In *Plessy v. Ferguson* (1896), the Supreme Court upheld separate but equal facilities. It overturned this ruling with *Brown v. Topeka Board of Education* in 1954 (A). The ruling that no black slave could be a citizen of the United States was the 1857 case *Dred Scott v. Sanford* (B). Various

Supreme Court decisions in the '50s, '60s, and '70s dealt with literacy tests (E) and Affirmative Action (D).

29. **(A)** The Spanish-American War showed the need of shifting naval forces rapidly between the Atlantic and the Pacific. There had never been much doubt about overcoming Latin American countries if that were necessary, or of dealing with any (highly unlikely) threat from Spain (D). The war did nothing to discredit opponents of the project (C), and such tropical diseases as malaria and yellow fever were not dealt with successfully (E) until during the actual building of the canal.

30. **(D)** Woodrow Wilson's most prized part of his Fourteen Points was the League of Nations. The Fourteen Points also included freedom of the seas (D), open diplomacy (A), and the right of self-determination— though not of a union of Germany and Austria in accord with such a right (C). Wilson would definitely have opposed either strengthening the Austrian Empire or restoring the balance of power (B).

31. **(A)** W. E. B. Du Bois founded the National Association for the Advancement of Colored People (NAACP). He was a leader of the Niagara Movement (C) and an outspoken critic of the Atlanta Compromise (B), which was the work of Booker T. Washington (E) whose teaching was that blacks should temporarily accommodate themselves to the whites (D).

32. **(D)** Northern voters simply lost interest and grew tired of Reconstruction. Leading Radicals in the North had never cared much whether Reconstruction was constitutional or not (C), but many of them were dead by 1877. Agitating wartime animosities was still a useful electoral tactic (E), but it did not necessarily need to be linked to reconstructing the South. The goals of the Radical Republicans had not been accomplished (B), but neither had the Southerners regained all the state governments (A).

33. **(C)** The Marshall Plan was an American economic aid program for Europe. The Truman Doctrine was the American commitment to help countries threatened by Communism (D). It was a post–World War II program and therefore had nothing to do with strategies for defeating Germany (A) or Japan (B). It also had nothing to do with American civil defense (E).

34. **(B)** Dewey was not concerned with strengthening a child's respect for parental or other traditional authority. He has been called the father of Progressive Education (E); he was influenced by the ideas of "Pragmatist" philosopher William James (D); he strove to alter the content and purpose of schooling (A) and to socialize the child through his peer group (C).

35. **(E)** Rather than presenting McKinley as a strong leader, this cartoon presents the president as being overwhelmed by a tidal wave of public and congressional opinion.

36. **(B)** he first policy toward the Plains Indians was simply to let them have the entire area, which was actually believed to be a desert. Later the policy changed to dividing the Indians between two large reservations (A), then to confining them to a number of small reservations (E), then to giving them their land in individual parcels (C), and then back to reservations again. The idea that Indians should be exterminated (D) was never a policy of the government but, unfortunately, was held by some individuals.

37. **(A)** Georgia O'Keeffe, Thomas Hart Benton, and Edward Hopper were all American painters of the 1920s (E). This was the age of jazz (B) and of skyscrapers (D). O'Keeffe was known for her abstract paintings of flowers and animal skulls against the background of the New Mexico desert (C).

38. **(E)** The Dumbarton Oaks Conference was one of the important meetings that led to the formation of the United Nations. Punishment of Nazi war criminals (A) was dealt with at the Nuremberg Trials. The map of Eastern Europe (D) was discussed at the Yalta Conference. The decision to drop the atomic bomb (B) was made by President Truman.

39. **(B)** The national unemployment rate soared to approximately 25% of the work force in early 1933. This meant that approximately 13 million workers were unemployed. While 25% was the national unemployment rate, in some cities the number of unemployed approached 90% (E). This was at a time when there were no welfare benefits or unemployment funds in most areas of the country. What made things worse was the sheer amount of time workers remained unemployed. By early 1937, unemployment had fallen to 14.3%, still representing 8 million unemployed workers. Then the recession of 1937 put an additional 2 million workers out of work again. The suffering of being unemployed as long as many of these workers is beyond description. Hobo camps and "Hoovervilles" popped up in virtually every American city.

Worse, even for those who kept their jobs, poverty became widespread. Crop prices for farmers dropped by 60% (D). Wages, for workers who still had jobs, dropped 40% (C). Banks continued to collapse, taking the personal savings of depositors down with them and leaving depositors with no savings to help them through this period. So, while 25% may not sound catastrophic at first, combined with the collapse of wages and crop prices, as well as the collapse of banks and the sheer amount of time many people were out of work, the nation's economy was close to total collapse.

40. **(D)** In early 1942, the Japanese high command, angered at air raids from American aircraft carriers, decided to force what was left of the American Pacific fleet into a decisive battle in which the American Navy and its carriers would be destroyed. They decided on an invasion of the American-held island of Midway. Midway was a logical choice. It was 1,100 miles northwest of Hawaii. More importantly, it had a seaplane base and an airstrip. In American hands it provided the United States with an observation post to monitor Japanese actions throughout the central Pacific. In Japanese hands, it would provide them with an airbase from which they could launch continuous air attacks on Pearl Harbor, making it unusable as an American base. If Japan invaded Midway, the Americans would have to send their fleet to defend it or face the loss of Pearl Harbor and Hawaii.

On paper, the plan seemed ideal. The Japanese could put up to ten aircraft carriers into the operation. They believed the Americans had only two available aircraft carriers (actually, the Americans had three usable carriers because the U.S.S. *Yorktown*, which the Japanese thought they had sunk at the Battle of Coral Sea (C), had survived and was repaired in time to fight at Midway). The Japanese had dozens of battleships and heavy cruisers. The Americans had only two battleships available, which they chose not to use, and only eight heavy cruisers. There seemed to be no way the Americans could win.

Unfortunately for the Japanese, the battle was not fought on paper. American cryptographers deciphered enough Japanese messages to uncover the plan. In addition, the overconfident Japanese, expecting to surprise a scattered American fleet, did not concentrate their forces into an overwhelming single attack force. Instead, they divided their fleet into four separate attack forces, each of which was vulnerable to American attack if caught off guard. When the Japanese arrived at Midway, a well-prepared, tightly concentrated American fleet was waiting. Despite a series of nearly catastrophic errors, the Americans caught the Japanese by surprise, sinking four of their largest aircraft carriers and killing 600 of Japan's best pilots. Without adequate air protection, the invasion was cancelled and the Japanese fleet returned to base. Midway was saved. At the time, American analysts thought they had just bought the United States some additional time until the Japanese regrouped and attacked again. In reality, the Japanese were so stunned by the defeat that they readjusted their war plans, switching to defensive operations. They never returned to Midway. With the Japanese now on the defensive, the United States was able to seize the initiative at Guadalcanal (E), beginning an island-hopping campaign that took America to Japan's outer islands. Midway was undoubtedly the turning point as it marked the first significant American victory over the Japanese and the end of major Japanese offensive operations in the central Pacific. The Japanese attack on Pearl Harbor in 1941 (B) brought the U.S. into the war. The Battle of Leyte Gulf in 1944 (A) preceded the American invasion of the Philippines.

41. **(E)**   *Brown v. Board of Education of Topeka* was the first legal shot in the war to desegregate America's public schools. Up to this time, many school districts, particularly in the South, had segregated schools for black and white schoolchildren under the doctrine of "separate by equal" enunciated by *Plessy v. Ferguson* (B). Sadly, most education facilities for black children were anything but equal. Blacks usually got dilapidated facilities, poorly trained teachers, and an inferior education. Frustrated black parents challenged the "separate but equal" doctrine in several states and those challenges were consolidated into one case to be presented before the United States Supreme Court in 1954. Previous court decisions had chipped away at the separate but equal doctrine in the realm of graduate and professional education, but the 1954 decision was a landmark one because it dealt with public education at the elementary and high school levels, thereby affecting a broad range of Americans. The 1954 decision had nothing to do with prayer in public schools (A), rights of minors (C), or aptitude tests (D),

42. **(B)**   There were many major changes resulting from the rapid industrial development in the United States from 1860 through 1900. First, there was a shift to building larger and larger industrial facilities to accommodate the new machine technologies coming into existence. Small factories could not absorb the cost of much of the machinery and did not produce enough to make the machinery profitable. So contrary to choice (D), there was an increase in large industrial plants and a relative decline in small factories and contrary to choice (E) an increase in worker productivity. Also, in the late nineteenth century there was little interest in health and safety issues (A). The major focus was on speed of production rather than quality of work (B).

43. **(A)**   After he was overthrown by revolutionary forces in 1978, the Shah of Iran, now residing in Mexico, asked for permission to enter the United States to receive cancer treatment. President Carter was warned that

admitting the Shah to the United States, for any reason, would look to the Iranians like America still supported the Shah's regime and would lead to trouble. However, other advisors told Carter that the United States owed the Shah a large debt of gratitude for the favors he had done for America and also for the lack of decisive support from the U.S. when his government was overthrown. Carter had previously refused to grant the Shah exile in the United States, but when he was told of the Shah's need for cancer treatment he decided to allow the Shah to enter the U.S. on humanitarian grounds. As predicted, the Iranians were infuriated by this. On November 4, 1979, young Iranian males, backed by their government and claiming to be students, seized the American embassy compound and took 76 hostages, 62 of whom were held for more than a year. It was the beginning of one of the worst nightmares in American foreign policy and it helped ruin Carter's presidency. The United States made no attempt to overthrow the government of Khomeini (E). The Israeli invasion of Lebanon (D) and air strikes against Libya (C) both took place after the hostage crisis. The Camp David Accords (B) were signed in 1978.

44. **(A)** The "Good Neighbor" policy sought to smooth over relations between the United States and Latin America by retreating from the blatant interventionism which dominated U.S. policy into the 1930s. The effects of interventionism had become increasingly costly to the point that the benefits derived were not worth the expense. In 1933, Franklin Roosevelt officially consolidated many changes already under way in U.S. policy toward Latin America under the heading of the "Good Neighbor" policy. Under this plan, the United States would pull back from the nearly constant use of military intervention to control Latin American nations. The U.S. government would cease acting unilaterally in Latin American affairs and would attempt to consult with and seek the approval of Latin American governments before intervening in the region. In addition, the United States would support Latin American governments headed by strong, independent leaders and would help train Latin American military forces so they could defend themselves. U.S. banks would also provide loans and other economic assistance to help stabilize fragile Latin American economies.

While the United States still dominated many aspects of Latin American life, with the adoption of the "Good Neighbor" policy that domination was handled more diplomatically, with somewhat more respect for local authorities. Many of the leaders who emerged at this time were military dictators who were trained by American military personnel as part of the effort to train Latin American military forces. These dictators owed their power to the United States and often stayed in power only as a result of U.S. backing. So, while the days of the "Big Stick" effectively ended with the "Good Neighbor" policy, U.S. domination of the region continued, albeit at a somewhat reduced level of visibility. Choices (B) through (D) were never part of American policy. Choice (E) refers to Lend-Lease, adopted in 1941.

45. **(A)** "Reaganomics" was the term coined for President Ronald Reagan's supply-side economic policies. Reagan believed that the way to repair the shattered economy he inherited from the Carter administration was to cut federal spending on domestic programs while at the same time cutting taxes for the wealthy and for corporations. The "supply-side" theory advocated by Reagan asserted that by cutting taxes to businesses and to the rich, money would be freed up for future investments and the creation of new jobs. This investment income would offset the initial loss of tax revenue caused by the tax cuts. Eventually, through the creation of new jobs and investments, the money freed up by tax cuts to the rich would "trickle down" to the middle-classes and the poor. While this sounded good on paper, it never worked out quite as well in real life. The tax cuts did spur investment, but the investments often didn't translate into jobs that paid well. The "trickle-down" was uneven and often quite limited. Many wealthy people pocketed the money rather than investing it. Still, new jobs were created and the nation began an economic expansion that lasted into the 1990s, but in the meantime the government experienced mounting budget deficits. Reagan rejected the ideas of a "planned economy" (D) advocated by many liberals in the 1930s and the "pump-priming" theory of John Maynard Keynes (E). "Controlled Growth" (B) refers to efforts to balance growth and inflation through monetary policy. There is no such thing as the "bubble up" theory (C).

46. **(B)** In January 1918, Woodrow Wilson proposed Fourteen Points that enunciated his goals for the peace that would follow World War I. These were idealistic goals based on notions of open diplomacy, the elimination of secret treaties, self-determination, arms reduction, open trade, and a League of Nations to serve as an international forum to prevent future wars. The thrust of the Fourteen Points emphasized fairness and openness in international relationships. By November 1918, the Germans faced military and political collapse, but they approached an armistice with the Allies convinced that the postwar treaty would be a fair one based upon Wilson's Fourteen Points. They reasoned that since the United States had turned the

tide and saved France and Britain from almost certain defeat, the United States would dominate the peace negotiations. Unfortunately, they reasoned incorrectly and the Treaty of Versailles reflected British and French desires for vengeance more than it reflected the Wilsonian principles elucidated in his Fourteen Points. The "New Freedom" policy (E) refers to Wilson's domestic agenda when elected president in 1912 and the Balfour Declaration (D) of 1917 promised British protection to Jewish settlers in Palestine. The Twenty-One Demands (A) were made by Japan on China in 1915. In the Sussex Pledge (C) of 1916, Germany promised not to sink unarmed merchant ships without warning.

47. **(B)**   The years between 1876-1900 were years of relative political equality between the Republicans and Democrats. It was also a time when most Americans were rejecting or resisting the cries for reform by political activists. Most people wanted the federal government to remain inactive and uninvolved as much as possible. The concept of laissez-faire leadership was flourishing. This resulted in little significant reform legislation from the Congress. It also led to the election of presidents who saw themselves as political caretakers of the office of the presidency, rather than advocates of social or political reform. The equality between the two parties at this time also made it difficult for any president to push for major changes because the political base of support was too evenly divided to provide the necessary votes in Congress for effective action. While none of these presidents were incompetent (B), they just did not see the presidency as an office appropriate for taking strong initiatives. They believed their major job was to insure Congressional legislation was effectively carried out and to veto any legislation in which they felt Congress had exceeded its powers. Such an attitude does not usually lead to inspirational, dynamic leadership. Their style was such that they believed the *less* they were noticed the better they were doing their job. This has left the long-term impression of them being "weak" presidents. Although Hayes, Garfield, Arthur, and Harrison each served one term or less, Cleveland served two non-consecutive terms and McKinley was elected in both 1896 and 1900 (A). Populism was a minority movement (E) and Congress passed no specific laws limiting the power of the president (C). Although Arthur (D) came out of machine politics, the others did not.

48. **(E)**   The print suggests that the contended, hard-working people on the right are on the right track to wealth, whereas those on the left are grasping for wealth through such means as gambling and stock speculation, represented by balloons forever out of their reach.

49. **(D)** Muckrakers got their name from Theodore Roosevelt, who compared the sensationalistic exposes of high-level corruption to "raking muck." Their stories tended to focus on the very worst behaviors of industrial leaders and politicians. The stories were designed to arouse the public and play to their "baser instincts." They explored all of the flaws in American society and provided a method of airing the nation's "dirty laundry." While political and industrial leaders were horrified by the tone and focus of the stories, the general public could not get enough. The stories confirmed in many people's minds what they had long suspected: rather than protecting the public interest, many public and private leaders were using their positions to further their own self-interest at the expense of everyone else. The stories led to an outcry for reform and provided Progressives with just the ammunition and public support they needed to insure passage of legal reforms.

50 **(D)** The 1920s were a mixture of both conservative and liberal trends. On the liberal side, women were granted the right to vote with ratification in 1920 of the Nineteenth Amendment to the Constitution (A). With new forms of credit and advertising, combined with increases in wages and productivity, consumerism became the new American ethic (C).

On the conservative side, prohibition was enacted with the passage of the Eighteenth Amendment to the Constitution in 1919 and when put into effect it unintentionally encouraged bootlegging and the rise of organized crime in America (B). The Ku Klux Klan, using new advertising techniques to market itself, reached a peak membership of 5 million people in 1925 (E), before sex scandals, corruption, poor leadership, and public revulsion at Klan activities broke its power base and discredited it as a major political force. Throughout the mid-1920s, however, the Klan was a force to be feared and accommodated, and Klan activities had a very intimidating effect on local and regional politics in the South, Midwest, and mid-Atlantic regions.

The only choice not characteristic of the 1920s is choice (D). The Progressive movement, so forceful before World War I, was eclipsed by the pro-business economic growth philosophies of Harding, Coolidge, Hoover, and the Republicans. Progressive reforms were rolled back throughout the 1920s, negating many gains previously made in regulating businesses and securing labor rights. These gains were sacrificed on the altars of economic growth and laissez-faire capitalism. Progressivism would not return to the fore until the enactment of Franklin Roosevelt's "New Deal" in the 1930s, where Progressive principles were carried far beyond anything hoped for at the turn of the century.

51. **(A)** The Farm Security Administration was created to help restore faith in America by sending photojournalists around the country to photograph Americans and American life. The focus of the resulting publications was on how people had survived, rather than succumbed to, the Great Depression. This program was designed as a public relations program, not as a jobs creation program. The Civil Works Administration (B) and Civilian Conservation Corps (C) were created in 1933 and the Works Progress Administration (D), and National Youth Administration (E) were established in 1935, all as job creating programs.

52. **(B)** The Plains Indians depended upon buffalo for almost every aspect of their survival. When they killed a buffalo, they used virtually every part of it, from the hide to the bones. In 1850, over 13 million buffalo meandered along the migration routes in the Great Plains. By 1890, fewer than 1,000 remained. Without the buffalo, the Plains Indians could not live according to their traditional ways. They were forced to either adapt to white rules (usually on reservations) or fight for their survival, as the Sioux and Cheyenne did in the 1870s. Fighting the whites was hopeless, but to many Indians, war was more honorable than dying in subjugation. While they managed a few victories such as at Little Big Horn, they were too badly outmanned and outgunned to have a long-term chance at victory. Without the buffalo, the entire Indian way of life was undermined and it led directly to the destruction of the Plains Indians' societies in a much broader way than any of the other choices listed in the question.

53. **(C)** The sharecropping system allowed poor tenant farmers and poor independent farmers to borrow seed, equipment, and supplies for planting and harvesting a crop. In return, sharecroppers had to pledge their crop, or a portion of their crop, as collateral. While this arrangement allowed sharecroppers to continue to farm the land and squeeze out a minimal survival, the costs charged to farmers for supplies and equipment as well as the exorbitant interest rates charged for loaning those supplies effectively kept sharecroppers in permanent debt. Interest rates ranged as high as 200%. Most sharecroppers never accumulated enough cash to work their way out from under the tremendous debt load they incurred trying to work their small plots of land (A). The only ones who got wealthy from this system were the landowners and the merchants who controlled the sharecroppers. This system did nothing to bring poor farmers into the middle class (B).

Neither did it expand the number of independently owned farms in the south. It had no restrictive effect on the power of former plantation owners or Northern business interests (D). Finally, it did nothing to enhance the relationship between blacks and whites as it did not force them to work side by side (E). In fact, in many ways it was used by Southern ruling elites to maintain the old social and racial order.

54. **(B)** During the 1880s and 1890s, America's railroads had a stranglehold on the transportation of goods, particularly agricultural goods, to the marketplace. In major markets where there were several competing rail lines, shipping costs were low. However, many farmers and manufacturers lived in areas served by only one major rail line or a "short line." On these noncompetitive lines, railroads charged exorbitantly high rates, often so high that the producers of goods could not make a profit on their goods. After bitter struggles in Congress and several Supreme Court challenges, the Interstate Commerce Act of 1887 was passed to curb pricing and other abuses by the railroad industry. In the related court cases, the Supreme Court ruled that only Congress had the right to regulate interstate commerce. This act created the Interstate Commerce Commission, whose major purpose was to keep an eye on railroad policies and to prevent further abuses.

55. **(E)** The Knights of Labor were founded in 1869 by workers in Philadelphia's garment district. They were the only broad-based union to survive the economic depression of 1873. They were also the only major union of their time to extend membership to blacks, women, and unskilled workers. They preached a long-term philosophy of achieving a society where employees and managers would work together cooperatively for all society's benefit. They reached the peak of their success in the mid-1880s, but following a series of failed strikes culminating in the disastrous Haymarket Square riot in 1886, the Knights began to splinter into small crafts unions and various other more radical workers groups. They never regained their dominance and were eventually supplanted by the AFL (C) in the 1890s as America's major labor union. The National Labor Union (A) was founded in 1866 but died out in the 1870s. The Industrial Workers of the World (B) was a radical union growing out of the Western Federation of Miners in the late nineteenth century but never became very large. The Congress of Industrial Organizations (D) grew out of the AFL in the mid-1930s.

56. **(E)** Political machines and the politics of political bosses dominated the workings of city governments in the late nineteenth century. Many of these organizations stayed in power through bribery, graft, and other corrupt

practices. In return, however, the machines took care of the interests of many of their most influential constituents. They provided many services that helped the poor survive in return for support at the polls. Many reformers, mostly from the middle and upper classes, demanding changes to end the corruption, found themselves stymied at the polls by large blocks of poor and immigrant voters who supported the political machines. The machines were often successfully able to portray themselves as protectors of the poor who fought against upper-class re-formers interested only in themselves.

While the political machines were able to enlist the support of some industrial leaders (A), and sometimes got indirect support from organized religion (B), they received little support from the middle class (D) and virtually no support from wealthy landowners living outside the city (C).

57. **(B)**   New Orleans in the 1890s provided the perfect opportunity for the European musical influences followed by wealthy Creoles (half white, half black) to intermingle with African musical influences dominating the culture of poor blacks. The result was a distinctly American musical form called jazz. Jazz players of turn-of-the-century New Orleans were among the highest paid "workers" in the South. The almost exclusively black performers were wealthier than virtually any other blacks in the country at the time. They also enjoyed a certain amount of respect and recognition denied to most other blacks. Eventually, these New Orleans jazz musician stook their music with them to other parts of the country. But it was in New Orleans that black musicians gave America its first truly original music form, jazz.

Blues (E) was and is a related musical form that developed in the rural South. Its development preceded jazz somewhat and was dominated by African musical influences. It never integrated the influences of European music with African musical traditions in the way jazz did, although even the sparse use of chords in blues owes its ancestry to Europe.

Gospel (A) and country (D) were later musical developments, both emerging in the late 1920s and 1930s, not directly connected with New Orleans. Folk (C) is a generic term for unschooled music that arises from the common people, but does not refer to any specific musical style.

58. **(E)**   The Tet Offensive, beginning on January 31, 1968, marked a turning point in the Vietnam War. Up until Tet, press coverage of the war, while raising some questions and more graphic than anything Americans had ever seen before, was mostly positive. American military leaders were talking

about seeing "light at the end of the tunnel." Many Americans still believed a military victory was possible. With the Tet Offensive, all illusions of a military victory ended.

What is ironic is that Tet was a military disaster for the North Vietnamese. Up until Tet, the Vietcong had stalled the American war effort by engaging in guerilla warfare which accented their advantages in the villages and jungle terrain and neutralized American superiority in conventional arms and equipment. They avoided the kind of massive pitched battles in which American technical superiority could be focused to destroy them. The repeated midnight attacks and "hit and run" raids on villages, convoys, and military bases kept the South Vietnamese and the Americans constantly off-balance and unable to use their forces effectively.

With Tet, the North Vietnamese scrapped this policy in favor of an all-out military assault on key bases and provincial capitals in South Vietnam. At first, caught by surprise, American and South Vietnamese forces reeled back at the ferocity of the North Vietnamese assaults. But soon, the Americans recovered and the North Vietnamese found themselves tied down in the very pitched battles that they could not hope to win. When it was over, the North Vietnamese had suffered over 400,000 casualties, which would take them more than four years to replace. It was the biggest American/ South Vietnamese military victory of the war. But it was also the biggest American political disaster of the war.

Tet came just as Lyndon Johnson was preparing to run for reelection in the 1968 political campaign. It called into question all the assurances by the government that the North Vietnamese were beaten and would collapse in the near future. People asked, "If they're beaten, how could they mount an offensive as large as this?" That the offensive had failed was irrelevant. Americans focused on the fact that it had taken place at all. Now many Americans began to see Vietnam as a tunnel with no way out, and press coverage became increasingly negative. Talk shifted from winning to just getting out. Johnson withdrew from the presidential campaign. The North Vietnamese, seeing the political effect, dug in their heels and were determined to outlast faltering American support for the war. After Tet, it was just a matter of how long it would be until America pulled out of Vietnam, and under what circumstances that pullout would take place.

The Gulf of Tonkin Incident (C) took place on August 2, 1964, and became the basis for escalation of the war. The Vietcong attacked American airfields at Pleiku (A) in February 1965 and Khe Sanh (D) in January,

1968. NLF (B) stands for National Liberation Front, the name for the political unit organized by the Vietcong to overthrow the South Vietnamese government.

59. **(C)**   In 1947, the British government told the American government that it could no longer afford the expense of economic and military aid to Greece and Turkey. At the time, both countries were locked in struggles against Communist insurgents. Greece was in virtual civil war and could not have won against Communist rebels without Western help. President Truman was determined that Greece should not be allowed to fall under Communist control. In response, he delivered a speech to Congress committing the United States to aid free people anywhere in the world in their struggle to preserve their freedom from foreign intervention or armed insurgents. This policy quickly became known as the Truman Doctrine. Congress approved aid to both Greece and Turkey, which both survived their respective Communist insurrections.

The aid to Greece and Turkey was just a first step in what became a massive aid program to noncommunist governments all over the world. Regrettably, many of the noncommunist governments receiving U.S. aid were led by brutal dictators every bit as evil as the Communist insurgents Truman wanted to suppress. American policy was so focused around Truman's effort to contain Communist expansion, however, even such rulers were seen as preferable to Communists.

Communists overthrew the government of Czechoslovakia (A) in 1948. The United States became concerned about Soviet influence in Iran (B) and helped sponsor a coup that brought Shah Resa Pahlavi to power in 1953. The Hungarian Revolution (D) against Communism took place in 1956. The Korean War (E) began in 1950.

60. **(E)**   All of these events relate to the Great Depression and New Deal eras. The order, from the earliest event to the most recent event, is as follows:

1. U.S. stock market crash (1929)

2. Hawley-Smoot tariff (1930)

3. election of Franklin D. Roosevelt (1932)

4. National Labor Relations Act (1935)

61. **(E)**   When Woodrow Wilson left Washington for the Paris Peace Conference, he had already taken steps to insure Senate opposition to whatever treaty emerged from the negotiations. The Senate was dominated by Republicans

and Wilson, a Democrat, neglected to ask any senators to accompany him to the negotiations. He also neglected to ask any Republicans to accompany him. These errors of omission guaranteed anger and resentment among Republicans in general and senators in particular. When the Treaty of Versailles was presented to the Senate, it found plenty of grist to grind in opposing the treaty. Contrary to Wilson pre-negotiation pledges, the treaty was punitive and failed to come close to approaching the principles of humanitarianism and self-determination that the president had so nobly espoused before and during the Paris Peace Conference. One senator prophetically called the treaty a "blueprint for another war."

Wilson made matters worse by refusing to compromise with the Senate on provisions senators found objectionable. Instead, he lectured them like a teacher would lecture some errant schoolchildren. Then, he embarked on a cross-county speaking tour by train to try to go "over the heads" of the senators and sell the treaty directly to the American people. During this trip he engaged in name-calling and direct attacks on the intelligence of the Senate. To a body of people as proud as those in the Senate, this was both insulting and infuriating, and their reaction was predictable. In addition, on his return to Washington, Wilson suffered a stroke which incapacitated him and he refused to negotiate further with treaty critics. Not surprisingly, when the treaty came up for ratification in November 1919, it was voted down. It came up for a vote again in March 1920, but Wilson still refused to compromise and the treaty was again voted down. The treaty was never ratified in its original form. The Unite States later signed a separate peace treaty with Germany.

62. **(C)**   Most Americans welcomed the economic growth and prosperity of the mid-1920s. However, some found the collapse of Progressivism, the subsequent dominance of materialistic consumerism, laissez-faire capitalism and its greed, corruption, and conspicuous consumption, as well as the emphasis on social conformity and dearth of spirituality, to be morally repugnant. This repugnance and cynicism regarding America's social framework were captured most poignantly in the works of several young American authors. F. Scott Fitzgerald, H. L. Mencken, Ernest Hemingway, and Sinclair Lewis wrote stories of heroes as flawed as the villains they sought to conquer. Their works raised question about traditional assumptions of right and wrong and often left those questions unanswered. They painted unsettling pictures of American society, frequently with a sharply critical, sometimes satirical portrayal of American hypocrisy and decadence.

Their unsettling works, with the inherent crying out at the loss of ideals, values, and purpose as well as the interwoven criticism of the current dominance of materialism, led critics and historians to label them the "Lost Generation." A whole generation of young writers faced what they believed to be a spiritually lost America, desperately needing to find new and meaningful goals and values. These writers' works attempted to point out the folly of 1920s America and rekindle the idealism and sense of deeper purpose they felt necessary for America to live up to its potential for all its citizens.

63. **(A)**   This cartoon presents Tweed as ruled by greed. The source of his money is not indicated.

64. **(D)**   Of the choices listed, a lack of available credit was the only choice that did not contribute to the Great Depression. In fact, just the opposite was true. Throughout the 1920s, to help spread the new ethic of consumerism, banks and industries made several new forms of credit and installment loans available to the public. This credit was essential because while industry was pushing people to consume, it was refusing to pay workers the wages they needed to buy the whole range of new consumer goods being made available. Credit was also essential to the farmers who could not earn enough from their crops, because of depressed crop prices, to break even. Without the new forms of credit being offered, consumers and farmers could not have sustained the economy as long as they did. Even with the new credit extensions, without wage increases and increases in crop prices, workers and farmers could not continue to purchase new goods and equipment indefinitely. Eventually, they reached their credit limits and often found they couldn't pay off their loans. The resulting foreclosures and bankruptcies weakened the entire banking system, making banks particularly vulnerable when the stock market crash began the final collapse of the economic boom of the 1920s. So, if anything, it was the easy availability of too much credit with too little screening to make sure those who borrowed could pay back the loans that contributed to the Great Depression.

65. **(B)**   The Indian Reorganization Act represented a reversal of previous government policy that had worked against Indian control of their lands and preservation of Indian traditions. Under the new law, Indian lands could not be divided up and parceled off in allotments that effectively broke up tribal reservations and allowed whites to move in and exploit Indian lands, as had been done by the General Allotment Act of 1887 (D). Further allotments were prohibited and Indians were provided funds with which they could purchase new land and regain control of land previously lost to allotments.

Indians were also given the right to draw up their own tribal constitutions, as separate tribal "nations," and establish their own tribal governments. Federal funds were offered to help Indian tribes construct schools, hospitals, and welfare agencies. Finally, the Act ended restrictions on the rights of Indians to practice tribal religions, rituals, and use tribal languages.

66. **(C)** Lyndon Johnson's "Great Society" was the collective name for several separate programs aimed at ending civil rights abuses and combating poverty. In the area of civil rights, the Civil Rights Act of 1964 was a piece of landmark legislation. It forbade discrimination based on race, color, religion, sex, or national origin in job hiring, promotion, and firing. It also forbade such discrimination in access to public accommodations and gave the federal government powers to cut funding to federally aided industries or agencies found guilty of discrimination. It also actively involved the United States government in attacking segregated school systems and forcing them to desegregate.

Related to this, the Voting Rights Act of 1965 gave the government the power to intervene and supervise voter registration in areas where minorities had been illegally restricted or discouraged from registering to vote in significant numbers. Economically, Johnson declared a war on poverty, backing several bills to combat poverty and its causes in the United States. Medicare, followed by Medicaid, was aimed at providing quality medical care to the elderly. Several programs were initiated to increase the quality of teachers and education in poverty-stricken areas. Most notably, Project Headstart, which attempted to provide quality pre-school training for impoverished preschoolers, involved the government in attacking the failure to succeed in school, which marked the lives of so many of the nation's poor.

Johnson also initiated the Neighborhood Youth Corps and the Job Corps to provide job training and experience for inner city youths. There were also tax cuts and economic aid programs to provide increased welfare benefits, especially to mothers with young children.

While the programs showed some initial success, and some pro-grams such as Project Head start were undeniably successful, many of the programs were tied to qualifications that helped lead to the destruction of the family unit among those seeking aid. Some economists argue that there is more poverty now than there was before the "Great Society" programs began. Many programs led to long-term dependence on government aid rather than fostering the independence needed to get off government support. While the civil rights aspects of the "Great Society" were quite successful in ending legal abuses to civil rights, many abuses continue today, albeit at a more subtle, insidious level. So, while the intentions of Johnson's "Great Society" programs were clearly good, the results were a mixed success.

67. **(D)**   In the 1880s and 1890s, the U.S. Supreme Court struck down desegregation laws and upheld the doctrine of segregated "separate but equal" facilities for blacks and whites. These laws became known as "Jim Crow" laws. Their impact was to allow racist governments in the south to set up "separate but unequal" facilities in which blacks were forced to sit in the rear of streetcars and buses, in the back rooms of restaurants, or were excluded completely from white businesses, and had to use separate and usually inferior public rest room facilities. These laws allowed white supremacists to "put blacks in their place" and effectively kept blacks from achieving anything near equal status. It was not until the 1950s and 1960s that new Supreme Court decisions finally forced the repeal of these laws. Poll taxes and literacy requirements were related laws that kept blacks from voting (A).

68. **(D)**   The Smoot-Hawley Tariffs were enacted in 1930, a time when the world economy had already been badly weakened and was still collapsing. These protectionist measures aided a few powerful industries but at high cost. Europeans called the measures an "economic declaration of war" and responded with their own retaliatory tariffs. What few jobs the Smoot-Hawley Tariffs initially saved were far outnumbered by the other jobs lost when European tariffs took effect. Additionally, Europeans now could not sell their goods to Americans, because of the high tariffs, and thus could not earn the money they needed to buy American products. At a time when trading doors needed to be opened wide and international trade expanded, Smoot-Hawley had the effect of closing those doors and stifling what little was left of international trade between Europe and the United States.

69. **(D)**   Most Americans were angered about the Iran-Contra Affair not because of the illegal funding of the Contra rebels in Nicaragua, but because of the shipment of arms to Iran for Iranian help in releasing American hostages in Lebanon. Despite the fact that the support for the Contra rebels involved direct violations of Congressional restrictions, which was a more serious legal concern than shipping arms to Iran, Congress had changed its

rules several times regarding aid to the Contras and many Americans felt they should be supported, regardless of what Congress said.

This is not to say that Americans were not upset by the illegal aid to the Contras. Many Americans opposed any aid to the Contras and to find out it had been done illegally by members of the government outraged them. But the level of rage and the numbers of people outraged did not come close to matching the anger felt over the "arms for hostages" aspects of the affair.

70. **(E)** The Great Plains saw the largest PERCENTAGE of population growth during this period. Immigrants from Europe and migrants from the East Coast and eastern Midwest were drawn to rich farmlands of the Great Plains by measures such as the Homestead Act (1862), which granted them 160 acres of land in return for promises to stay and farm the land. Railroad developers gave settlers tracts of land in return for developing the land adjacent to railroad rights of way. Finally, state and territorial governments, hungry for more residents to help develop local economies and help broaden and stabilize the economic structure of the state or territory, set up land grants and programs to encourage settlement. While virtually every area of the country experienced some population growth during this period, it was the Great Plains region with its vast tracts of undeveloped farmlands that experienced the greatest PERCENTAGE of growth.

71. **(B)** Many legal scholars consider the Fourteenth Amendment to the Constitution the most important amendment. It mandates that the federal government must provide equal protection under the law for every American citizen. This amendment was drawn up by Congress during Andrew Johnson's administration in an attempt to guarantee that civil rights legislation would be enforced. At the time, Johnson was accused, accurately, of not enforcing laws designed to protect the rights of freed blacks and former slaves. By passing this amendment, Congress hoped to guarantee enforcement of these laws. To ensure that the returning southern states would not block overall ratification of the amendment, Congress mandated that states seeking readmission must ratify the amendment before their governments would be recognized.

The Thirteenth Amendment prohibited slavery (A), while the Fifteenth Amendment guaranteed the right to vote (C). The Nineteenth Amendment gave women the right to vote (D) and the Sixteenth Amendment authorized the income tax (E).

72. **(D)**   What got Nixon into trouble was his involvement in covering up White House involvement with the entire Watergate Affair. What began as a second-rate burglary by a group of unknowns became a national scandal when the burglars' connections with the White House became public. Nixon actively involved himself in trying to prevent knowledge of White House involvement in Watergate from reaching the public, and it was this effort that ruined his presidency.

Had Nixon admitted White House involvement from the beginning, fired those involved, and made a public apology for the "excesses" of his underlings, he probably would have completed a successful second term. However, he and his advisors felt that the damage from Watergate could be contained if White House involvement was kept secret. Documents were shredded, records were changed, people were paid off, and Nixon was involved every step of the way. When the press finally began unraveling the mystery, Nixon continued to deny involvement and continued the cover up. When it was revealed that the White House had a taping system that had recorded Nixon's conversations during the period in question, he refused to release the tapes. Eventually, in April 1974, under increasing pressure and surrounded by growing stacks of incriminating evidence, Nixon released an edited version of the tapes. This moves parked even more controversy because the edited portions of the tapes included suspicious gaps where crucial conversations should have been.

Finally, under Supreme Court order, Nixon handed over unedited tapes, which, combined with the other evidence, confirmed Nixon's involvement in a massive, illegal cover up of the Watergate Affair. Nixon, facing impeachment, was forced to resign in disgrace. Later, he was pardoned before being brought to trial, by new president Gerald Ford.

73. **(A)**   The Atlantic Charter was the end product of a meeting between Winston Churchill and Franklin Roosevelt in August 1941, aboard the American *Augusta* off the coast of Newfoundland, Canada. The document pledged Britain and the United States to mutual cooperation in working for the defeat of Hitler. This was significant because America was still officially neutral, but Roosevelt's signing of the Atlantic Charter made the United States and Britain de facto allies. Roosevelt was convinced that it was now just a matter of time before the United States would have to fight Hitler's Germany, and he was determined not to let the British fall before the United States could become fully engaged. The Atlantic Charter cemented these beliefs and laid out long-term military and political goals

in a combined Anglo-American war effort. The Charter was the foundation of the extremely successful coordination of operations between the two countries for the remainder of the war.

It did not exchange American destroyers for British bases (D), which had taken place in 1940. Nor did it repeal the Neutrality Acts(1935–37) (B) and allow cash-and-carry sales of arms to Britain (E), which occurred in 1939. It said nothing about Latin America specifically; the Declaration of Panama in 1939 established Latin American neutrality (C).

74. **(A)**   Pearl Harbor was the worst defeat ever suffered by the American Navy. To be caught as unprepared as the commanders at Pearl Harbor were was unbelievable to most Americans. American racism against the Japanese led many people to believe that the Japanese could never have pulled off their stunning raid without "inside help" of some sort. Suspicions immediately turned to Washington where Roosevelt's desire to bring America into World War II was well known. To these people, a conspiracy by Washington to let the Japanese get away with the attack, stirring up American anger and bringing America into the war, answered so many questions about the Japanese success that many felt it had to be the real reason Pearl Harbor had succeeded for the Japanese.

Evidence indicates that there was no plot. While American intelligence analysts knew the Japanese were about to attack somewhere, they did not know where. Since Japanese ships had been spotted sailing south, it was natural to assume that they were going to attack Southeast Asia or the Philippines, where British and American naval strength were too weak to effectively deter them. Military leaders sold themselves on this idea to the point that they ignored evidence indicating Pearl Harbor was also a target.

In addition, prejudice against the Japanese played a large role in the base being unprepared. Commanders at the base refused to focus on what the Japanese were capable of doing and instead focused on what seemed to make sense for them to do (D). To these commanders, a Japanese attack on Pearl Harbor was senseless. The odds involved with attacking the bulk of the American Pacific Fleet, in its home harbor with the hundreds of defensive aircraft and antiaircraft guns, were so high that to Americans it seemed suicidal for the Japanese to attempt an attack. Americans felt that the Japanese would not dare try it and ignored the fact that they had the capability to pull it off if they got lucky. Based on these assumptions, base commanders prepared only for the immediate threat of sabotage from local Japanese-Americans in Hawaii (B). They never seriously considered preparation for a full-scale Japanese assault, in spite of repeated war warnings from Washington, until the bombs actually began to fall.

While a message warning Pearl Harbor was sent before the attack, it went over commercial telegraph services rather than priority military lines (C) and did not arrive until after the attack, too late to make a difference. Some historians question if the telegram would have changed the result even if it had arrived on time, so convinced were Pearl's commanders that the Japanese would not dare attack.

Finally, one of the major contributors to the belief in a government conspiracy was the amount of intelligence gathered before the attack which clearly indicated Pearl Harbor was at risk. In hindsight, the failure to effectively use this intelligence was shocking. Unfortunately, the intelligence was gathered in bits and pieces by several different intelligence agencies within the Army and Navy. At the time the two services did not share their intelligence with each other, due to inter service rivalry and other logistical factors (E). As a result, each intelligence service had only some of the necessary "bits" of information needed to piece the entire picture together. It was only AFTER the attack that all the intelligence was put together and the obviousness of Pearl Harbor as a target became clear.

75. **(C)**   Open-range ranching was a technique in which a rancher would purchase a relatively small plot of land, usually located near a stream, that bordered on public domain land which was open to public use. The ranchers along this land would then let their cattle graze in the vast open ranges of public domain land bordering their property. Since no one else was using the land, this was at first a very cost-effective method of raising cattle. However, as development of the Western states continued, more and more people crowded into the territories and competed to use this open range land. Sheepherders, "sodbusters" or crop farmers, and others all took their share of the land at the expense of the cattle ranchers. This process did not always occur peacefully. Several "range wars" broke out between cattle ranchers and farmers leading to many injuries and deaths. Farmers started fencing in their lands denying access to the cattle. Cattle ranchers began fencing in large tracts of public domain land to protect land they needed for their herd to graze. Eventually, the pressures of overgrazing and competition eliminated or greatly curtailed the practice of open range ranching, a process accelerated by the harsh winter of 1886–87, which killed large numbers of cattle. Ranching became more industrialized and large cattle companies

dominated the cattle industry. By the mid-1890s, the age of open range ranching was over.

The other choices are incorrect. Low beef prices did not affect open range ranching (A) as it was one of the most cost-effective ways to raise cattle, if the open range was available for grazing. While cattle did occasionally wander off (E), use of branding limited ranchers' losses and the losses rarely reached unacceptable levels. The government never en-acted laws giving sheepherders priority use of the land (B). Finally, cattle ranchers never, on a wide scale, adopted sharecropping techniques (D), which would have been inappropriate for most cattle-raising operations.

76. **(C)** Pulitzer believed that newspapers should be targeted at the masses. In this vein, his newspaper, *New York World*, used a combination of sensationalist stories, muckraking, and a publishing style designed to make the news read like a soap opera, to popularize newspapers among the middle class and the poor. His tactics worked. Using banner headlines, emphasizing the most scandalous or gory aspects of a story, exaggerating stories or making up details designed to arouse the reader, all served to catch people's attention and bring them back for more. Since his paper used a cheap yellow ink in printing a popular comic strip of the time, the term "yellow journalism" came to symbolize this early form of "tabloid" style news reporting. Pulitzer's techniques were so effective in increasing his newspaper's readership, that soon newspaper publishers throughout the nation were copying his style and "yellow journals" were springing up in nearly every major U.S. city. William Randolph Hearst's chain of papers was the most successful in imitating Pulitzer's approach.

77. **(C)** In 1885, the federal government had enacted tariffs on more than 4,000 separate manufactured items. While this protected the manufacturers of these items, it also needlessly raised prices paid by consumers. Democrats began a major push at this time to enact "free trade" legislation, charging that most tariffs benefitted the industrialists while hurting poor and middle-class consumers. They also charged that since nearly all the tariffs protected manufactured goods and few tariffs protected agricultural products, that farmers were being hurt by tariffs. Farmers had to pay the inflated prices for imported manufactured goods (or inflated prices for domestic goods because many American manufacturers raised their prices to levels near the artificially high import prices, making a huge profit) but could not get inflated prices for their unprotected agricultural products. Despite their efforts, high tariffs remained in effect throughout the period. Republican

claims that the tariffs were necessary to protect American industries were strongly supported by the business leaders of the country, and Democratic reforms were defeated or so watered down as to be useless.

78. **(B)** When the United States declared war on Germany and entered World War I, a massive mobilization effort was needed to prepare the nation for wartime requirements. Procedures for drafting, training, and transporting soldiers had to be quickly organized. Industrial production had to be regeared for wartime production needs. At first, this mobilization effort was headed by a number of industrial committees that advised the government on selection and cost of equipment. However, it soon became apparent that many of the businessmen running these committees had more than the nation's interests at heart. Many were using the committees as vehicles to quick wartime riches. Press reports of the corruption quickly led to public demands for reform. Wilson responded by disbanding the various committees and replacing them in July 1917 with the War Industries Board (WIB). The WIB coordinated war production for the remainder of the war.

79. **(B)** The Scopes "Monkey Trial" was instigated when in 1925 a Dayton, Tennessee, biology teacher, John Scopes, challenged a state law prohibiting the teaching of evolution. His trial that summer became a national news story as the state brought in former Secretary of State William Jennings Bryan as an expert witness. The defense was led by well-known trial lawyer Clarence Darrow. The case took on a circus atmosphere with vendors and crowds of reporters milling about the courtroom and the surrounding environs.

Bryan's unswerving defense of the literal truth of the Bible was attacked as foolish and ignorant. He was made a laughingstock in the national press. Despite the fact that Scopes admitted breaking the law and was found guilty, defense attorneys claimed victory in that they had pointed out the intolerance of religious fundamentalism and showed it to be out of place in modern society.

Observers of the trial saw it to be a clash between reactionary social elements trying to resist the onslaught of changing values, life-styles, and technology by desperately clinging to antiquated belief systems, and modernists trying to replace traditional thought with newer secular ideas based on individualism and supported by scientific evidence. While the fundamentalists won the verdict, it was a Pyrrhic victory in that the trial painted them in such a bad light that they lost ground in their efforts to sway society from becoming increasingly secular.

80. **(D)** In post-World War II Europe, Berlin was a headache for both the United States and the Soviet Union. The city was jointly occupied by the French, British, Americans, and the Soviets. It was situated about 100 miles inside the Soviet zone of occupation in eastern Germany. For the Western Allies, Berlin was a headache because in the event of Soviet aggression the city was virtually indefensible. It was also vulnerable to supply cutoffs because everything had to be transported through Russian-controlled East Germany. At the same time, a Western pullout from the city was politically unacceptable in the supercharged Cold War atmosphere of the time.

Berlin was a headache for the Russians because it sat right in the middle of their occupation zone in eastern Germany. It provided the Americans with an ideal observation post from which to monitor Soviet troop movements. It also sat on one of the main supply routes needed by Soviet forces if they were forced to fight the Western Allies. Soviet leaders called it a "bone in the throat" of Russia.

In June 1948, Stalin decided to drive the Westerners permanently out of Berlin. Rather than force the issue by starting a war, Stalin decided to blockade the city, cutting off its land supply routes. In this way, if a war started, the undermanned forces of the Western Allies would have to start it. Stalin knew the Allies' conventional military forces were not capable of winning a war at this time against Soviet forces in Germany. He also doubted that Truman would initiate a nuclear war over Berlin. *Without resorting* to war, there seemed to be no way for the West to maintain its forces in western Berlin. Stalin also hoped to pressure the West Germans and the Americans into ceasing their efforts to create a separate sovereign state of West Germany. If nothing else, cutting off Berlin might force a compromise that would prevent a new West German state.

While Stalin's blockade was capable of closing the highways and rail roads into the city, the World War II agreements regarding the occupation of Berlin had given the Allies use of air space on several approaches to Berlin. Stalin could not blockade this air space without himself resorting to war, which he did not want to do. With this loophole in mind, President Truman initiated a massive airlift to keep the city supplied. For 11 months the planes flew back and forth to supply the beleaguered Berliners. While the Berliners did not live well, they survived. When it be-came apparent that Truman would maintain the airlift no matter how long it took, Stalin decided that the cost to the Soviets' international image was not worth it and he ordered the blockade lifted.

81. **(E)**   During the 1932 election campaign, Franklin Roosevelt promised the American people a "New Deal." This "New Deal" pledged to replace the detached, inactive, and seemingly insensitive government of Herbert Hoover and the Republicans with an expanded government that would take an activist role in changing the conditions that had led to the great Depression. Roosevelt promised massive federal public works pro-grams and relief programs, modeled on those he had pioneered as governor of New York State. While Roosevelt was often vague on the specifics of how this "New Deal" would be paid for, people were so desperate for the government to do *something* that few concerned themselves about the payment issue. While Hoover emphasized what the government could not do, because of the need to keep the budget balanced, Roosevelt gave lip service to the balanced budget and hammered away at all the things a caring, involved government could do and would do if he was elected. Roosevelt understood that his programs would require running large federal deficits, although he was never comfortable with them, as well as expanding the size of the federal government. He also knew that people did not want or need to hear about the cost of his programs; they needed to have hope that the government was going to do something to help them get back on their feet.

While some people accused Roosevelt of planning to destroy capitalism and replace it with a socialist system in which the government ran the entire economy, he never intended to go that far with his reforms. His plan was to restore confidence in America, put people back to work no matter what it took to get them there, then work to reform the abuses by banks, business, and industry which had caused the depression. He did not want to replace capitalism with socialism; he just wanted reform forcing capitalism to "clean up its act" and protect the weaker members of American society.

82. **(E)**   The Taft-Hartley Labor Act of 1947 reflected the culmination of increasing public and government disaffection with labor unions. A series of strikes in the steel industries, coal mines, automobile factories, and the railroads had left Truman and many others feeling that unions were acting beyond the legitimate interests of workers and were engaging in actions which could endanger the nation. Truman led the attack with calls for laws giving the government greater authority to control striking unions and punish their members.

In the 1946 election, conservative Republicans gained control of Congress. They were even more anti-union than Truman. Led by Republican Robert Taft, conservatives passed the Taft-Hartley Act over the veto of

President Truman, who felt that it went too far in controlling unions. The law prohibited unions from running "closed shops" in which workers had to join the union to keep their jobs. It also gave the president the power to call for a "cooling off" period in strikes which threatened the national security. It forced union leaders to sign affidavits certifying they were not Communists. Finally, it reduced the ability of unions to actively participate in elections by restricting union contributions to election campaigns.

83. **(A)**   While each of the choices was an element in Truman's decision to drop the atomic bomb, the major factor was Truman's belief that it would shorten the war and save lives. Germany had already surrendered, and Americans wanted the war to end. Thus far, the Japanese had been fighting fanatically, usually to the last man, to defend the islands approaching Japan itself. Casualties had been heavy for both sides. It looked as if the only way the Japanese would surrender was through an all-out invasion of the Japanese home islands. Given the ferocity of Japanese defenses of the outlying islands, predictions of casualties ranged up to 2 million Americans dead and 10 million Japanese dead in such an assault. Given that the United States had lost only 300,000 servicemen throughout the entire war thus far, 2 million dead American servicemen was a politically unacceptable cost to Truman if it could possibly be avoided. The atomic bomb gave him a tool to avoid that cost. Predictions also emphasized that the invasion could take from one to four more years to eliminate major centers of Japanese resistance, and the United States could face a protracted struggle against Japanese partisans. A Japanese surrender before a full-scale invasion could prevent this. Again, the atomic bomb gave Truman a tool to avoid an invasion. Therefore, if it worked it would shorten the war and save American lives.

84. **(A)**   Jane Addams was a leading Progressive who was most well-known for her work in settlement houses. Her work was part of the social reform movement of this time in which religious activists sought to apply their religious principles by helping the poor. These people believed that Christian principles dictated that those who were well off had a Christian duty to help those less fortunate. This "Social Gospel" movement led many middle- and upper-class adults to build churches and settlement houses in the inner city slums. These settlement houses were places where middle-class social workers could live and hopefully provide the poverty stricken around them with an example of how to improve their lives. From these settlements, workers could make direct contact with the poor and work with them to

improve their education, their cultural knowledge, their religious faith, and their ability to get themselves "on their feet" economically. They also provided child-care to allow parents to work and helped people learn job skills. Finally, they provided temporary shelter for some and helped others find better long-term housing arrangements. Our modern social work system essentially evolved from the goals established by these early settlement houses and workers like Jane Addams.

85. **(B)**   The primary reason for the internment of Japanese American citizens by the United States was that they were Japanese (B). There was tremendous anger at Japan because of the Pearl Harbor attack. The Japanese were also victims of unabashed racism. American attitudes toward Japan were much different than they were toward Germany and Italy. Public opinion polls at the time suggested that while most Americans felt that the Germans and Italians were good people who had been taken advantage of by corrupt and evil leaders, they believed that Japan and its people were just plain evil. Americans saw the Japanese and their leaders as one and the same. Thus, hostility at anyone of Japanese descent was much greater than that aimed at German or Italian Americans.

   Japanese Americans were never found to be involved in treasonous activities (A). Most were appalled at the Japanese government's attack on Pearl Harbor and very few openly supported Japanese government policy (D). Many were insulted that they would be expected to take an oath of loyalty to the United States, but there is no evidence that they would have refused to do so (E). In fact, many Japanese Americans joined the American military where, organized into an independent infantry unit, they fought extremely well in Italy against the Germans. While there were many businessmen who took advantage of the Japanese internment to buy up valuable property for almost nothing from the internees (C), this was not the primary motive for interning them. The major motive was based on prejudice, anger, and to a minor degree, a desire to protect them from attacks by angry, racist Americans who had already attacked some Japanese Americans several times.

86. **(E)**   This cartoon portrays a rather passive role for President Grant suggesting that southerners need only heed his advice to accept the new social reality and all will be well. There is no hint that the federal government might need to bring its weight to bear upon the situation (D). Though the road to reconciliation will be difficult, there is no guarantee that it will not occur or that blacks do not want to be reconciled with southern whites (A), (B), and (C).

87. **(C)** From the protests of organized labor and former presidential candidates Pat Buchanan and Ross Perot to the cheers of Republican and business interests, the North American Free Trade Agreement was a widely debated measure. Originally negotiated by the Bush administration, NAFTA loosened trade restrictions between Canada, Mexico, and the United States. SALT (Strategic Arms Limitation Talks) (A) and START (Strategic Arms Reduction Talks) (B) dealt with limiting arms production, WIN (Whip Inflation Now) (D) was Gerald Ford's voluntary anti-inflation program. SDI (Strategic Defense Initiative) (E) was a plan to implement a space based missile defense system.

88. **(D)** President Reagan chose the conservative jurist Sandra Day O'Connor to be the first woman to sit on the Supreme Court. Ruth Bader Ginsberg (B) was the second woman to sit on the court. Madeleine Albright (C) became the first female Secretary of State. Ann Richards (A) was governor of Texas, and Margaret Chase Smith (E) was the first woman elected U.S. Senator.

89. **(E)** Frank Lloyd Wright served a seven-year apprenticeship in the Chicago office of Louis Sullivan. Wright established himself at Oak Park, Illinois, where he practiced radical innovations and introduced methods of building that stressed harmony with natural surroundings. Virgil Thomson (B) and Victor Herbert (C) were composers, while Ernest Hemingway (A) and James T. Farrell (D) were writers.

90. **(A)** William Marcy Tweed or "Boss Tweed" led the powerful Democratic political machine that was able to control or crush the opposition. In two years (1869-71) Tweed milked the City of New York of approximately $100 million. Tweed eventually was sent to prison in 1872; he died four years later.

91. **(B)** Marcus Garvey, a West Indian, was the leading force in the Universal Negro Improvement Association. In the early 1920s the association attracted hundreds of thousands of followers. Garvey had nothing but contempt for whites, for light-skinned blacks, and for the National Association for the Advancement of Colored People (NAACP) that sought to bring white and blacks together to fight segregation and other forms of prejudice. He preached that the black man must "work out his salvation in his motherland," Africa.

92. **(A)** During his second term, Franklin Roosevelt decided to ask Congress to shift the balance on the Supreme Court to pro-New Deal justices. He thinly disguised his proposal by making it part of a general reorganization

of the judiciary. Roosevelt's plan provided for the retirement of Supreme Court justices at the age of 70 with full pay. If a justice chose not to retire, the president was to appoint an additional justice up to a maximum of six, to ease the work load for the aged justices who remained on the court. Congress failed to pass Roosevelt's plan.

93. **(E)** Early in his presidency, Theodore Roosevelt faced the Venezuelan debt crisis. Venezuela owed sizable debts to European and American creditors. Germany and Great Britain attempted to collect their debts in December 1902 by force. Roosevelt joined the Venezuelan president in urging arbitration, and the British and Germans agreed. In this crisis, Roosevelt made it clear that he would not permit European powers to intervene in Western Hemisphere affairs in any way that might endanger American interests.

   After the settlement of the crisis, Roosevelt continued to be concerned about the intervention of European powers in Latin America. He believed that such intervention could be prevented only if the U.S. assumed responsibility for maintaining political and economic stability in the region. Therefore, in his annual message to Congress in May 1904, Roosevelt asserted that not only did the U.S. have the right to oppose European intervention in the Western Hemisphere, but it also had the right to intervene in the domestic affairs of the Western Hemisphere states to maintain order and to prevent intervention of others.

94. **(A)** In February 1950, shortly after the conviction of Alger Hiss for perjury, Republican Senator Joseph R. McCarthy of Wisconsin claimed that he had a list of Communists and Communist sympathizers in the United States Department of State. He repeated his charge and leveled others about Communist influence in government but never produced any significant evidence to substantiate them.

95. **(B)** The Lend-Lease Act (1941) gave the president the authority to lend or lease equipment to any nation "whose defense the President deems vital to the defense of the United States." During World War II, the United States provided $50 billion in lend-lease aid to its allies, and the British received over $31 billion of the total.

96. **(C)** In the presidential election of 1876, the Democrats nominated Samuel Tilden, governor of New York and a symbol of honest government. The Republicans nominated Rutherford B. Hayes, governor of Ohio and also a symbol of honest government. Tilden carried states with 184 votes in the

electoral college, one short of the necessary majority. Hayes received 165 undisputed electoral votes; but the votes of South Carolina, Florida, and Louisiana were in dispute. To avert any possibility of violence, Congress created a special commission of 15 to pass judgment upon the disputed electoral votes. After a series of maneuvers and compromises, the commission voted to award the disputed electoral votes to Hayes. Therefore, Hayes won the election by one electoral vote. It should be noted that the Constitution does not require a candidate to receive a majority of the popular vote.

97. **(D)** Helen Hunt Jackson's book *A Century of Dishonor* (1881) recounted the long record of broken treaties and gross injustices against the Native Americans. She sent a copy to all the members of Congress.

98. **(D)** In 1890, the two major women's groups combined as the National American Women's Suffrage Association (NAWSA). NAWSA made women's suffrage its main objective and concentrated on a state-by-state approach. By 1896, Wyoming, Utah, Colorado, and Idaho had been won over to women's suffrage, and California voted for women's suffrage in 1911. The suffragists then shifted the campaign back to the national level. By 1920, three-quarters of the states had ratified the Nineteenth Amendment.

99. **(C)** Calvin Coolidge made this statement. Reagan took a similar attitude in his handling of the 1981 air traffic controllers' strike (E). Hayes and Cleveland also took uncompromising attitudes toward such labor disturbances as the Great Railroad Strike of 1877 (A) and the Pullman Strike of 1894 (B). Senator Robert A. Taft was co-sponsor of the Taft-Hartley Act of 1947 (D), aimed at restraining the excesses of labor unions.

100. **(D)** Under the crop lien system, a farmer mortgaged his next harvest to a merchant in order to buy seed and supplies and support his family through the year. It was a system under which a farmer was likely neither to diversify his crops (C) nor get out of debt anytime soon (E). He would hardly be buying more land (A). Some of those who felt trapped in the system expressed through the Farmers' Alliances of the 1880s their desire that the government should loan them money against the previous year's harvest, which would be stored in warehouses until the market was favor-able for selling (B), but nothing came of this.

101. **(C)** The Reconstruction Finance Corporation was not part of the New Deal but was created in 1932, during the presidency of Herbert Hoover, as an attempt to expand credit by extending loans to distressed businesses. This was part of Hoover's response to the Depression. The National Industrial

Recovery Act (A) (1933), the Tennessee Valley Authority (B) (1933), the Agricultural Adjustment Act (D) (1933), and the Works Progress Administration (E) (1935) were all part of Roosevelt's New Deal program.

102. **(D)** The "New Immigration" of 1880–1900 predominantly con-sisted of immigrants from eastern and southern Europe, rather than northern and western Europe. The "New Immigrants" were largely unskilled day laborers (A) and came from non protestant religions (C); as a result, quotas were established in the 1920s to keep these "inferior" immigrants out. Immigration did increase steadily in the late nineteenth century (B), although the Chinese remained excluded (E) from the immigration boom by the Chinese Exclusion Act of 1882, which was renewed upon its expiration in 1892 and remained in effect for the rest of the century.

103. **(A)** The Tonk in Gulf Resolution of 1964, which granted President Johnson vast powers in pursuing the Vietnam War, best exemplifies the post–World War II trend toward executive-directed foreign policy in which Congress plays only a small role. The Civil Rights Act (B), while it enhanced the reputation of President Johnson, was an act of domestic, not foreign, policy. Both the Boland Amendments (C), which forbade the president from providing monetary aid to overthrow the Nicaraguan government, and the War Powers Act of 1973 (D), which limited the president's war-making powers to 60 days without congressional approval, represent congressional attempts to curtail executive foreign policy-making power. The Good Neighbor Policy (E) was a complex set of initiatives toward Latin American nations that was part of Franklin D. Roosevelt's foreign policy.

104. **(C)** Those who held large amounts of government securities, pay-able in gold, would not have favored bimetallism since, by monetizing silver at an artificially high, fixed rate relative to gold, it would tend to drain the government's gold reserves and endanger its ability to meet its obligations to pay those securities. Those who thought inflation would benefit the economy (A), those who owned stock in silver mines (B), those who were deeply in debt (D), and those who came from predominantly agricultural states (E), particularly in the South and Great Plains areas, would have seen bimetallism as likely to benefit them financially and favored it.

105. **(B)** Novelist and essayist Baldwin (B), born in 1924 in Harlem, was too young to have played a part in the Renaissance, which was cut short by the Great Depression, although he embodied many of its values in his work.

Major figures in the Harlem Renaissance movement, which flowered during the 1920s, were poet and essayist Langston Hughes (C), poet Countee Cullen (A), and poet Alain Locke (D). Novelist and anthropologist Zora Neale Hurston (E) was a contemporary of most Harlem Renaissance writers and spent time in Harlem during the Renaissance, even collaborating with Hughes on a play.

106. **(E)** Reconstruction came to an end in 1877, primarily because the Northern electorate had grown tired of the effort to remake Southern society. Many leading Radical politicians in the North had died (B), but it was the electorate's fatigue with Reconstruction (E) that prevented others from rising to take their place. The violence of organizations such as the Ku Klux Klan (D) actually increased after the withdrawal of federal troops from the South, and it was the end of Reconstruction that allowed the nation to shift its interest from racial and sectional issues to economic ones. (C).

107. **(B)** The purpose of Roosevelt's 1941 "Four Freedoms" speech was to gain public support for his recently announced Lend-Lease program, giving the Allies fighting against Hitler's Germany "all aid short of war." The speech did say much about the kind of world Roosevelt wanted to create after the war, but it did not herald American entry into the conflict.

108. **(B)** Wealthy American planters overthrew Hawaii's monarchy in 1893, but the islands were not annexed until the 1898 Spanish-American War. Alaska (A) was purchased from Russia in 1867. Cuba (C), though the site of Spanish-American hostilities, was not annexed but granted independence. California (D) was ceded to the U.S.A. in 1848, as was New Mexico (E).

109. **(A)** The book *The Shame of the Cities*, originally published by Steffens as a series of articles for periodicals, denounced corruption in big-city politics and the reign of the big-city political machines.

110. **(D)** The urban riots of the mid-1960s, such as the famous 1965 Watts riot in Los Angeles, were primarily triggered by racial tensions (D). The Vietnam War (A) became a cause for rioting in the late 1960s and early 1970s. The need for food and clothing (B), opposition to run away government spending (C), and the conflicting concerns of the counterculture and traditional society (E), while often subsidiary reasons, were not primary causes of the urban riots of the mid-1960s.

111. **(A)** The "Crime of '73," so called by factions desiring an inflationary monetary policy, was the Grant administration's demonetization of silver

(A) and return to a straight gold standard. The assassination of President Garfield (C) took place in 1881, not 1873. Neither the incursion of whites into Sioux territory in the Black Hills (B), the failure of Congress to pass civil service legislation (D), nor the attempts by Gould and others to corner the gold market (E) were ever known as the "Crime of '73."

112. **(B)** "Waving the bloody shirt," or invoking the memory of the Civil War, was something the Democrats, the "party of disunion," rarely succeeded with. Northern—and Republican—success in the Civil War accounts at least in part for Republican domination of presidential elections in this era (D), which occurred despite in fighting between the Stalwart and Half-Breed factions that occasionally produced "compromise" candidates such as Presidents Hayes and Garfield (C). Only twice did the Democrats manage victory, both times with Grover Cleveland. The Populist party was a third-party option in 1892, but the Democratic party ultimately absorbed the Populist agenda and most of its supporters (E) with the candidacy of William Jennings Bryan. On two occasions, in 1876 (Hayes over Tilden) and 1888 (Harrison over Cleveland), the winner of the popular vote lost the electoral vote (A).

113. **(D)** The Immigration Acts of 1921 and 1924 were a watershed in immigration law because they were the first to set limits on the immigration of certain groups, including natives of Eastern Europe, Africa, Asia, and Oceania. Qualitative requirements (C), such as fitness of health and character, had previously been determinants of immigration levels. Under the laws of 1921 and 1924, however, the overall quota of immigrants was to be 150,000 by 1927, and quotas for individual groups were to be set at the percentage of the 150,000 figure that each group constituted in the total population. Western Hemisphere immigrants, including Mexicans and Canadians (A), were, however, exempt from these quotas, thus the actual immigration figures of these years regularly exceeded 150,000. The McCumber-Walter Act of 1952 (E) simplified the quota formula so that the limit was one-sixth of one percent of the population, which usually amounted to about 160,000. In 1965, the United States began to admit nuclear relatives of citizens, returning resident aliens, certain former citizens, and families of Western Hemisphere countries as "special immigrants" (B) who were exempt from numerical ceilings.

114. **(E)** Despite friction with Britain over oil rights, the Harding and Coolidge administrations apparently preferred Middle Eastern lands to remain in the hands of European powers, and secured such rights via the negotiations

of Secretary of State Charles Evans Hughes. The United States generally took an "isolationist" line toward European political conflicts, such as the Ruhr Crisis, during this time (B). But it also had to contend with Allied war debts (D), which it did not forgive, and were slow to restructure. In the Five-Power Naval Treaty of 1921–1922, the United States negotiated naval parity with Britain and superiority to Japan (C) based on a 5-5-3 ratio. The Coolidge years are also notorious for armed intervention and occupation of the Dominican Republic, Haiti, Mexico, and Nicaragua (A) at various times.

115. **(A)** The cartoonist sees agrarian, labor, and other "radical" movements as a "Platform of Lunacy." Because the Democratic party in the 1890s leaned toward Populism, the cartoonist was most likely a Republican.

116. **(C)** Henry Kissinger was secretary of state under Presidents Nixon and Ford from 1973 to 1977. One of his most notable accomplishments, in addition to negotiating an end to the war in Vietnam, was drafting Nixon's policy of détente with the Soviet Union. This policy combined a series of scientific and economic incentives for the Soviets with political moves designed to move China out of the Soviet "sphere of influence" and into a close relationship with the United States, with the purpose of making the Soviets more dependent on the West economically and isolating them politically. Kissinger's hope was that he could establish a rapprochement between the superpowers that could end the Cold War. While détente failed to end the Cold War, it did ease tensions between the super powers for a few years until a combination of Soviet moves in Africa and Afghanistan and a harder American attitude under the Reagan administration effectively ended it by 1982. While Kissinger was noted for negotiating a peace agreement that allowed the United States to withdraw from the war in Vietnam, he was not publicly associated with Nixon's "Vietnamization" of the war (A). He was not associated with the development of "flexible response," which was a Kennedy administration policy (B). Although he was involved in setting up Nixon's official visit to China in 1974 that opened the door to rapprochement with China (D), the actual rapprochement is associated much more with Nixon himself than with Kissinger, since much of Kissinger's work was done secretly. Finally, Henry Kissinger was one of the few high-level members of Nixon's administration who was not tarnished by the Watergate scandal (E), and therefore he is not usually associated with it.

117. **(E)** The state governments during Reconstruction were not in effective and actually did a surprisingly good job, beginning the herculean task of

rebuilding the South's infrastructure. Housing, roads, railroads, and industry all needed to be rebuilt, almost from scratch. The plantation system was in ruins, as was the entire southern economy. Reconstruction governments founded the South's first adequate public education systems and helped establish a whole range of public services, such as facilities to care for the poor and the mentally ill. Voting rights were expanded for the first time, resulting in poor and middle class voters electing representatives from their own economic class. While these governments were not demonstrably superior to those that preceded them (D), they were certainly no less efficient, and managed to accomplish much that pre–Civil War governments did not (E). Many of the problems that kept Reconstruction governments from doing a better job stemmed from active resistance to needed reforms by Southern whites, who resented being represented by Yankees or blacks. Many of the notable reforms enacted by these governments were eliminated by the conservative white Democrats who regained power after Reconstruction ended. Reconstruction office holders were just as qualified, albeit less experienced, as those who preceded them, and while white Democrats portrayed all of their problems as resulting from illiterate blacks running the government, the evidence does not support this racist argument (A). While greed and corruption certainly existed in Reconstruction governments (C), there is no evidence that it was worse than the corruption that existed in Southern state governments before or during the Civil War, or that it made Reconstruction governments less efficient. Finally, there is no evidence that tight restrictions associated with Union military control prevented Reconstruction governments from operating effectively (B).

118. **(A)**   The industrialization of the Old South is the only effect listed that was not a direct result of the railroad building in the last half of the nineteenth century. Most railroad construction linked factories and consumers in the northeast with Midwest farmers and Far West miners and farmers. Railroad construction lagged in the South by comparison. The South remained primarily a rural agricultural region well into the twentieth century; industrialization would not flourish there until the rail industry had passed its peak and was beginning its mid-twentieth century decline. The completion of America's rail network was a feat of monumental proportions, leading to dramatic changes in the lives of most Americans. Goods could now be shipped from the most distant corner of the land to virtually anywhere else in the country within a few days (B). This allowed farmers access to markets that would otherwise have been denied them. It allowed for more efficient distribution of goods throughout the country. It also made the country

smaller in that one could now travel from coast to coast in just six to ten days (D), whereas the trip could take weeks or months by horse and wagon. Before the railroads, time was kept by individual communities according to the position of the sun overhead. This led to confusion as a traveler went from one community to the next, and made it nearly impossible for the railroads to draw up workable timetables fort heir trains. In response, the railroads developed plans for a national system of time zones, in which every community within a specific zone would share the same local time (E). Eventually this system was universally adopted and evolved into the four time zones which exist today. Finally, railroad construction and development led to some important technical improvements in areas like boiler construction, air brakes, automatic coupling devices, steel construction techniques, and bridge building (C).

119. **(C)**   The Washington Conference of 1921-22 resulted in agreements between European powers, the United States, China, and Japan that established a ratio for capital ships among the five great naval powers (I) (United States, Great Britain, Japan, France, Italy), stabilized the postwar title to islands previously held by Germany (II), and reaffirmed the integrity and independence of China (IV). There was no agreement to recognize Manchuria as a Japanese sphere of influence (V) and the conference was not identified with the standards of the Reparations Commission established at the Versailles Peace Conference (III).

120. **(D)**   When Russia signed a separate peace with Germany in January 1918, the Allies felt betrayed. The Bolshevik government, responsible for the pull-out, was ostracized by Western Europe and the United States. In 1919, the Bolsheviks announced the formation of the Communist International Movement (Comintern) to spread the revolution worldwide. This spread fear throughout non-Communist industrial nations and led to suspicions of Communist subversion whenever domestic problems arose, especially when those problems involved labor, where Communist organizers were believed to be most active. In the United States in 1919, many management-labor disputes held in check during the war now boiled to the surface. Workers who did not feel free to challenge the government or industry while the nation was at war now felt justified in pushing for resolution of their grievances. As a result, more than 4,000,000 workers walked off the job in over 3,000 strikes. Bombs were mailed to several business and political leaders and threats were sent to hundreds more. While the vast majority of these walkouts were due to labor complaints about wages and working

conditions, there was just enough involvement by known leftists and Communists to confirm suspicions that all the strikes were part of a massive plot by Communists and anarchists to bring down the U.S. government and economic system. The Federal Bureau of Investigation was created to crush the "insurrection." Working together with state and local police agencies, the FBI arrested thousands of suspected Communists and charged them with sedition. Hundreds of foreign nationals living in the United States were deported, often on very flimsy evidence. However, when alleged plots and predictions of terrorism proved unfounded, the leaders of the anti-Communist crackdown slowly but steadily lost their credibility, and the crackdowns ceased.

PRACTICE TEST 2

CLEP History of the United States II: 1865 to the Present

Also available at the REA Study Center (*www.rea.com/studycenter*)

This practice exam is also available at the REA Study Center. To closely simulate your test-day experience with the computer-based CLEP exam, we suggest that you take the online version of the practice test. When you do, you'll also enjoy these benefits:

- **Timed testing conditions** – helps you gauge how much time you can spend on each question
- **Automatic scoring** – find out how you did on the test, instantly
- **On-screen detailed explanations of answers** – gives you the correct answer and explains why the other answer choices are wrong
- **Diagnostic score reports** – pinpoint where you're strongest and where you need to focus your study

PRACTICE TEST 2

CLEP History of the United States II: 1865 to the Present

(Answer sheets appear in the back of the book.)

TIME: 90 Minutes
120 Questions

DIRECTIONS: Each of the questions or incomplete statements below is followed by five possible answers or completions. Select the best choice in each case and fill in the corresponding oval on the answer sheet.

1. Place the following in the correct chronological order, from the earliest event to the most recent.

   I. Reconstruction Act
   II. Amnesty Act
   III. impeachment of President Johnson
   IV. Fourteenth Amendment

   (A) IV, II, I, III
   (B) II, IV, I, III
   (C) III, II, IV, I
   (D) IV, I, III, II
   (E) I, II, III, IV

2. As advertising developed in the late nineteenth and early twentieth centuries, some marketers used fear to sell products. Which of the following disease-sounding words was created to sell Listerine?

   (A) Hepatitis
   (B) Psoriasis
   (C) AIDS
   (D) Bacterium
   (E) Halitosis

3. The agency that resettled tens of thousands of Civil War refugees, built dozens of hospitals, and issued millions of rations to the poor and hungry was

   (A) the Freedmen's Bureau
   (B) the Thirteenth Amendment Foundation
   (C) the Women's Loyal League
   (D) the Bureau for Resettlement
   (E) the League for Southern Negroes

4. The Fifteenth Amendment, ratified in 1870, was finally enforced by which of the following efforts of the 1960s?

   (A) The Civil Rights Act of 1964
   (B) The Black Power movement
   (C) The hippie movement
   (D) The Voting Rights Act of 1965
   (E) The Equal Rights Amendment

5. Comprising the introduction of the black vote and the subsequent failure of Reconstruction, the years between 1865 and the mid-1870s included the

   (A) rise and fall of Republican state governments in the South
   (B) rise and fall of Democratic state governments in the South
   (C) rise and fall of President Grant
   (D) great success of the Republican party in the South
   (E) great success of the women's movement in the South

6. The famous Model T Ford automobile was first built in

   (A) 1900
   (B) 1908
   (C) 1920
   (D) 1930
   (E) 1937

7. In the Haymarket Square Riot of 1886, what occurred?

(A) Labor demonstrated for a shorter work day and the police shot several of them.
(B) Children were trampled in a factory fire and their parents rioted in protest.
(C) Bread prices skyrocketed and many people rioted.
(D) Anarchists demonstrated and a bomb exploded, killing several people.
(E) While protesting the end of Reconstruction, many disenfranchised blacks rioted.

8. What were President Clinton's tax plans soon after winning the election of 1992?

(A) Raising taxes for the middle class, the rich, and corporations
(B) Lowering taxes for the middle class
(C) Maintaining the status quo but reducing government spending
(D) Lowering corporate taxes as an incentive to hire more workers
(E) He had no tax plan until 1996.

9. By 1890 Standard Oil Company of New Jersey controlled a virtual monopoly of oil refining and distribution in the U.S. It was owned and operated by

(A) Andrew Carnegie
(B) John D. Rockefeller
(C) J.P. Morgan
(D) Jacob Schiff
(E) Henry George

10. A general definition of Social Darwinism is

(A) survival of the fittest is an outdated idea
(B) the working masses have the most power
(C) all citizens should be equal in every way
(D) only superior people are able to gain wealth and power
(E) the poor should receive charity

11. What general led the U.S. offensive in the Pacific theater during World War II?

(A) General George S. Patton
(B) General Dwight Eisenhower
(C) General Douglas MacArthur
(D) General George Marshall
(E) General Erwin Rommel

12. The political cartoon shown below relates to which controversy of the late nineteenth century?

Source: Prints & Photographs Division, Library of Congress, LC-DIG-ppmsca-25455

(A) the revaluation of Confederate currency
(B) the legalization of the income tax by Democrats
(C) the corruption in the Republican Grant administration
(D) the economic costs of the Spanish-American War
(E) the Populist demands for free coinage of silver

13. Who was William Levitt?

(A) Union leader
(B) Revolutionizer of American religion
(C) Son of Eisenhower and a leading businessman
(D) Chicago politician
(E) Builder of planned communities

14. The heaviest casualties in the Spanish-American War came as a result of

 (A) the sinking of the *Maine*
 (B) Spanish bullets
 (C) hand-to-hand combat with Filipinos
 (D) tropical diseases
 (E) the battle of Manila Bay

15. The description below is of which of the following events?

 "A revolution was staged, it was bloodless, they declared independence in 1903. It was then that the treaty was signed, the treaty later called outrageously unfair."

 (A) The building of the Panama Canal
 (B) The Sino-American war
 (C) The Alaskan purchase
 (D) The annexing of Hawaii
 (E) The expulsion of the Spanish from Cuba

16. Which of the following people was a spokesperson for the Niagara movement, author of *The Souls of Black Folk*, and a founder of the NAACP?

 (A) Booker T. Washington
 (B) Ida B. Wells
 (C) W. E. B. Du Bois
 (D) Frederick Douglass
 (E) Frederick Jackson Turner

17. Which of the following sponsored buffalo hunts in the mid- to late nineteenth century?

 (A) Railroads—Indians and the buffalo that they depended on were seen as hindrances to westward expansion.
 (B) The Census Bureau—it feared it could not reliably count all the existing buffalo.
 (C) The Indian Rights Association—the buffalo were sick and needed to be destroyed.
 (D) Pioneering farmers—they were afraid roving buffalo herds would trample their crops.
 (E) The Earp brothers—they were gamblers who enjoyed buffalo hunts as sport.

18. What is the name of Booker T. Washington's famous school for blacks in the South?

    (A) Merced Institute
    (B) Atlanta University
    (C) Howard College
    (D) Tuskegee Institute
    (E) Hampton University

19. One of the accomplishments of President Theodore Roosevelt was

    (A) rescinding the pure food and drug laws
    (B) creating dozens of labor unions
    (C) halting the sale of Alaska
    (D) creating the Peace Corps
    (E) setting aside millions of acres for national parks

20. Which Republican won the presidential election of 1908?

    (A) Theodore Roosevelt
    (B) William Howard Taft
    (C) Woodrow Wilson
    (D) Warren G. Harding
    (E) William Jennings Bryan

21. What did the "Roosevelt Corollary" to the Monroe Doctrine state?

    (A) European militaries could not interfere in the Western Hemisphere.
    (B) Latin America needed to stabilize or be policed by the U.S.
    (C) Cuba had to be capitalistic or be invaded by the U.S.
    (D) England had to stay out of India.
    (E) African nations were warned to stabilize.

22. The term "muckrakers" refers to

    (A) Native American civil rights advocates
    (B) "turn of the century" musicians
    (C) slum lords
    (D) journalists who exposed corruption
    (E) farmers

23. Why was the Dawes Severalty Act of 1887 such a disaster for Native Americans?

   (A) It mandated that all Native Americans convert to Christianity.
   (B) It only gave land to individual families, thereby breaking up the tribal system.
   (C) It disallowed ownership of land for any Native American.
   (D) It allowed the killing of the buffalo.
   (E) It granted statehood to North Dakota.

24. What May 7, 1915 event generated a great deal of U.S. public support for the Allied cause?

   (A) The sinking of the *Maine*
   (B) The assassination of Archduke Francis Ferdinand
   (C) The death of President Wilson's wife, Ellen Wilson
   (D) The sinking of the *Lusitania*
   (E) The presidential election campaign of 1916

25. When did the period known as Reconstruction officially end?

   (A) With the birth of the Ku Klux Klan
   (B) With the Thirteenth Amendment
   (C) When the Confederates set the Alamo on fire
   (D) It never officially ended
   (E) When all federal troops left the South

26. What was the "Zimmermann telegram"?

   (A) An intercepted telegram from Germany offering Mexico much U.S. territory if Mexico joined Germany against the U.S. in World War I
   (B) A telegram revealing the spy codes used by the Germans
   (C) An intercepted telegram from the British offering to switch sides of the war if Germany would grant them additional territory
   (D) A telegram from the U.S. to the Italians giving secrets to new weapons
   (E) A telegram from Israel to the U.S. asking if they should join in the war

27. What does the following statement refer to?

"About 150,000 WAC members and nearly as many WAVES served in World War II."

(A) Juvenile army units
(B) Men over 50 years of age serving in the armed forces
(C) Planes
(D) Specialized submarines
(E) Women serving with the armed forces

28. Which president stated the following in his campaign for the presidency? "The Congress will push me to raise taxes and I'll say no...I'll say to them, 'Read my lips; no new taxes.'"

(A) Ronald Reagan
(B) Andrew Jackson
(C) George Washington
(D) Bill Clinton
(E) George H. W. Bush

29. Wilson's famous "Fourteen Points" included which of the following?

(A) The U.S. military draft
(B) The integration of African Americans into the army
(C) The rationing of nonessential goods
(D) The creation of female divisions in the army
(E) The creation of the League of Nations

30. What was decided in the U.S. Supreme Court case of *Roe v. Wade*?

(A) Individual states could bar abortion.
(B) Abortion was only legal in the first 10 weeks of pregnancy.
(C) Anti-abortion activists could not protest in front of an abortion clinic.
(D) Individual states could not outlaw abortion.
(E) Girls under 16 years of age needed a parent's consent for an abortion.

31. Who was Marcus Garvey?

(A) A radical Native American leader of the 1920s
(B) An upper middle-class white advocate of rights for blacks
(C) A radical black activist of the 1920s
(D) A leader in the labor movement of the 1920s
(E) A big-business advocate in the Harding administration

32. In 1940 Japan signed the Tri-Partite Pact with which other countries?

    (A) French Indochina and Italy
    (B) Germany and the Soviet Union
    (C) Ethiopia and China
    (D) Poland and Hungary
    (E) Germany and Italy

33. Who uttered the famous phrase, "The chief business of the American people is business"?

    (A) Calvin Coolidge
    (B) Theodore Roosevelt
    (C) Herbert Hoover
    (D) Warren G. Harding
    (E) Eugene Debs

34. The marchers shown in this photograph sought which of the following?

Source: Library of Congress, Prints & Photographs Division, Theodor Horydczak Collection, LC-H823-14S8

    (A) A guaranteed role in future wars
    (B) A college plan for their children
    (C) Early payment of veterans' bonuses due to the depression
    (D) Three months' mortgage per veteran during the depression
    (E) Medals for bravery in World War I

35. What event precipitated the "Iranian hostage crisis"?

    (A) American reporters in Iran had their licenses revoked.
    (B) The Shah overthrew the Muslim government.
    (C) The Shah, who was in exile, went to the U.S. for medical aid.
    (D) The Ayatollah became very ill.
    (E) Iranian prisoners mysteriously died in U.S. prisons.

36. An ongoing event in the 1920s that focused on finding communists hidden in the U.S. was called

    (A) McCarthyism
    (B) Progressivism
    (C) the Red Scare
    (D) patriotism
    (E) the Scare

37. The year 1968 was marred by the assassinations of two important public figures; Martin Luther King, Jr., and

    (A) Robert Kennedy
    (B) Malcolm X
    (C) John F. Kennedy
    (D) Medgar Evers
    (E) George Wallace

38. The trial of Sacco and Vanzetti demonstrated

    (A) strong anti-foreign and anti-radical fear in the American government
    (B) specifically anti-Italian feelings in America
    (C) that the criminal trial process in America was fair and just
    (D) the new information gathering techniques employed by America's police
    (E) the need for child labor laws

39. One of the reasons for the despair brought on by the stock market crash of 1929 was

    (A) most Americans owned stock
    (B) Hoover had just been assassinated
    (C) Europeans, in comparison, did extremely well
    (D) many investors had been buying on margin
    (E) all American businesses were doing poorly at the time

40. The "New Deal" was to Franklin Roosevelt what the "Great Society" was to

    (A) Lyndon Johnson
    (B) Herbert Hoover
    (C) John Kennedy
    (D) Richard Nixon
    (E) Theodore Roosevelt

41. Which religious movement's success most refutes the trend shown in this graph?

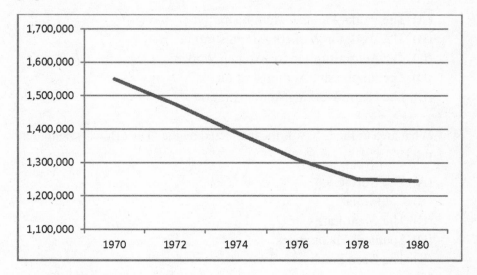

    (A) Evangelical Christianity
    (B) Mormonism
    (C) Nation of Islam
    (D) Quakerism
    (E) Catholicism

42. Which candidate for president in the election of 1992 won the most popular votes for an independent party in several decades?

    (A) Edward Kennedy
    (B) Clarence Thomas
    (C) Ross Perot
    (D) Al Gore
    (E) Ralph Nader

43. An example of the new literature of the 1920s that demonstrated a mistrust of the society and materialism was

    (A) *Uncle Tom's Cabin*
    (B) *The Affluent Society*
    (C) *The Birth of a Nation*
    (D) *The Great Gatsby*
    (E) *The Feminine Mystique*

44. Which of the following was part of the New Deal?

    (A) The Works Progress Administration
    (B) The Work for Workers Administration
    (C) The Administration for Women Workers
    (D) The Progressive Administration
    (E) The Negro Working Administration

45. What area of the U.S. was most affected by the "Dust Bowl" phenomenon of the 1930s?

    (A) The Northeast
    (B) California
    (C) The Great Lakes
    (D) Southern Plains states
    (E) The Deep South

46. The diplomatic strategy employed by Franklin Roosevelt that aimed to strengthen American influence in Latin America was called

    (A) the Latin American Strategy
    (B) the Latin Policy
    (C) the Mexican/Venezuelan Neighbor Policy
    (D) the Pan-American Strategy
    (E) the Good Neighbor Policy

47. The labor organization that avoided the militant rhetoric of socialism and worker solidarity but instead lobbied for immediate goals like higher wages, shorter working hours, and workmen's compensation was

    (A) the Knights of Labor
    (B) the Haymarket Riot
    (C) the American Federation of Labor
    (D) the Industrial Workers of the World
    (E) the Pullman Union

48. What did members of the Committee to Re-elect the President do to start what we now call the Watergate Scandal?

    (A) Harrassed a leading Democrat and his wife
    (B) Destroyed important Republican documents
    (C) Lied about army war crimes during the Vietnam era
    (D) Broke into Democratic headquarters and placed listening devices there
    (E) Bribed numerous Congressmen to support the President

49. In the election of 1876

    (A) Samuel J. Tilden won the popular vote and the election
    (B) Samuel J. Tilden was assassinated
    (C) Ulysses S. Grant was re-elected
    (D) Benjamin Harrison won the election
    (E) Samuel J. Tilden won the popular vote but lost the election

50. Who founded the "Share our Wealth Society" in the 1930s?

    (A) Francis Townsend
    (B) Eleanor Roosevelt
    (C) Huey Long
    (D) Harry Truman
    (E) Dwight Eisenhower

51. In which year did the Nineteenth Amendment grant women the right to vote?

    (A) 1911
    (B) 1915
    (C) 1918
    (D) 1920
    (E) 1922

52. Where did Puerto Ricans tend to settle in 1950s America?

    (A) New Hampshire
    (B) California
    (C) Arizona
    (D) Texas
    (E) New York

53. The movie industry thrived during the Great Depression. Which of the following films opened in the 1940s and dealt with issues of economic depression in a serious manner?

    (A) *Gone with the Wind*
    (B) *The Grapes of Wrath*
    (C) *Duck Soup*
    (D) *Snow White and the Seven Dwarfs*
    (E) *It Happened One Night*

54. What prompted the Cuban Missile Crisis?

    (A) The construction of medium-range nuclear missile launch sites in Cuba
    (B) A failed disarmament meeting between Kennedy and Khruschev
    (C) Six new airports being built in Cuba
    (D) The U.S. built a missile site in Florida.
    (E) The construction of a plutonium processing plant in Cuba

55. In the infamous Scottsboro case, who were the accusers?

    (A) Nine black men
    (B) Two white children
    (C) Three Mexican-American teens
    (D) Two white women
    (E) Two black women

56. Which of the following men does this sentence describe?

    "In 1934, at the age of 10, his father lost the family farm in Arizona and the members of the family became migrant workers in California."

    (A) Cole Porter
    (B) W. E. B. Du Bois
    (C) Cesar Chavez
    (D) Ronald Reagan
    (E) Franklin D. Roosevelt

57. What did the men of the New Deal's CCC do?

   (A) Soil conservation, flood control, and similar projects
   (B) American artifact conservation
   (C) Teach about energy conservation
   (D) Teach about conserving wild animal populations
   (E) Recruit army members

58. Progressivism was a movement concerned with many issues including child labor laws, rights for blacks and women, and

   (A) the temperance movement
   (B) aiding the movie industry
   (C) the animal rights movement
   (D) aid for Italy
   (E) vegetarianism

59. The Neutrality Act of 1935 was in response to which of the following fears?

   (A) American commercial ships could be vulnerable to attack during trade with a nation at war.
   (B) American planes were being shot down when nearing European shores.
   (C) The Spanish Civil War was creating enormous tensions in the U.S.
   (D) The Nazi-Soviet Pact included a pact to attack California in 1940.
   (E) Trade with a nation at war would stop if the U.S. didn't get goods to Europe in a more timely manner.

60. Place the following in the correct chronological order, from the earliest event to the most recent.

   I. Tet Offensive
   II. Gulf of Tonkin Resolution
   III. Geneva Accords
   IV. War Powers Resolution

   (A) I, II, III, IV
   (B) II, IV, I, III
   (C) III, II, I, IV
   (D) II, I, IV, III
   (E) III, I, II, IV

61. Who presented the greatest threat to the status quo in the 1930s?

    (A) Benito Mussolini
    (B) Adolf Hitler
    (C) Haile Selassie
    (D) Francisco Franco
    (E) HidekiTojo

62. Lend-Lease allowed the U.S. to do what?

    (A) Finally create the League of Nations
    (B) Break the Neutrality Act by selling arms to Great Britain
    (C) Uphold the Neutrality Act
    (D) Lease the Panama Canal for 99 years
    (E) Restrict American citizens from entering combat areas

63. Which war was fought during the time period indicated on this timeline?

    (A) World War I
    (B) Vietnam War
    (C) World War II
    (D) Korean War
    (E) Spanish-American War

64. One of the lasting changes in American labor due to World War II was that

    (A) universal health care for workers was implemented
    (B) women participated in the labor force in higher numbers
    (C) women started to earn the exact same wage as men
    (D) African-Americans received worse treatment in the workplace
    (E) labor unions no longer had any effectiveness

65. Why was Dr. Benjamin Spock's 1946 *Common Sense Book of Baby and Child Care* a new kind of parent advice book?

    (A) It advised fathers to spank their children.
    (B) It said that breast-feeding was detrimental to a baby's health.
    (C) Mothers were encouraged to have only one child.
    (D) It offered advice for black families and Latino families.
    (E) Mothers were encouraged to pick up a crying baby and be nurturing.

66. "Zoot suit" refers to

    (A) German spies during World War II
    (B) Japanese immigrants in the 1930s
    (C) corrupt politicians in the 1940s
    (D) a clothing style worn mostly by male Latino teens in the 1940s
    (E) garments women wore in the workplace during World War II

67. The largest armada ever assembled was at

    (A) Pearl Harbor, Hawaii
    (B) London, England
    (C) Berlin, Germany
    (D) Iwo Jima, Japan
    (E) Normandy, France

68. The heaviest U.S. casualties in the Pacific during World War II were sustained at

    (A) Okinawa
    (B) Marshall Islands
    (C) Pearl Harbor
    (D) Midway
    (E) Guadalcanal

69. Which of the following met at the famous Yalta conference in 1945?

    (A) Roosevelt, Churchill, Stalin
    (B) Churchill, Stalin, Tojo
    (C) Truman, Churchill, Stalin
    (D) Stalin, Tojo, Hitler
    (E) Roosevelt, Truman, Churchill

70. Which of the following was one of the leading scientists of the Manhattan Project?

    (A) Thomas Edison
    (B) Marie Curie
    (C) Antoine Bequerel
    (D) J. Robert Oppenheimer
    (E) Guglielmo Marconi

71. The American diplomat usually associated with the Cold War policy of containment is

    (A) Eleanor Roosevelt
    (B) Jan Masaryk
    (C) George F. Kennan
    (D) George C. Marshall
    (E) V. M. Molotov

72. In 1983, which of the following did President Reagan refer to as the "Evil Empire"?

    (A) China
    (B) Vietnam
    (C) The Ottoman Empire
    (D) Iran
    (E) The Soviet Union

73. What was the conclusion of the Berlin blockade and airlift?

    (A) The situation in Czechoslovakia distracted both sides.
    (B) The Germans started using their own modes of importing goods.
    (C) The Soviets stopped the blockade.
    (D) The Americans militarily intervened and liberated Berlin.
    (E) The Germans had a civil war and the non-communists won.

74. Under what circumstances did President Nixon leave office?

    (A) He was impeached and convicted.
    (B) He died of a heart attack before he could be impeached.
    (C) He finished his term and retired from public life.
    (D) He resigned after being impeached but before facing trial for conviction.
    (E) He was impeached, but not convicted, and then finished out his term of office.

75. What is the "Servicemen's Readjustment Act of 1944" more commonly known as?

    (A) The GI Bill
    (B) The Housing Act
    (C) The draft
    (D) The reserves
    (E) The FDIC

76. Who broke the "color line" in baseball in 1947?

   (A) Satchel Paige
   (B) Jackie Robinson
   (C) Willie Mays
   (D) Cool Papa Bell
   (E) Henry Aaron

77. What did the New Deal's TVA do?

   (A) Provide food for people in Virginia
   (B) Provide jobs for blacks
   (C) Provide cheap electricity to people in the Tennessee Valley
   (D) Provide glass, plastic, and aluminum to businesses
   (E) Provide free radio programs to people living in the Toledo area

78. What was NOT one of the major decisions of the Yalta conference in 1945?

   (A) India would become an autonomous nation.
   (B) A Soviet sphere of influence would be allowed in Eastern Europe.
   (C) The United Nations would be created.
   (D) Germany would be divided into four zones.
   (E) Free elections would be held in Eastern Europe.

79. HUAC's hearings and the prosecution of the "Hollywood Ten" were driven by fear of which of the following?

   (A) Economic meltdown
   (B) Communism
   (C) Liberalism
   (D) The influence of sex in the entertainment industry
   (E) Recidivism of parolees

80. Which nations shown on the map below were most significantly affected by the Vietnam War?

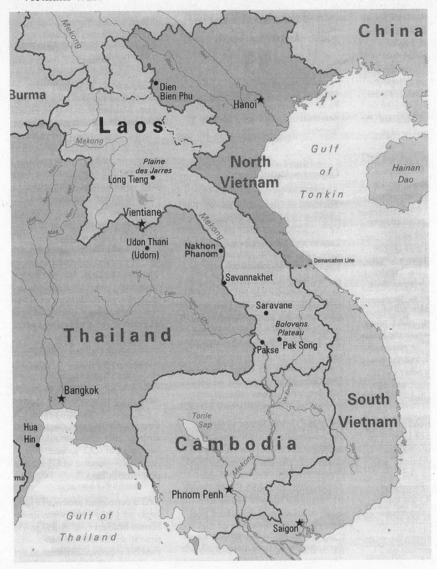

Source: Central Intelligence Agency

(A) China and Thailand because of their shared communist ideologies

(B) Thailand and Cambodia, because of their location on the Gulf of Thailand

(C) Laos and Cambodia, because they bordered a great deal of disputed territory

(D) Laos and Burma, because both had anti-American governments

(E) China and Cambodia, because each supported an opposing side in the war

81. How can President Eisenhower's political stance during his first term best be described?

    (A) Communistic
    (B) Liberal Democratic—part of the wave of "New Deal" liberals
    (C) Extreme liberalism
    (D) Modern Republicanism—between liberal and conservative
    (E) Extreme conservatism

82. What was the impact of the Tonkin Gulf Resolution?

    (A) Off-shore oil development was prohibited.
    (B) Whaling was banned in U.S. waters.
    (C) Military intervention in Vietnam escalated dramatically.
    (D) The CIA was ordered not to overthrow foreign governments.
    (E) Congress granted the President unlimited authority to negotiate trade agreements.

83. *Sputnik* caused a panic among some Americans because it demonstrated

    (A) Japanese-American anger over the internment camps of World War II
    (B) Soviet advances in the space race
    (C) German advances in industry
    (D) the youth of America's unwillingness to conform
    (E) the raw power of the movie industry

84. The man who succeeded Stalin and with whom Eisenhower had to deal was

    (A) Michail Gorbachev
    (B) Leon Trotsky
    (C) Georgi Malenkov
    (D) Nikita Khrushchev
    (E) Vladimir Lenin

85. The name of the American spy plane shot down over the U.S.S.R. was

    (A) U1
    (B) U2
    (C) B1
    (D) B2
    (E) XR2

86. What was argued in John Kenneth Galbraith's *The Affluent Society* (1958)?

    (A) Poverty was not even considered by most Americans in power, as they didn't think poor people existed in large numbers.
    (B) Wealthy people were giving more to charity than middle-class people.
    (C) The consumption of consumer goods was ruining America's youth.
    (D) Black Americans would never catch up to whites in terms of personal finances.
    (E) Churches were getting more donations than ever due to high moral standards.

87. Who was the NAACP's chief counsel in the *Brown v. Board of Education* (1954) case?

    (A) W. E. B. Du Bois
    (B) Jonas Salk
    (C) Thurgood Marshall
    (D) Rosa Parks
    (E) Rev. Ralph Abernathy

88. The Twenty-sixth Amendment to the U.S. Constitution was passed in 1971. What did it do?

    (A) Allowed re-districting in the South
    (B) Protected minorities at polling places
    (C) Gave women the vote
    (D) Legalized alcohol
    (E) Lowered the voting age to 18

89. The famous erroneous headline in the *Chicago Tribune* at the close of the 1948 election read

    (A) "Roosevelt defeats Truman"
    (B) "Dewey defeats Truman"
    (C) "Truman defeats Warren"
    (D) "Warren defeats Thurmond"
    (E) "Thurmond defeats Roosevelt"

90. What was the ending to the Montgomery Bus Boycott?

    (A) Martin Luther King, Jr., was arrested and jailed and the boycotters were forced to give up.
    (B) The race riots of 1956 ensued.
    (C) The Supreme Court refused to hear the case and the boycotters gave up.
    (D) The Supreme Court ruled that segregation on buses was illegal and the city was forced to comply.
    (E) The Supreme Court ruled that segregation on buses was legal and the black community was forced to comply.

91. Which of the following issues forced President Eisenhower to take a stand on civil rights?

    (A) The slow economy of the day
    (B) The downfall of Joseph McCarthy
    (C) The desegregation of Central High School in Little Rock, Arkansas
    (D) The formation of the KKK
    (E) The formation of the National Association for the run on of White People

92. Who ran for president in the famous election of 1960?

    (A) Eisenhower and Nixon
    (B) Truman and Eisenhower
    (C) Nixon and Eisenhower
    (D) Nixon and Kennedy
    (E) Kennedy and Johnson

93. What was the U.S. plan for the Bay of Pigs invasion?

    (A) Cubans who had been sending the U.S. information would attempt to help U.S. planes land at the bay.
    (B) Armed Cuban exiles launched from offshore U.S. boats would land on the beach and encourage the Cuban people to rise up and revolt against Castro.
    (C) U.S. military personnel would assassinate Castro.
    (D) U.S. spies would plant listening devices in Castro's boats.
    (E) Using Puerto Rico as a base, the Navy would invade Cuba.

94. Until about 1880 most immigrants came to the United States from Great Britain, Ireland, and Germany. However, as of 1890, many immigrants were

    (A) Italians and Eastern European Jews
    (B) Africans
    (C) Danes and Norwegians
    (D) Indians
    (E) from China and Japan

95. The Marshall Plan has been called one of the most important pieces of foreign policy in U.S. history. What did the plan do?

    (A) Installed U.S. troops along the border with Poland
    (B) Halted Soviet aggression in Cuba
    (C) Helped elect Democratic leaders in Italy
    (D) Aided in the revolutions of India, Pakistan, and Algeria
    (E) Provided $13 billion in loans to Western Europe's recovery effort

96. What Republican was elected to the Presidency in 1920?

    (A) Herbert Hoover
    (B) Charles Curtis
    (C) Calvin Coolidge
    (D) Warren G. Harding
    (E) Woodrow Wilson

97. In what year was John F. Kennedy assassinated?

    (A) 1963
    (B) 1964
    (C) 1965
    (D) 1966
    (E) 1967

98. Which issues were the major focus of Lyndon Johnson's Great Society?

    (A) Arts and sports programs
    (B) Making America safer
    (C) Protecting big business
    (D) Building America's industry
    (E) Social and economic welfare programs

99. What did the Eisenhower Doctrine assert?

   (A) The British had to stay out of Latin American affairs.
   (B) The U.S. would assist any Middle Eastern nation against communism.
   (C) The U.S. would assist any Middle Eastern nation against fanatical Islamic governments.
   (D) The U.S. would assist any Middle Eastern nation against Zionism.
   (E) The British had to stay out of Middle Eastern affairs.

100. AIM is an acronym for what group of militants that seized the deserted Alcatraz island in 1969 and kept it until 1971?

   (A) Allied Indian Marchers
   (B) American Indian Movement
   (C) African and Indian Mobilization
   (D) American International Movement
   (E) Alcatraz Indian Mobilization

101. In what year was the famous Tet offensive of the Vietnam War?

   (A) 1968
   (B) 1967
   (C) 1968
   (D) 1969
   (E) 1970

102. Why did President Lyndon Johnson not run for reelection in 1968?

   (A) The Democratic party voted to nominate Hubert Humphrey, instead of Johnson.
   (B) Anti-war protesters threatened to assassinate him and he was genuinely afraid for his life.
   (C) He was limited by the Constitution to two terms in office.
   (D) He did not want to further divide the country over his war politics.
   (E) He was very ill.

103. In 1992 President George H. W. Bush sent peacekeeping troops to what African country in a mission that ended in disaster in 1993?

    (A) Kenya
    (B) Somalia
    (C) Ethiopia
    (D) South Africa
    (E) Uganda

104. One of the major aspects of Nixon's domestic policy was revenue sharing. How can this be described?

    (A) The sharing of the responsibility of welfare between the states and federal government
    (B) The sharing of cigarette tax income between states
    (C) The sharing of export revenue between Northern and Southern states
    (D) Philanthropy was encouraged by the nation.
    (E) The sharing of alcohol tax income by the states to the federal government

105. In the My Lai incident, Lt. William Calley was sentenced to life imprisonment (but later pardoned) for what crime?

    (A) Lying to the army about his past drug use
    (B) The use of agent orange
    (C) The murder of Vietnamese villagers
    (D) The rape of a North Vietnamese woman
    (E) The murder of his commanding officer

106. During World War II, how were U.S. citizens of German, Italian, and Japanese heritage treated by the U.S. government?

    (A) Except in isolated incidents, they were treated like any other U.S. citizen.
    (B) U.S. citizens of German ancestry were barred from positions in the federal government.
    (C) Japanese Americans residing in west coast states were rounded up and imprisoned in concentration camps.
    (D) U.S. citizens of German and Italian heritage were barred from traveling to and from Europe.
    (E) They could serve in the U.S. military but could not fight against countries of their heritage because of fears that they would become spies.

107. Nixon nominated three justices to the U.S. Supreme Court, all of whom were considered to be conservative. Therefore, he was surprised when the famous *Roe v. Wade* case was handed down, as it was considered a liberal ruling. The judge who wrote the decision was

(A) Sandra Day O'Connor
(B) Harry Blackmun
(C) Louis Brandeis
(D) Thurgood Marshall
(E) Byron White

108. In the area of foreign relations, President Carter is most known for the

(A) independence of Indonesia
(B) Camp David accords between Israel and Egypt
(C) peace agreement between Panama and Colombia
(D) Camp Carter agreement between Zimbabwe and Great Britain
(E) selling of the Panama Canal to the U.S.

109. Why did the U.S. refuse to participate in the 1980 Olympic games in Moscow?

(A) The Soviets again built nuclear missile sites in Cuba.
(B) The Soviets had imposed an oil and grain embargo on the U.S.
(C) The SALT II talks had been stopped by the Soviets.
(D) The Soviets had executed American prisoners.
(E) The Soviets had invaded Afghanistan.

110. A book called *The Feminine Mystique* galvanized the feminist movement in the 1960s. It was written by

(A) Phyllis Schlafly
(B) an anonymous author
(C) Betty Friedan
(D) Gloria Steinem
(E) Geraldine Ferraro

111. A nickname often used for President Ronald Reagan is

(A) the "Great Liar"
(B) the "Big Man on Campus"
(C) the "Great Acto"
(D) the "Great Communicator"
(E) the "Incredible Liberal"

112. What did the Voting Rights Act of 1965 do for voters?

    (A) Ended literacy tests and placed the registration process under federal watch
    (B) Allowed Native Americans and Chinese Americans to vote
    (C) Ended the poll tax
    (D) Disallowed KKK members from voting or harassing voters
    (E) Ended the practice of the write-in ballot in federal elections

113. Reagan's Economic Recovery Act of 1981 did what?

    (A) Raised taxes in order to provide for more military spending
    (B) Significantly reduced federal income taxes for all taxpayers
    (C) Greatly increased welfare benefits
    (D) Gave only single mothers and the elderly a tax cut
    (E) Aided illegal immigrants

114. Reagan ordered the invasion of what small island nation in 1983 in order to prevent it from becoming communist?

    (A) Curacao
    (B) Cuba
    (C) The Bahamas
    (D) The Channel Islands
    (E) Grenada

115. What group of voters did Nixon directly appeal to in the 1968 presidential race?

    (A) Liberals from the Northeast
    (B) Staunch Conservatives from the deep South
    (C) Women
    (D) The "silent majority"
    (E) The "Americans for Democratic Action"

116. In 1990 the Senate voted whether to authorize the president to take military action against Iraq for its invasion of Kuwait. What was the result of that vote?

    (A) Nearly unanimous for war
    (B) A slim majority of votes were given for war
    (C) Nearly unanimous for not going to war, but President Bush ordered intervention anyhow
    (D) The vote was tied at 50/50 and the vice president cast the final vote to break the tie in favor of war.
    (E) No vote was taken in the Senate.

117. During the early Cold War, what did NSC-68 recommend?

    (A) Changing the Constitution to allow for more searches
    (B) New U.S. taxes to finance new military growth
    (C) Changing the military age to 15
    (D) Investment in the burgeoning computer industry
    (E) Halting the development of the hydrogen bomb

118. What was the important legislation passed in 1990 that covered most employees in the country and all businesses with over 25 employees?

    (A) The Americans with Disabilities Act
    (B) The Minimum Wage Act
    (C) The No New Taxes Act
    (D) The Equal Opportunity Amendment
    (E) The Employee Aid Act

119. In his first inaugural address, Franklin Roosevelt famously said which of the following?

    (A) "With hard work, America can be strong again."
    (B) "Do not ask what your country can do for you—ask what you can do for your country."
    (C) "Let me assert my firm belief that the only thing we have to fear is fear itself."
    (D) "I have a dream."
    (E) "Read my lips—no new taxes."

120. Which political group, led by Thaddeus Stevens, refused to recognize Southern Confederate members of Congress during Reconstruction?

    (A) Republicans
    (B) Radical Republicans
    (C) Reconstruction party
    (D) Radical Democrats
    (E) Whigs

PRACTICE TEST 2

Answer Key

1.	(D)	31.	(C)	61.	(B)	91.	(C)
2.	(E)	32.	(E)	62.	(B)	92.	(D)
3.	(A)	33.	(A)	63.	(D)	93.	(B)
4.	(D)	34.	(C)	64.	(B)	94.	(A)
5.	(A)	35.	(C)	65.	(E)	95.	(E)
6.	(B)	36.	(C)	66.	(D)	96.	(D)
7.	(D)	37.	(A)	67.	(E)	97.	(A)
8.	(A)	38.	(A)	68.	(A)	98.	(E)
9.	(B)	39.	(D)	69.	(A)	99.	(B)
10.	(D)	40.	(A)	70.	(D)	100.	(B)
11.	(C)	41.	(A)	71.	(C)	101.	(C)
12.	(E)	42.	(C)	72.	(E)	102.	(D)
13.	(E)	43.	(D)	73.	(C)	103.	(B)
14.	(D)	44.	(A)	74.	(D)	104.	(A)
15.	(A)	45.	(D)	75.	(A)	105.	(C)
16.	(C)	46.	(E)	76.	(B)	106.	(C)
17.	(A)	47.	(C)	77.	(C)	107.	(B)
18.	(D)	48.	(D)	78.	(A)	108.	(B)
19.	(E)	49.	(E)	79.	(B)	109.	(E)
20.	(B)	50.	(C)	80.	(C)	110.	(C)
21.	(B)	51.	(D)	81.	(D)	111.	(D)
22.	(D)	52.	(E)	82.	(C)	112.	(A)
23.	(B)	53.	(B)	83.	(B)	113.	(B)
24.	(D)	54.	(A)	84.	(D)	114.	(E)
25.	(E)	55.	(D)	85.	(B)	115.	(D)
26.	(A)	56.	(C)	86.	(A)	116.	(B)
27.	(E)	57.	(A)	87.	(C)	117.	(B)
28.	(E)	58.	(A)	88.	(E)	118.	(A)
29.	(E)	59.	(A)	89.	(B)	119.	(C)
30.	(D)	60.	(C)	90.	(D)	120.	(B)

PRACTICE TEST 2

Detailed Explanations of Answers

1. **(D)** All of these events relate to Reconstruction-era government and politics. The order, from the earliest event to the most recent event, is as follows:

   1. Fourteenth Amendment (1865)

   2. Reconstruction Act (1867)

   3. impeachment of President Johnson (1868)

   4. Amnesty Act (1872)

2. **(E)** "Halitosis" was a term coined to describe the "disease" of bad breath and was employed in ads promoting Listerine as a cure. The other choices are medical terms of more legitimate origins.

3. **(A)** Only the Freedmen's Bureau, created by Congress in 1865, accomplished these things before its demise. Its official name was the "Bureau of Refugees, Freedmen, and Abandoned Lands." With the help of many Northern volunteers, it assisted the resettlement of tens of thousands of Southern blacks on Southern land. However, it failed to reorganize Southern society enough to guarantee the rights of freed slaves.

4. **(D)** The Fifteenth Amendment prohibited denying the vote to a man based on race, color, or having previously been a slave. The Voting Rights Act of 1965 authorized the U.S. attorney general to intervene where blacks were not being allowed their right to vote. The Civil Rights Act of 1964 banned discrimination in public places, the Black Power and hippie movements do not relate to the right to vote, and the Equal Rights Amendment was aimed to ensure equal rights for women but has never been ratified.

5. **(A)** The Republican governments in the South tried to aid the reconstruction process and were considered the more liberal party. When Reconstruction failed the Democrats, then the more conservative party and the party of the Old South, regained its dominance.

6. **(B)** The Ford Motor Company, which revolutionized mass production, started operations in 1903, and the first Model Ts were introduced in 1908.

7. **(D)** Anarchists were demonstrating in Chicago in Haymarket Square when a bomb exploded as police began dispersing the crowd. The bomb

and ensuing riot killed 11 people. Eight protesters were convicted of inciting violence and four were hanged even though no evidence linked them to the bomb. After several years in prison, the surviving protesters were pardoned.

8. **(A)** Faced with a poor economy and high unemployment rate, Clinton's graduated tax plan called for raising taxes for the middle class and even higher for the rich (people earning over $250,000). He also raised corporate taxes. Clinton also ordered a reduction in military and other government spending in order to reduce $5 trillion in government debt and to bring the budget into balance.

9. **(B)** John D. Rockefeller created Standard Oil of New Jersey by using horizontal integration, a device that allowed him to buy many refineries without violating anti-trust laws. In 1911, the company was found to be in violation of anti-trust laws and was dissolved by the U.S. Supreme Court. Andrew Carnegie was involved with steel, Morgan and Schiff were investment bankers, and George was a reformer.

10. **(D)** Social Darwinism can be explained as the "survival of the fittest" slogan used as an economic model. In this theory, the fittest, most capable, most hard working become successful and the poor are destined to be so because they are not capable of being otherwise. All of the other answer choices contradict the Social Darwinist ideal.

11. **(C)** MacArthur led the Allied offensive against the Japanese in the Pacific. Eisenhower commanded the Allies in Europe. Patton led the Third Army through France and Germany. Marshall was Chief of Staff in the war, but was not specifically in charge of the Pacific offensive. Rommel was a German general in command of the Afrika Corps.

12. **(E)** The Populist party was an agrarian movement hoping to help non-industrialists, farmers, and other people left out of the new industrial economy. In the early 1890s, low prices on cotton and wheat threatened the income of many farmers, leading to their interest in Populism. But by 1896, the Democrats, led by William Jennings Bryan, appropriated the free coinage of silver theme (and focused on it more than the Populists had due to the Democrats' silver mining industry backers). With rising farm prices, the Populists rapidly declined in influence.

13. **(E)** Levitt developed what are referred to as "Levittowns," which were planned suburban communities with house designs based on a few models,

so that they were similar in design. In this way, affordable homes could be built quickly helping to alleviate the post–World War II housing shortage. These communities were built in New York, New Jersey, Pennsylvania, and other areas. Levitt demonstrated that new suburban communities could be successfully developed independent of urban settings.

14. **(D)** Tropical diseases killed an estimated 5,000 U.S. soldiers. The sinking of the *Maine* killed 262 and Spanish bullets killed 385. The Battle of Manila Bay is included in the total for Spanish bullet deaths, and there are no specific numbers for hand-to-hand combat with Filipinos because the number of killed were very few.

15. **(A)** The proposed location for the Panama Canal was in a province of Colombia called Panama. The Panamanian nationalists, with the help of American money, staged a bloodless revolution and Panama declared independence. Americans then arranged a treaty giving the U.S. the rights to build and operate the future canal. It was called the "treaty that no Panamanian signed."

16. **(C)** Du Bois was a black scholar, writer, professor, and historian who aimed to end racial discrimination and promote racial equality in America. Washington advocated black assimilation, though not necessarily racial equality. Wells was a black author who ran an anti-lynching campaign. Douglass was an ex-slave who advocated abolition through political activism. Turner was a white historian.

17. **(A)** From the 1860s until the 1880s railroads often sponsored buffalo hunts. In some cases, men shot at the buffalo from slowly moving trains and the carcasses were left in the fields by the thousands. The railroads feared that Indian tribes would impede westward expansion, and therefore, the expansion of the railroad and its ensuing profits. Because the buffalo were a necessary part of the life of the Plains Indians tribes, killing the buffalo effectively destroyed their culture.

18. **(D)** The Tuskegee Institute was led by Washington and embodied his beliefs. It was aimed at promoting "industrial education"—education for the sake of learning a trade or skill, not for higher knowledge. Washington wanted the students to have the advantage of melding into white society by possessing useful skills. His critics believed he was aiming too low by not advocating a traditional academic education.

19. **(E)** Roosevelt was a conservationist who believed in resource management and habitat protection. He did not halt the pure food and drug laws,

but helped them get passed. He was pro-big business, not pro-labor. The Peace Corps was created by President Kennedy. The sale of Alaska occurred in 1867 during the administration of Andrew Johnson.

20. **(B)** Roosevelt, Taft, and Harding were all Republican presidents. Taft won the election of 1908 against Bryan, a Democrat. T. Roosevelt was elected in 1900 and 1904. Harding was elected in 1920. Wilson, a Democrat, became president in 1912, and was reelected in 1916.

21. **(B)** Answer choice (A) is a short explanation of the Monroe Doctrine itself, not the Roosevelt Corollary. Answer choice (B) is a short explanation of the Roosevelt Corollary. The other answers are false.

22. **(D)** Muckrakers like Ida Tarbell and Lincoln Steffens exposed corruption in city government, big business, and other places. The muckrakers were an important part of what is called the Progressive Era. All of the other answers are false.

23. **(B)** The Dawes Severalty Act ended all rights to tribal lands and instead gave land only to individual nuclear families. It also granted citizenship only to those who accepted these family allotments. In addition to aiding in the death of tribal life, this act had a negative impact on the Native Americans because some of them were convinced to sell their land to whites to make a quick profit and then ended up with nothing.

24. **(D)** The sinking of the British ship known as the *Lusitania* by a German U-boat generated a great deal of U.S. public support for the Allied cause. One hundred twenty-eight Americans were among the 1,195 people who died on board the luxury ship when it sank. The sinking of the *Maine* prompted the Spanish-American War. The assassination of Archduke Ferdinand sparked World War I but not U.S. involvement. President Wilson's wife did pass away, and the election of 1916 would be close, but neither was a reason for pulling the U.S. into the war. The predominant public opinion was in staying out of the war, not joining in it.

25. **(E)** With the withdrawal of federal troops, Reconstruction ended in 1877. At this point, the old order of the South was in power again. Black codes and other racist laws kept the black population of the South underemployed, underpaid, undereducated, and out of the political process.

26. **(A)** In January 1917 the British intercepted a coded message from German Foreign Minister Arthur Zimmermann to the German minister in Mexico City. The Germans offered to return all U.S. territories Mexico had

lost in 1848, including Texas and Arizona, in return for its involvement in the war. The Mexicans never received the telegram but when it was published in U.S. newspapers, the incident enflamed public opinion to join the war. None of the other answers are true.

27. **(E)** WAC is the acronym for Women's Army Corps and WAVES were Women Accepted for Volunteer Emergency Services. Women were not allowed to serve in combat roles, but they were assigned jobs that were occasionally close to the front lines and were dangerous. A total of 350,000 women served in the WACs or WAVES during the war.

28. **(E)** George H. W. Bush, in his 1988 campaign against Michael Dukakis, stated that "no new taxes" would be raised under his administration. Two years after his election he did ask for a tax increase, making this quote ironically famous.

29. **(E)** Wilson's Fourteen Points contained his political and philosophical ideals regarding peace after World War I. They addressed issues such as freedom of the seas, autonomy for certain European regions, and his hope for an international body called the League of Nations. While a military draft was instituted, black soldier divisions did exist (but not integrated in the military), and goods needed to be rationed, Wilson did not address these issues in his Fourteen Points. No women were permitted in the army.

30. **(D)** *Roe v. Wade* (1973) made abortion legal in all states in the U.S. as it struck down individual state laws that had made abortion illegal. It also made abortion legal except in the last trimester of pregnancy, at which time a state could stop abortions.

31. **(C)** Garvey was the publisher of *Negro World*, which advocated separating from white society and espoused a "back to Africa" movement. He was also a founder of the Universal Negro Improvement Association.

32. **(E)** Japan signed the Tri-Partite Pact with Germany and Italy in 1940 expanding the Axis alliance. The U.S. responded by cutting off all trade with Japan. Japan would attack the U.S. at Pearl Harbor in 1941, forcing the U.S. to declare war on Germany and Italy, as well as Japan.

33. **(A)** Coolidge believed in unfettered big business and that the U. S. government should stay out of business affairs. Debs was a socialist who believed the American people should have a government that promotes the interests of the people. The others, while certainly supportive of big business, did not utter this famous quote.

34. **(C)** During the depths of the Great Depression, over 15,000 World War I veterans marched on Washington in 1932 to set up a "tent city" on federal grounds. The marchers demanded payment of their bonus certificates for having served the U.S. military during the war. President Hoover ordered U.S. troops to oust the veterans from their encampment. The violent action resulted in a calamity that became a public relations fiasco for the Hoover administration.

35. **(C)** After the ouster of the U.S.-backed Shah of Iran in a fundamentalist Islamic revolution, President Carter offered him temporary asylum in the U.S. to undergo cancer treatment in 1979. Iranians, angry that the Shah would not stand trial, stormed the American embassy in Teheran and took hostages. The U.S. deadlocked negotiations and the hostages were held in captivity for over a year. The hostage dilemma, along with a declining economy, contributed to Reagan's landslide victory over Carter in 1980. The hostages were released on the day of Reagan's inauguration.

36. **(C)** The Red Scare was sparked by labor strikes after World War I and the Bolshevik Revolution. Many workers who advocated change were labeled as communist when they were not. The Red Scare culminated in an event referred to as the Palmer Raids.

37. **(A)** The assassination of both Robert Kennedy and Martin Luther King, Jr., occurred in 1968. President Kennedy was assassinated in 1963, Malcolm X in 1965. Civil rights activist Medgar Evers was murdered in 1963 and Alabama governor George Wallace was shot in an assassination attempt but not killed.

38. **(A)** Sacco and Vanzetti, two Italian immigrant anarchists, were convicted and executed for murder in a trial marked by the presiding judge's prejudicial nativist statements. The prosecution relied extensively on attacking their radical beliefs. The case brought to public attention inequities of the criminal justice system that needed to be modernized.

39. **(D)** Many, if not most, of the people invested in the market in 1929 had been buying on margin, which means that they had borrowed in order to buy the stock. When the market crashed they not only lost the investment in the stocks, but also could not pay back their creditors. It is not true that "most Americans owned stock"—in fact, only a small percentage of Americans did. Hoover was not assassinated. The European market followed the Americans plunging into an economic depression.

40. **(A)** The New Deal was Franklin Roosevelt's plan for getting America through the Great Depression of the 1930s and 1940s by using government resources and money to improve impoverished social conditions, especially unemployment. The Great Society was Lyndon Johnson's economic plan for aiding low-income Americans through welfare programs and other forms of public assistance in the 1960s. The term "Great Society" does not apply to any of the other presidents.

41. **(A)** Evangelical Christianity was not a new movement but gained a large following in the 1970s. Preachers like Jerry Falwell, Billy Graham, and Pat Robertson used the medium of television to raise large sums of money in spreading their form of Christianity.

42. **(C)** Ross Perot, a billionaire Texan, ran for president as an independent. He received nearly 20% of the popular vote but did not win any electoral votes. Edward Kennedy is a Democrat senator from Massachusetts and did not run for president in 1992. Thomas is a Supreme Court Justice. Gore won the 1992 election as President Clinton's vice president and ran for the presidency in 2000. Nader was the Green party presidential candidate in 1996 and 2000.

43. **(D)** The answer is *The Great Gatsby* by F. Scott Fitzgerald. *Uncle Tom's Cabin* by Harriet Beecher Stowe was written prior to the Civil War. John Kenneth Galbraith's book was written in the 1950s. *The Birth of a Nation*, which premiered with the title *The Clansman*, was an explicitly racist 1915 film, not a piece of literature. Betty Friedan's book, which explored the issues faced by modern women in traditional roles, was published in 1963. Of these works, only Fitzgerald's evinces a specific mistrust of society and materialism.

44. **(A)** The Works Progress Administration (WPA) provided work to 8 million people over its lifespan. It employed people during the Great Depression building and repairing bridges, hospitals, and power plants, and had many other projects.

45. **(D)** The Dust Bowl, an environmental crisis of fierce dust storms whipped up from drought-dried, overgrazed farmland soil, mostly affected the Southern Plains prairie states of Kansas, Missouri, and Oklahoma. The other geographic areas were not affected.

46. **(E)** The Good Neighbor Policy provided agreements with several Latin American countries. These agreements focused on American trade and economic agreements in order to ensure American influence in the region.

47. **(C)** When considering these answer choices, only the AFL advocated higher wages, shorter workdays, and safer conditions. The Knights of Labor and IWW wanted worker solidarity and other ideals considered very radical at the time. The Haymarket Riot was an event, not a labor organization, and there was no Pullman Union.

48. **(D)** The Democratic headquarters was in the Watergate hotel. Members of the Committee to Re-elect the President were caught breaking into the headquarters and placing listening devices. This incident unraveled a series of scandals affecting many members of the Nixon administration. During congressional investigative hearings, it was revealed that President Nixon secretly taped conversations in the Oval Office. The tapes contained incriminating information, which led to Nixon's resignation.

49. **(E)** In 1876 Democrat Samuel J. Tilden of New York won the popular vote but lost the election to Republican Rutherford B. Hayes of Ohio. There were disputed electoral college votes in several states, and in 1897 a special congressional commission was created to settle the issue. The commission, composed of eight Republicans and seven Democrats, voted on strict party lines and gave all the disputed states to Hayes, handing him the presidency by one electoral college vote.

50. **(C)** Louisiana Governor and U.S. Senator Huey Long was a socialist who believed that taxes on the wealthy should be significantly raised and redistributed to programs for lower income Americans. He founded the Share our Wealth Society and was preparing to run for president when he was assassinated in 1935. Townsend was an advocate for the elderly. None of the other famous figures started the society mentioned above.

51. **(D)** Women organized for more than 60 years to win the right to vote in general elections in the United States. In the 1910s some Western states had allowed women to vote in state elections, but most states, especially those in the South, did not allow women to vote in any elections until the Nineteenth Amendment was passed in 1920.

52. **(E)** In the 1950s, Puerto Rican immigrants tended to settle in New York, mostly in New York City. Most settled in the area known as Spanish Harlem. By 1960 over 600,000 Puerto Ricans lived in the area.

53. **(B)** Steinbeck's novel *The Grapes of Wrath* and the movie adapted from it dealt with the Great Depression in a realistic manner. For the movie-going public, this was an anomaly because most of the Hollywood movies produced during this time were comedies, musicals, or other escapist fantasies from the harsh realities of the depression. Answer choice (A) is a romance novel set during the Civil War, (C) is a Marx brothers comedy, (D) is a Disney animated fairy tale, and (E) is also a comedy.

54. **(A)** U.S. reconnaissance flights over Cuba took pictures of missile sites under construction by the Soviets. Considering the proximity of Cuba to Florida, this posed a major threat to U.S. security. On October 22, 1962, President Kennedy ordered a naval "quarantine" (a word used to avoid saying "blockade," which is an act of war) of Cuba and demanded the immediate removal of the missiles. War between the two superpowers loomed, but a week later the Soviets promised to remove the missiles in exchange for the U.S.'s promise not to invade Cuba.

55. **(D)** In the Scottsboro case (1931) two white women accused nine young black men of raping them on a freight train passing through Alabama. The nine were found guilty in Alabama courts and were sentenced to death or life in prison. The U.S. Supreme Court twice reversed their convictions on procedural grounds and ordered new trials. In the second trial, one of the women recanted her testimony, yet the men were still convicted. In 1937 charges were dropped against five of the men and three others were freed in the 1940s. The last escaped from prison in 1948 to Michigan, which refused extradition. Alabama pardoned him in 1976.

56. **(C)** Cesar Chavez and his family became migrant workers when young Cesar was 10 years old. He would later become a very influential and important labor leader, organizing a famous lettuce boycott in support of migrant workers. Porter was a songwriter and singer; Du Bois was a black scholar and leader. Franklin Roosevelt was from a wealthy family, and he and Reagan never were migrant workers.

57. **(A)** The Civilian Conservation Corps was established by Congress during the Great Depression to provide work and job training for unemployed young men in programs designed to protect the nation's natural resources (soil conservation, reforestation, development of national parks, flood control, etc.). Most of the men's pay was sent back home to support their families. The CCC ran from 1933 until it was abolished by Congress in 1942.

58. **(A)** Progressive groups like the Anti-Saloon League started the modern-day temperance movement. They wanted the sale of alcohol outlawed in the U.S. due to its negative influence on American society, especially the poor and working class. None of the other answers are true.

59. **(A)** The Neutrality Act of 1935 was passed to keep the U.S. out of a possible war in Europe by ensuring the safety of American ships. Shipment of military material by U.S. ships to nations engaged in war was banned and U.S. citizens were prohibited from traveling on belligerent ships. No American planes were being shot down, the Spanish Civil War began in 1936 and did not produce great tensions in the U.S., the Nazi-Soviet Pact included no agreements mentioning the U.S., and getting goods to Europe in a more timely manner was not an issue.

60. **(C)** All of these events relate to the Vietnam War and its effects on U.S. government. The order, from the earliest event to the most recent event, is as follows:

    1. Geneva Accords (1954)

    2. Gulf of Tonkin Resolution (1964)

    3. Tet Offensive (1968)

    4. War Powers Resolution (1973)

61. **(B)** While Italy's Mussolini and Spain's Franco posed a fascist threat to peace in Europe, and Japan's Tojo would soon order the attack on the U.S. at Pearl Harbor, it was Germany's Hitler who was the biggest threat to the world's status quo. Germany had amassed an enormous technically advanced army for Hitler's dream of world domination. Hitler could exploit the political instability and economic hardship of the Great Depression in Europe to terrorize other nations. Selassie was the Emperor of Ethiopia, which was overtaken by the Italians in World War II.

62. **(B)** Lend-Lease allowed the U.S. to supply arms to Great Britain while circumventing the restrictions of the Neutrality Act. During World War II the U.S. later expanded the program to include lending, leasing, or otherwise providing arms to other Allied nations, including the Soviet Union.

63. **(D)** The Korean War started in June 1950 and ended in July 1953. Much of the war was a stalemate along the 38th parallel, and at the war's end North and South Korea were divided near that line. Over 54,000 American soldiers died in the war.

64. **(B)**   Women joined the work force in large numbers, especially in the defense industry, during the war. Their pay was a small portion of the pay that a man would earn in the same role, but the women both needed the paycheck and wanted to do their patriotic duty. Right after the war many returned home, but a general trend of women in the workplace had begun and would change the American labor force until this day.

65. **(E)**   Dr. Spock broke away from the rigid parenting philosophy of the 1940s and 1950s by advising mothers to show affection for their children and respond to their needs. Previously, for example, it had been believed that picking up a crying baby would spoil him or her.

66. **(D)**   This fashion style was mostly worn by Latino teens, but was also worn by white and black teens, as well. It could be seen in large metropolitan areas like Los Angeles, Detroit, and New York. It was comprised of an oversized jacket or coat with wide lapels and heavily padded shoulders, and baggy, tight-cuffed pants.

67. **(E)**   The beaches of Normandy, France, were the spot for "Operation Overlord," the D-Day Allied invasion of Europe on June 6, 1944. More than 5,000 ships transported 9 divisions of troops with 130,000 men landing on 50 miles of beaches. Over 12,000 planes dropped supplies and 3 airborne divisions of paratroopers.

68. **(A)**   The battles for Okinawa and Iwo Jima were two of the costliest battles for the U.S. in the Pacific theater. At Okinawa American deaths totaled 7,600 and Japanese deaths were estimated to be over 20,000.

69. **(A)**   The "Big Three" at Yalta were Roosevelt, Churchill, and Stalin. Roosevelt was in poor health and died shortly after the conference.

70. **(D)**   The Manhattan Project was the $2 billion wartime effort that developed the atomic bomb in 1945. J. Robert Oppenheimer was the director of the laboratory at Los Alamos, New Mexico, where the design and the building of the bombs took place. None of the other scientists was alive at the time.

71. **(C)**   Kennan, known only as "X," wrote in *Foreign Affairs* that the Soviet Union was planning a communist takeover of much of the world and needed to be contained by America and her allies. None of the other answer choices formulated this policy. Roosevelt was involved with women's issues among other causes, Masaryk was a Czech leader, and Marshall was Secretary

of State and formulated the Marshall Plan. Molotov was a Soviet foreign minister.

72. **(E)** The United States and the U.S.S.R. were still considered to be in a Cold War in 1983. Reagan was an ardent anti-communist who believed that the U.S.S.R. would stop at nothing to achieve world domination.

73. **(C)** After World War II the Soviets, in response to the non-communist Allied government in West Berlin, halted all modes of transportation to and from the area, thereby cutting off food and other supplies. The U.S. and allies, in return, began airlifting supplies to the area. The blockade proved ineffective and eventually the Soviets relented.

74. **(D)** Three articles of impeachment were brought against Nixon in July 1974. In August 1974, Nixon faced a loss of public support and almost certain conviction by Congress, and he resigned from office. He was the first president to ever do so. One month later, Nixon's successor, Gerald Ford, pardoned him.

75. **(A)** The GI Bill, as the act is usually called, gave financial assistance and other types of aid to returning World War II veterans. It helped rebuild the economy by allowing the returning servicemen to easily purchase a home, go to college, or start a business.

76. **(B)** Jackie Robinson joined the Brooklyn Dodgers in 1947, becoming the first black baseball player in the major leagues. In 1962 he also became the first African American to be inducted into the Baseball Hall of Fame; he died ten years later.

77. **(C)** The Tennessee Valley Authority created a series of dams and other projects in order to provide the seven-state area with cheap electricity and bring it into the modern age. Not only did this provide the people with electricity in their homes, but it also encouraged businesses to move into the area. It also provided health and education programs to the region.

78. **(A)** The fate of India and Great Britain's other territories was a point of tension between the U.S. and England at the conference. India was finally declared an autonomous nation in 1947. All of the other points were true, even that Stalin agreed to holding free elections, although they never actually occurred.

79. **(B)** HUAC, or House Committee on Un-American Activities, searched for communists that could pose a threat to the U.S. This fear of communism

is also referred to as McCarthyism (after Senator Joseph McCarthy—one of the most aggressive anti-communists) or the "Great Fear." The "Hollywood Ten" were actors, writers, and producers accused of being commuists and who went to jail for refusing to testify. It is now believed that none of these Hollywood figures were actually communists.

80. **(C)** U.S. President Lyndon B. Johnson authorized the bombing of North Vietnam and neighboring Laos in the mid-1960s. In 1970, President Richard Nixon sent U.S. troops into Cambodia to attack communist Vietnamese forces that used the neighboring territory as a base of operations. Thus, both nations' proximity to disputed territory drew them directly into the Vietnam War.

81. **(D)** Eisenhower, a Republican, was known as someone who preferred not to take political risks. Regarding the delicate issues of the time, he moved cautiously and quietly, rarely in an outspoken manner. His policies are considered to be "modern Republicanism," a middle ground between the two poles of liberalism and conservatism. In his second term he took a firmer position on issues like civil rights and the Cold War, but still remained moderate in his rhetoric.

82. **(C)** After U.S. ships in the Gulf of Tonkin were allegedly attacked by North Vietnamese gunboats, President Lyndon Johnson asked Congress to grant him the authority to respond to further military aggression. The Tonkin Gulf Resolution was passed by near unanimous vote on August 7, 1964, giving Johnson uncontested authority to use "all necessary measures" to deal with the civil war in Vietnam.

83. **(B)** *Sputnik* was the first space satellite and it was launched by the Soviets in 1957. In the era of the Cold War, any advantage of the Soviets over the Americans caused panic. Partially in response to *Sputnik*, the National Aeronautics and Space Administration (NASA) was created in 1958.

84. **(D)** Nikita Khrushchev became Stalin's successor after an internal Soviet struggle for leadership. He, in some ways, seemed fair-minded and liberal, as in his denouncement of the crimes of Stalin. In other ways, however, he was a staunch communist who would stop popular uprisings in Hungary and Poland. He was the Soviet Premier during the days of Eisenhower, and on through Kennedy and the Cuban Missile Crisis.

85. **(B)** The name of the plane was the U2; it was shot down over Soviet territory and its pilot, Francis Gary Powers, was captured. The tension caused

by the event caused a summit between Eisenhower and Khrushchev to be cancelled.

86. **(A)** Even though millions of Americans were poor, Galbraith believed that important people like politicians, city planners, and economists were not taking them into account. Galbraith asserted that the wealthy considered poverty a thing of the past.

87. **(C)** Marshall was the NAACP's chief counsel. Du Bois was involved with international matters and was not an attorney. Salk was the creator of the polio vaccine; Parks would become the symbol of the Montgomery Bus Boycott. Abernathy helped Martin Luther King, Jr., found the Southern Christian Leadership Conference.

88. **(E)** The Twenty-sixth Amendment lowered the voting age to 18. This worried Republicans regarding their reelection campaign in 1972, as younger people tended to vote Democratic.

89. **(B)** The headline read "Dewey defeats Truman" when it was Truman who defeated Dewey in the election of 1948. Truman received 3 million more popular votes and 113 more electoral votes. Strom Thurmond, of the State's Rights Party, won 39 electoral votes.

90. **(D)** The Supreme Court decided in favor of the boycotters. The city of Montgomery, Alabama, had to allow blacks to sit wherever they wanted on the city's buses (and not be forced to sit in the back or give up seats to whites). The case was decided in 1956.

91. **(C)** In 1954 the U.S. Supreme Court struck down racial segregation in public schools. While the city of Little Rock made efforts to comply with integration, in 1957 the governor ordered the Arkansas National Guard to surround the school and prevent blacks from entering. After a federal court injunction, Eisenhower responded by federalizing the Arkansas National Guard and sending U.S. army troops to enforce desegregation.

92. **(D)** In this famous election, power shifted from the Republicans to the Democrats with Kennedy's win over Nixon. In the first televised debates, Kennedy used the media well, appearing handsome, well spoken, and self-assured while Nixon was less telegenic and appeared angry and surly. This election demonstrated the importance of the new media in influencing votes.

93. **(B)** In the U.S. plan for the Bay of Pigs, Cuban exiles trained in the U.S. would covertly land on the beach and incite the Cuban people to revolution. It was a disastrous failure. Most of the Cuban exiles were captured, along with American CIA members who went with them. Cubans did not revolt against their popular leader.

94. **(A)** Nearly 40% of the "new immigrants" came from Italy or were Eastern European Jews. They tended to settle in big cities like New York, Chicago, and Philadelphia, and worked in factories and other low-wage jobs. The other groups were small minority immigrant populations for this time period.

95. **(E)** The Marshall Plan was designed to help Western Europe quickly recover from the devastation of World War II. It aimed to halt the further spread of communism by healing Western Europe's economic wounds, as it was believed that economic troubles could lead to communist takeovers.

96. **(D)** Harding was elected in 1920. Wilson, a Democrat, had served two terms as President but became incapacitated in 1919 after a massive stroke and did not run again. Republican Coolidge was Harding's vice president and became president in 1923 upon Harding's death in office; Republican Hoover was elected president in 1928. Curtis was Hoover's vice president.

97. **(A)** John F. Kennedy was assassinated on November 22, 1963, while riding in an open car in Dallas, Texas. Kennedy had served less than three years as president. Texas governor John Connally was also wounded in the motorcade.

98. **(E)** Medicare, welfare and other assistance for the poor, and civil rights were the crux of the Great Society programs.

99. **(B)** British influence and power was waning in the Middle East and there was great fear regarding the future of Middle Eastern oil exports to the U.S. The Doctrine allowed the president to get more involved in the region.

100. **(B)** The American Indian Movement's cause represented poor and forgotten Native Americans, who were victims of the U.S. government's racist and misguided policies. This group modeled itself after militant black power movements in the U.S., as well as Mexican-American activists.

101. **(C)** The Tet offensive was launched by the North Vietnamese on the eve of Tet (the Vietnamese Lunar New Year) in 1968. In this offensive, the North Vietnamese used tanks, cannons, and other Soviet equipment to

attack Saigon and other cities in South Vietnam. Although it was a military failure, the heavy combat marked a turning point in the Vietnam War. The offensive convinced many anti-war critics that American losses were not worth the cost of protecting South Vietnam.

102. **(D)** Some historians point to Johnson's not running for reelection as a sign that he knew he could not get reelected, as the country was seriously divided over the war and support for him was waning even among Democrats. Others claim that he wanted to do what was best for the country and believed that he had become too divisive a leader to be able to lead effectively. The Democratic party nominated Humphrey as their presidential candidate after Johnson withdrew from consideration. Technically, Johnson did not serve two complete terms as he assumed the presidency after Kennedy's assassination. Johnson was not ill at the time.

103. **(B)** A civil war in Somalia caused chaos, with rival warlords controlling different parts of the country. The U.S. maintained interest in Somalia as an important military base for operations in the Middle East. With famine reaching epidemic proportions, Bush sent U.S. troops to bring relief supplies to the starving people. Later, the troops were placed under U.N. control. Warlords in the city of Mogadishu began guerrilla attacks to force U.N. peacekeepers out. After an ambush in which 25 Pakistani U.N. peacekeeping troops were killed a retaliatory raid by American troops in October 1993 resulted in disaster. Eighteen U.S. troops and many hundreds of Somalis died. President Clinton subsequently withdrew U.S. involvement in Somalia.

104. **(A)** Although never passed, Nixon's revenue-sharing plans aimed to help both the states and the poor by streamlining the welfare process and creating a federal agency to distribute welfare. The size of the welfare checks would be decreased.

105. **(C)** In 1971, 374 unarmed Vietnamese peasants, mostly women and children, were massacred by U.S. troops in the alleged Viet Cong stronghold of My Lai. Although the military kept the incident secret, the story became public when one soldier refused to remain silent. Five U.S. soldiers were court-martialed and Lt. Calley was convicted. A federal court overturned the conviction in 1974.

106. **(C)** Following the Japanese attack on Pearl Harbor in December 1941, the United States was gripped by war hysteria. This was especially strong along the Pacific Coast of the U.S. where more Japanese attacks were greatly

feared. As a result, in February 1942 President Roosevelt signed an executive order authorizing the military to forcibly relocate people of Japanese ancestry from their homes to internment camps in isolated inland areas. Japanese Americans in the Hawaiian Islands were also interned. Incarcerated were more than 120,000, of whom over two-thirds were U.S. citizens and half children. No action was taken against U.S. citizens of German or Italian heritage. Roosevelt rescinded the executive order in 1944, and the last of the camps was closed in March 1946. Even so, many families lost their homes, possessions, and livelihoods.

107. **(B)** Nixon appointee Blackmun wrote the *Roe v. Wade* decision that legalized abortion in the U.S. While O'Connor is considered conservative, she was appointed by President Reagan and thus was not on the court at the time. Brandeis was appointed by Woodrow Wilson and served on the Supreme Court from 1916 to 1939. Marshall was appointed by Lyndon Johnson and was the court's first African American. White did tend to side with the conservative point of view but he was appointed by President Kennedy and retired in 1993.

108. **(B)** On March 26, 1977, Carter helped the Israelis and Egyptians reach a peace agreement. The meetings were held at Camp David, the famous retreat of U.S. presidents.

109. **(E)** The Soviets began a war with neighboring Afghanistan in 1979 in order to aid a communist revolution. The U.S. provided military assistance to the opposing Islamic fundamentalists. The war would drag on for many years until the Soviets were forced to back out. After the Cuban Missile Crisis in 1962, the Soviets never again put nuclear missiles in Cuba. The U.S. imposed a grain embargo on the U.S.S.R. after the Afghanistan war began. The SALT II agreement was never ratified by the Senate due to the war.

110. **(C)** Betty Friedan wrote the book in 1963 and was one of the founders of the National Organization for Women. In the book, Friedan explained her theories on why women were depressed and lost in the world of the 1960s, as they could not ultimately be happy in the narrow roles of housewife and mother. Schlafly was a conservative, not a feminist, and she called for a return to traditional family values. Steinem was a feminist and founded *Ms. Magazine*. Ferraro was a congresswoman and the first female candidate for vice president from a major political party.

111. **(D)** Reagan has been called the "Great Communicator" because of his persuasive public speaking skills. His long-time experience as a movie actor honed talents for delivering a powerful speech, but he was also quick with one-liners and making his audience feel that he was both relaxed and in charge.

112. **(A)** The Voting Rights Act of 1965 was a great achievement for Lyndon Johnson. When added to the Twenty-fourth Amendment to the U.S. Constitution, which ended the federal poll tax, it allowed a much larger segment of the black population to both register to vote and vote.

113. **(B)** This act included a tax cut for all Americans, reducing taxes by 25% over a three-year period. Also, corporate taxes were dramatically cut and other incentives were provided for big business. This was part of the economic plan referred to as "Reaganomics," which was designed to stimulate business investment and increase consumer spending to jumpstart the sagging economy. In theory, the benefits of expanded wealth would "trickle-down" to lower income groups.

114. **(E)** On October 13, 1983, the Grenadian Army staged a bloody coup and established a Marxist regime allied to Castro's Cuba. Ten days later, American foreign policy suffered a terrible shock when a Muslim suicide bomber destroyed barracks in Beirut, Lebanon, killing 240 U.S. Marines, and forcing the U.S. to retreat from the country during its civil war. The perceived threat to nearly 1,000 American medical students in Grenada provided President Reagan cause to eliminate communist expansion in the Caribbean. The intervention was successful, and with the loss of only 19 U.S. soldiers, it would prove helpful in diverting attention from the setback in Lebanon.

115. **(D)** Nixon appealed to "the silent majority" of American citizens who did not engage in protest during a violent and rebellious era of antiwar demonstrations, race riots, civil rights protests, and counter-culture activism. According to Nixon the silent majority was the average patriotic citizen who was hard working, conservative, and middle class. For this reason, Nixon emphasized "law and order" in his campaign speeches.

116. **(B)** The vote in the Senate was 52–47 to authorize military action. President Bush's administration had to lobby vigorously to gain support for the war against Iraq. The U.S. took several months to build up its military presence in the Middle East. The combat fighting of "Operation Desert Storm"

began on January 16, 1991, and ended with Iraq's unconditional surrender six weeks later.

117. **(B)** NSC-68, or National Security Council Report 68, strongly favored enhancing America's military capabilities because of the threat imposed by the Soviet Union. While it did not call for the lowering of military age to 15, it did ask for taxes to pay for a larger peacetime armed forces. It also recommended putting more investment in the development of the hydrogen bomb.

118. **(A)** The Americans with Disabilities Act (ADA) covers most employees and is specifically designed to prohibit job discrimination against those who are deaf, blind mentally retarded, or physically handicapped. Answer choices (B) and (D) have never been passed. The other two are not real acts.

119. **(C)** This was Franklin Roosevelt's attempt to make Americans feel confident at the time of his first inauguration and during some of the worst months of the Great Depression. Answer choice (A) is not a real quote, answer choice (B) is a quote by John F. Kennedy, answer choice (D) comes from Martin Luther King, Jr., and answer choice (E) is from George H. W. Bush.

120. **(B)** The Radical Republicans tried to truly Reconstruct the South following the Civil War. They passed the Reconstruction Acts and helped pass the Fourteenth Amendment to the U.S. Constitution. They impeached Johnson when he impeded their progress, but failed to have enough votes to convict him.

ANSWER SHEETS

Practice Test 1
Practice Test 2

PRACTICE TEST 1

Answer Sheet

1. Ⓐ Ⓑ Ⓒ Ⓓ Ⓔ	27. Ⓐ Ⓑ Ⓒ Ⓓ Ⓔ	53. Ⓐ Ⓑ Ⓒ Ⓓ Ⓔ
2. Ⓐ Ⓑ Ⓒ Ⓓ Ⓔ	28. Ⓐ Ⓑ Ⓒ Ⓓ Ⓔ	54. Ⓐ Ⓑ Ⓒ Ⓓ Ⓔ
3. Ⓐ Ⓑ Ⓒ Ⓓ Ⓔ	29. Ⓐ Ⓑ Ⓒ Ⓓ Ⓔ	55. Ⓐ Ⓑ Ⓒ Ⓓ Ⓔ
4. Ⓐ Ⓑ Ⓒ Ⓓ Ⓔ	30. Ⓐ Ⓑ Ⓒ Ⓓ Ⓔ	56. Ⓐ Ⓑ Ⓒ Ⓓ Ⓔ
5. Ⓐ Ⓑ Ⓒ Ⓓ Ⓔ	31. Ⓐ Ⓑ Ⓒ Ⓓ Ⓔ	57. Ⓐ Ⓑ Ⓒ Ⓓ Ⓔ
6. Ⓐ Ⓑ Ⓒ Ⓓ Ⓔ	32. Ⓐ Ⓑ Ⓒ Ⓓ Ⓔ	58. Ⓐ Ⓑ Ⓒ Ⓓ Ⓔ
7. Ⓐ Ⓑ Ⓒ Ⓓ Ⓔ	33. Ⓐ Ⓑ Ⓒ Ⓓ Ⓔ	59. Ⓐ Ⓑ Ⓒ Ⓓ Ⓔ
8. Ⓐ Ⓑ Ⓒ Ⓓ Ⓔ	34. Ⓐ Ⓑ Ⓒ Ⓓ Ⓔ	60. Ⓐ Ⓑ Ⓒ Ⓓ Ⓔ
9. Ⓐ Ⓑ Ⓒ Ⓓ Ⓔ	35. Ⓐ Ⓑ Ⓒ Ⓓ Ⓔ	61. Ⓐ Ⓑ Ⓒ Ⓓ Ⓔ
10. Ⓐ Ⓑ Ⓒ Ⓓ Ⓔ	36. Ⓐ Ⓑ Ⓒ Ⓓ Ⓔ	62. Ⓐ Ⓑ Ⓒ Ⓓ Ⓔ
11. Ⓐ Ⓑ Ⓒ Ⓓ Ⓔ	37. Ⓐ Ⓑ Ⓒ Ⓓ Ⓔ	63. Ⓐ Ⓑ Ⓒ Ⓓ Ⓔ
12. Ⓐ Ⓑ Ⓒ Ⓓ Ⓔ	38. Ⓐ Ⓑ Ⓒ Ⓓ Ⓔ	64. Ⓐ Ⓑ Ⓒ Ⓓ Ⓔ
13. Ⓐ Ⓑ Ⓒ Ⓓ Ⓔ	39. Ⓐ Ⓑ Ⓒ Ⓓ Ⓔ	65. Ⓐ Ⓑ Ⓒ Ⓓ Ⓔ
14. Ⓐ Ⓑ Ⓒ Ⓓ Ⓔ	40. Ⓐ Ⓑ Ⓒ Ⓓ Ⓔ	66. Ⓐ Ⓑ Ⓒ Ⓓ Ⓔ
15. Ⓐ Ⓑ Ⓒ Ⓓ Ⓔ	41. Ⓐ Ⓑ Ⓒ Ⓓ Ⓔ	67. Ⓐ Ⓑ Ⓒ Ⓓ Ⓔ
16. Ⓐ Ⓑ Ⓒ Ⓓ Ⓔ	42. Ⓐ Ⓑ Ⓒ Ⓓ Ⓔ	68. Ⓐ Ⓑ Ⓒ Ⓓ Ⓔ
17. Ⓐ Ⓑ Ⓒ Ⓓ Ⓔ	43. Ⓐ Ⓑ Ⓒ Ⓓ Ⓔ	69. Ⓐ Ⓑ Ⓒ Ⓓ Ⓔ
18. Ⓐ Ⓑ Ⓒ Ⓓ Ⓔ	44. Ⓐ Ⓑ Ⓒ Ⓓ Ⓔ	70. Ⓐ Ⓑ Ⓒ Ⓓ Ⓔ
19. Ⓐ Ⓑ Ⓒ Ⓓ Ⓔ	45. Ⓐ Ⓑ Ⓒ Ⓓ Ⓔ	71. Ⓐ Ⓑ Ⓒ Ⓓ Ⓔ
20. Ⓐ Ⓑ Ⓒ Ⓓ Ⓔ	46. Ⓐ Ⓑ Ⓒ Ⓓ Ⓔ	72. Ⓐ Ⓑ Ⓒ Ⓓ Ⓔ
21. Ⓐ Ⓑ Ⓒ Ⓓ Ⓔ	47. Ⓐ Ⓑ Ⓒ Ⓓ Ⓔ	73. Ⓐ Ⓑ Ⓒ Ⓓ Ⓔ
22. Ⓐ Ⓑ Ⓒ Ⓓ Ⓔ	48. Ⓐ Ⓑ Ⓒ Ⓓ Ⓔ	74. Ⓐ Ⓑ Ⓒ Ⓓ Ⓔ
23. Ⓐ Ⓑ Ⓒ Ⓓ Ⓔ	49. Ⓐ Ⓑ Ⓒ Ⓓ Ⓔ	75. Ⓐ Ⓑ Ⓒ Ⓓ Ⓔ
24. Ⓐ Ⓑ Ⓒ Ⓓ Ⓔ	50. Ⓐ Ⓑ Ⓒ Ⓓ Ⓔ	76. Ⓐ Ⓑ Ⓒ Ⓓ Ⓔ
25. Ⓐ Ⓑ Ⓒ Ⓓ Ⓔ	51. Ⓐ Ⓑ Ⓒ Ⓓ Ⓔ	77. Ⓐ Ⓑ Ⓒ Ⓓ Ⓔ
26. Ⓐ Ⓑ Ⓒ Ⓓ Ⓔ	52. Ⓐ Ⓑ Ⓒ Ⓓ Ⓔ	78. Ⓐ Ⓑ Ⓒ Ⓓ Ⓔ

(Continued)

PRACTICE TEST 1

Answer Sheet

79. Ⓐ Ⓑ Ⓒ Ⓓ Ⓔ
80. Ⓐ Ⓑ Ⓒ Ⓓ Ⓔ
81. Ⓐ Ⓑ Ⓒ Ⓓ Ⓔ
82. Ⓐ Ⓑ Ⓒ Ⓓ Ⓔ
83. Ⓐ Ⓑ Ⓒ Ⓓ Ⓔ
84. Ⓐ Ⓑ Ⓒ Ⓓ Ⓔ
85. Ⓐ Ⓑ Ⓒ Ⓓ Ⓔ
86. Ⓐ Ⓑ Ⓒ Ⓓ Ⓔ
87. Ⓐ Ⓑ Ⓒ Ⓓ Ⓔ
88. Ⓐ Ⓑ Ⓒ Ⓓ Ⓔ
89. Ⓐ Ⓑ Ⓒ Ⓓ Ⓔ
90. Ⓐ Ⓑ Ⓒ Ⓓ Ⓔ
91. Ⓐ Ⓑ Ⓒ Ⓓ Ⓔ
92. Ⓐ Ⓑ Ⓒ Ⓓ Ⓔ

93. Ⓐ Ⓑ Ⓒ Ⓓ Ⓔ
94. Ⓐ Ⓑ Ⓒ Ⓓ Ⓔ
95. Ⓐ Ⓑ Ⓒ Ⓓ Ⓔ
96. Ⓐ Ⓑ Ⓒ Ⓓ Ⓔ
97. Ⓐ Ⓑ Ⓒ Ⓓ Ⓔ
98. Ⓐ Ⓑ Ⓒ Ⓓ Ⓔ
99. Ⓐ Ⓑ Ⓒ Ⓓ Ⓔ
100. Ⓐ Ⓑ Ⓒ Ⓓ Ⓔ
101. Ⓐ Ⓑ Ⓒ Ⓓ Ⓔ
102. Ⓐ Ⓑ Ⓒ Ⓓ Ⓔ
103. Ⓐ Ⓑ Ⓒ Ⓓ Ⓔ
104. Ⓐ Ⓑ Ⓒ Ⓓ Ⓔ
105. Ⓐ Ⓑ Ⓒ Ⓓ Ⓔ
106. Ⓐ Ⓑ Ⓒ Ⓓ Ⓔ

107. Ⓐ Ⓑ Ⓒ Ⓓ Ⓔ
108. Ⓐ Ⓑ Ⓒ Ⓓ Ⓔ
109. Ⓐ Ⓑ Ⓒ Ⓓ Ⓔ
110. Ⓐ Ⓑ Ⓒ Ⓓ Ⓔ
111. Ⓐ Ⓑ Ⓒ Ⓓ Ⓔ
112. Ⓐ Ⓑ Ⓒ Ⓓ Ⓔ
113. Ⓐ Ⓑ Ⓒ Ⓓ Ⓔ
114. Ⓐ Ⓑ Ⓒ Ⓓ Ⓔ
115. Ⓐ Ⓑ Ⓒ Ⓓ Ⓔ
116. Ⓐ Ⓑ Ⓒ Ⓓ Ⓔ
117. Ⓐ Ⓑ Ⓒ Ⓓ Ⓔ
118. Ⓐ Ⓑ Ⓒ Ⓓ Ⓔ
119. Ⓐ Ⓑ Ⓒ Ⓓ Ⓔ
120. Ⓐ Ⓑ Ⓒ Ⓓ Ⓔ

PRACTICE TEST 2

Answer Sheet

1. (A) (B) (C) (D) (E)
2. (A) (B) (C) (D) (E)
3. (A) (B) (C) (D) (E)
4. (A) (B) (C) (D) (E)
5. (A) (B) (C) (D) (E)
6. (A) (B) (C) (D) (E)
7. (A) (B) (C) (D) (E)
8. (A) (B) (C) (D) (E)
9. (A) (B) (C) (D) (E)
10. (A) (B) (C) (D) (E)
11. (A) (B) (C) (D) (E)
12. (A) (B) (C) (D) (E)
13. (A) (B) (C) (D) (E)
14. (A) (B) (C) (D) (E)
15. (A) (B) (C) (D) (E)
16. (A) (B) (C) (D) (E)
17. (A) (B) (C) (D) (E)
18. (A) (B) (C) (D) (E)
19. (A) (B) (C) (D) (E)
20. (A) (B) (C) (D) (E)
21. (A) (B) (C) (D) (E)
22. (A) (B) (C) (D) (E)
23. (A) (B) (C) (D) (E)
24. (A) (B) (C) (D) (E)
25. (A) (B) (C) (D) (E)
26. (A) (B) (C) (D) (E)

27. (A) (B) (C) (D) (E)
28. (A) (B) (C) (D) (E)
29. (A) (B) (C) (D) (E)
30. (A) (B) (C) (D) (E)
31. (A) (B) (C) (D) (E)
32. (A) (B) (C) (D) (E)
33. (A) (B) (C) (D) (E)
34. (A) (B) (C) (D) (E)
35. (A) (B) (C) (D) (E)
36. (A) (B) (C) (D) (E)
37. (A) (B) (C) (D) (E)
38. (A) (B) (C) (D) (E)
39. (A) (B) (C) (D) (E)
40. (A) (B) (C) (D) (E)
41. (A) (B) (C) (D) (E)
42. (A) (B) (C) (D) (E)
43. (A) (B) (C) (D) (E)
44. (A) (B) (C) (D) (E)
45. (A) (B) (C) (D) (E)
46. (A) (B) (C) (D) (E)
47. (A) (B) (C) (D) (E)
48. (A) (B) (C) (D) (E)
49. (A) (B) (C) (D) (E)
50. (A) (B) (C) (D) (E)
51. (A) (B) (C) (D) (E)
52. (A) (B) (C) (D) (E)

53. (A) (B) (C) (D) (E)
54. (A) (B) (C) (D) (E)
55. (A) (B) (C) (D) (E)
56. (A) (B) (C) (D) (E)
57. (A) (B) (C) (D) (E)
58. (A) (B) (C) (D) (E)
59. (A) (B) (C) (D) (E)
60. (A) (B) (C) (D) (E)
61. (A) (B) (C) (D) (E)
62. (A) (B) (C) (D) (E)
63. (A) (B) (C) (D) (E)
64. (A) (B) (C) (D) (E)
65. (A) (B) (C) (D) (E)
66. (A) (B) (C) (D) (E)
67. (A) (B) (C) (D) (E)
68. (A) (B) (C) (D) (E)
69. (A) (B) (C) (D) (E)
70. (A) (B) (C) (D) (E)
71. (A) (B) (C) (D) (E)
72. (A) (B) (C) (D) (E)
73. (A) (B) (C) (D) (E)
74. (A) (B) (C) (D) (E)
75. (A) (B) (C) (D) (E)
76. (A) (B) (C) (D) (E)
77. (A) (B) (C) (D) (E)
78. (A) (B) (C) (D) (E)

(Continued)

PRACTICE TEST 2

Answer Sheet

79. Ⓐ Ⓑ Ⓒ Ⓓ Ⓔ	93. Ⓐ Ⓑ Ⓒ Ⓓ Ⓔ	107. Ⓐ Ⓑ Ⓒ Ⓓ Ⓔ
80. Ⓐ Ⓑ Ⓒ Ⓓ Ⓔ	94. Ⓐ Ⓑ Ⓒ Ⓓ Ⓔ	108. Ⓐ Ⓑ Ⓒ Ⓓ Ⓔ
81. Ⓐ Ⓑ Ⓒ Ⓓ Ⓔ	95. Ⓐ Ⓑ Ⓒ Ⓓ Ⓔ	109. Ⓐ Ⓑ Ⓒ Ⓓ Ⓔ
82. Ⓐ Ⓑ Ⓒ Ⓓ Ⓔ	96. Ⓐ Ⓑ Ⓒ Ⓓ Ⓔ	110. Ⓐ Ⓑ Ⓒ Ⓓ Ⓔ
83. Ⓐ Ⓑ Ⓒ Ⓓ Ⓔ	97. Ⓐ Ⓑ Ⓒ Ⓓ Ⓔ	111. Ⓐ Ⓑ Ⓒ Ⓓ Ⓔ
84. Ⓐ Ⓑ Ⓒ Ⓓ Ⓔ	98. Ⓐ Ⓑ Ⓒ Ⓓ Ⓔ	112. Ⓐ Ⓑ Ⓒ Ⓓ Ⓔ
85. Ⓐ Ⓑ Ⓒ Ⓓ Ⓔ	99. Ⓐ Ⓑ Ⓒ Ⓓ Ⓔ	113. Ⓐ Ⓑ Ⓒ Ⓓ Ⓔ
86. Ⓐ Ⓑ Ⓒ Ⓓ Ⓔ	100. Ⓐ Ⓑ Ⓒ Ⓓ Ⓔ	114. Ⓐ Ⓑ Ⓒ Ⓓ Ⓔ
87. Ⓐ Ⓑ Ⓒ Ⓓ Ⓔ	101. Ⓐ Ⓑ Ⓒ Ⓓ Ⓔ	115. Ⓐ Ⓑ Ⓒ Ⓓ Ⓔ
88. Ⓐ Ⓑ Ⓒ Ⓓ Ⓔ	102. Ⓐ Ⓑ Ⓒ Ⓓ Ⓔ	116. Ⓐ Ⓑ Ⓒ Ⓓ Ⓔ
89. Ⓐ Ⓑ Ⓒ Ⓓ Ⓔ	103. Ⓐ Ⓑ Ⓒ Ⓓ Ⓔ	117. Ⓐ Ⓑ Ⓒ Ⓓ Ⓔ
90. Ⓐ Ⓑ Ⓒ Ⓓ Ⓔ	104. Ⓐ Ⓑ Ⓒ Ⓓ Ⓔ	118. Ⓐ Ⓑ Ⓒ Ⓓ Ⓔ
91. Ⓐ Ⓑ Ⓒ Ⓓ Ⓔ	105. Ⓐ Ⓑ Ⓒ Ⓓ Ⓔ	119. Ⓐ Ⓑ Ⓒ Ⓓ Ⓔ
92. Ⓐ Ⓑ Ⓒ Ⓓ Ⓔ	106. Ⓐ Ⓑ Ⓒ Ⓓ Ⓔ	120. Ⓐ Ⓑ Ⓒ Ⓓ Ⓔ

BIBLIOGRAPHY

The following United States history textbooks are used in introductory college courses and will be useful to you in preparing for the CLEP examination. The editions listed are current as of this writing, but note that publishers issue new editions every few years and sometimes a textbook moves from one publisher to another.

Divine, Robert A.; T. H. Green; George M. Frederickson; and R. Hal Williams, *The American Story* (New York: Longman, Penguin Academics, 2002).

Garraty, John A. and Mark C. Carnes, *The American Nation: A History of the United States,* 11th ed. (White Plains: Longman Publishing Group, 2002).

Gillon, Steven M. and Cathy D. Matson, *The American Experiment: A History of the United States* (Boston: Houghton Mifflin, 2002).

Goldfield, David; Carl Abbott; Virginia DeJohn Anderson; JoAnn E. Argersinger; Peter H. Argersinger; William L. Barney; and Robert M. Weir, *The American Journey: A History of the United States* (Upper Saddle River, NJ: Prentice Hall, 1998).

Norton, Mary Beth; David M. Katzman; David W. Blight; Howard P. Chudacoff; Thomas G. Paterson; William M. Tuttle, Jr, and Paul D. Escort., *A People and a Nation: A History of the United States,* 6th ed. (Boston: Houghton Mifflin Co., 2001).

Tindall, George B. and David Shi, *America: A Narrative History,* 5th ed. (New York: W. W. Norton, 2001).

Woods, Randall B. and Willard B. Gate wood, *The American Experience: A Concise History* (New York: Harcourt Brace, 2000).

Glossary

ABC Programs: those implemented by Franklin Delano Roosevelt during the Great Depression to give relief to the unemployed

Affirmative Action: programs designed to overcome past discriminatory actions such as providing employment opportunities to members of a group that were previously denied employment because of racial barriers

Amendment: the modification of the constitution or a law

Appeasement: the act of making concessions to a political or military rival

Big Stick Diplomacy: Using American military power to fortify the diplomatic policies of the United States

Big Three: leaders of the three major allied powers (Roosevelt, Churchill and Stalin)

Bill of Rights: the first ten amendments to the Constitution

Bipartisan: politics that emphasizes cooperation between the major parties

Black Tuesday: October 29, 1929, the day the stock market fell about 40 points with 16.5 million shares traded

Block grants: federal money provided to a state or local government for a general purpose, such as reducing crime or improving education, with relatively few requirements on how the states can spend the money

Brown vs. Board of Education of Topeka: the Supreme Court declared the doctrine of "separate but equal" unconstitutional

Cabinet: the heads of the various departments in the Executive branch who aid in the decision-making process

Capital Punishment: the execution of an individual by the state as punishment for heinous offenses

Caucus: a closed meeting of Democratic Party leaders to agree on a legislative program

Civil Rights Act of 1964: legislative act that removed racial barriers in all places vested with a public interest

Class Action Suit: a lawsuit filed on behalf of a group of persons with a similar legal claim against a party or individual

Cloture: parliamentary procedure for ending debate and calling for an immediate vote on a pending matter

Conference: a meeting between committees of the two branches of the legislature to reconcile differences in pending bills

Conglomerate: a corporation that has many businesses in unrelated fields

Containment: strategy that called for containing communism and preventing it from spreading any further

Contras: Right-wing guerillas who fought the leftist Sandinista government of Nicaragua

Court Packing: the act of placing members of the same political party on the bench so that opinion of the court will be consistent with the political party's (seen most dramatically with Franklin Delano Roosevelt)

Crime of '73: What pro-inflation forces called the demonetization of silver

De Facto Segregation: segregation that results from nongovernmental action; i.e., administered by the public

De Jure Segregation: legally established segregation

Democrat: any member of the Democratic Party, one of two major parties in the U.S.; party's lineage traces to Jefferson's Democratic Republican Party (1792)

Deregulation: the act of reducing or eliminating economic controls

Desegregation: the removal of racial barriers either by legislation or judicial action

Dixiecrats: Southern Democrats who opposed Truman because of his support of civil rights; nominated Strom Thurmond for president in 1948 campaign

Dred Scott vs. Sanford: the Supreme Court upheld the right of a slave owner to reclaim his property after the slave had fled into a free state

Eminent Domain: the power of a government to seize private property for public use, usually with compensation to the owner

Ethnocentrism: a belief that one's ethnic group is superior

Executive Agreement: informal agreements made by the executive with a foreign government

Filibuster: a senator who gains the floor has the right to go on talking until the senator relinquishes the floor to another

Foreign Policy: treaties, agreements, and programs focusing on the relations between the United States and other nations

Franchise: the right to engage in the electing of public office holders

Gerrymander: redrawing of congressional districts in order to secure as many representative party votes as possible

Gideon vs. Wainwright: case decided by the U.S. Supreme Court in 1963 that established the right to legal representation for all defendants in criminal cases

GOP: the Republican Party

Hoovervilles: empty spaces around cities where the homeless would set up empty shacks in which to live

Impeachment: the process used to remove certain officials, including the President, from office. Similar to a trial, impeachment does not necessarily mean that an official will be removed from office; he or she must be found guilty of an impeachable offense

Interest Group: group of persons who share some common interest and attempt to influence elected members of the government

Iran-Contra: the selling of arms to Iran so that the profits from these sales could be used to fund the *contras* in El Salvador

Jim Crow Laws: laws designed to promote racial segregation

Kennedy, John F.: in 1960 became youngest man elected president of the United States; established the Peace Corps in 1961; issued challenge to NASA to land a man on the moon; assassinated in 1963

King, Jr., Martin Luther: civil rights leader who fought for the rights of minorities by the use of peaceful civil disobedience

Lame Duck: a defeated office holder after that person has lost their re-election, but is still in office until the newly elected official is sworn in

League of Nations: international organization to promote peaceful resolution of international conflicts; called on all members to protect the territorial integrity and political independence of all nations; replaced by United Nations

Line-Item Veto: the objection by the president to a single item in a piece of legislation; this authority, signed into law by President Clinton in 1996, was unsuccessfully challenged as unconstitutional by six members of Congress, with the U.S. Supreme Court saying the plaintiffs had no legal standing to bring a case

Lobbying: activities aimed at influencing public officials and the policies they enact

Malcolm X: radical Muslim leader who wanted a total separation of the races

Mapp vs. Ohio: the Supreme Court recognized that evidence seized without a search warrant cannot be used

McCarthyism: the act of seeking out subversives without cause or need (seen during the 1950s when Senator Joseph McCarthy stoked fear of Communism)

Miranda vs. Arizona: 1966 case in which the U.S. Supreme Court decided that all persons who are detained or arrested must be informed of their rights

Moral Majority: Christian conservatives, led by the Rev. Jerry Falwell, who favored prayer and teaching of creationism in public schools, opposed abortion and pornography, and backed a strong national defense

Muckrakers: investigative journalists and authors who exposed corruption in business and government

NATO: North Atlantic Treaty Organization; pledged that an attack against one was an attack against all

Naturalization: process by which persons acquire citizenship

New Deal: legislation championed by Franklin Delano Roosevelt during the Great Depression that provided a safety net (e.g., Social Security) for all members of society

Nixon, Richard M.: the only president of the United States to resign after being confronted with impeachment (because of his alleged actions in the Watergate scandal)

Nonproliferation Treaty: an agreement not to distribute nuclear arms to countries that do not have them

Open Door Policy: declared that trade with China should be open to all nations

Original Intent: a doctrine of Constitutional interpretation that says Supreme Court Justices should base their interpretations of the Constitution on its authors' intentions

Partisan: political opposition drawn along party lines

Plessy vs. Ferguson: Supreme Court ruling that established the rule of "separate but equal" as being constitutional

Political Question: constitutional question that judges refuse to answer because to do so would encroach upon the authority of Congress or the president

Poll Tax: the requirement of a person to pay for the right to vote

Populist: a political coalition of agrarians with urban workers and the middle class; goals included monetization of silver, a graduated income tax, public ownership of railroads, telegraph, telephone systems, an eight-hour workday, and a ban on private armies used to break up strikes

Progressivism: political movement calling for rejuvenation of free enterprise capitalism and the destruction of illegal monopolies; also called for civil service reform and honest and efficient government

Public Opinion: the beliefs, preferences, and attitudes about an issue that involves the government or society at large

Reagan, Ronald W.: two-term president during the 1980s whose economic policies followed supply-side theory

Referendum: the process whereby a legislative proposal is voted upon by popular vote

Republican: any member of the Republican Party, one of the U.S.'s two major political parties; the GOP came into being 1854–1856, unifying anti-slavery forces

Roe vs. Wade: the Supreme Court decision establishing a woman's right to an abortion

Roosevelt, Franklin Delano: president of the United States during the Depression and World War II; most noted for his enactment of New Deal programs such as the Social Security Act

Scalawags: Southerners who supported Reconstruction programs

Social Darwinism: application of Darwin's theory of evolution, survival of the fittest, to justify unequal distribution of wealth by claiming that God granted wealth to the fittest

Supply-Side Economics: economic theory that says if government policies leave more money in the hands of the people, they will invest it and stimulate the economy

Symbolic Speech: nonverbal communication of a political idea

Tariff: any tax levied on imported goods

Truman Doctrine: President Truman's assertion that the United States must support free peoples who were resisting Communist domination

United States vs. Nixon: the Supreme Court ruled that material vested with a public interest could not be withheld from evidence under the rule of executive privilege

War Powers Act: the act requires Congress to approve stationing American troops overseas for more than 90 days

Watergate: the illegal entry and phone monitoring in 1972 of Democratic headquarters in the Watergate complex in Washington by members of the Republican Party

Index